THE BOOK

OF

ESTHER.

THEOLOGICALLY AND HOMILETICALLY EXPOUNDED,

BY

FR. W. SCHULTZ,

PROFESSOR IN ORDINARY OF THEOLOGY AT BRESLAU, PRUSSIA.

TRANSLATED, ENLARGED, AND EDITED

BY

JAMES STRONG, S.T.D.,

PROFESSOR OF EXEGETICAL THEOLOGY IN DREW THEOLOGICAL SEMINARY,
MADISON, N. J.

Wipf & Stock
PUBLISHERS
Eugene, Oregon

Wipf and Stock Publishers
199 W 8th Ave, Suite 3
Eugene, OR 97401

The Book of Esther
an Exegetical and Doctrinal Commentary
By Schultz, Frederick William
ISBN 13: 978-1-55635-406-9
ISBN 10: 1-55635-406-1
Publication date 4/4/2007
Previously published by Charles Scribner, 1877

THE BOOK OF ESTHER.

INTRODUCTION.

§ 1. CONTENTS AND COMPOSITION.

THIS book, which in the subscription of many of the old manuscripts of Alexandria (as subjoined to chap. ix. 26) is designated as ἡ ἐπιστολὴ τῶν Φουρίμ, and briefly as אֶסְתֵּר, 'Εσθήρ or as מְגִלַּת אֶסְתֵּר, and by the rabbins is called simply מְגִלָּה [*the roll*], stands peculiar in more than one respect in the Old Testament canon. Compared with the historical books of the Canon, it towers far above them, if we examine its composition—which may be said to be nearly perfect—while it falls behind them, if viewed as to the spirit of its statement. First, then, let us consider its composition. The history which it portrays, appears like a well-planned drama; developing scene after scene in rapid succession, and progressing by fascinating movements, to a consummation which we may compare to the tying of a knot. But when the ἀκμή is reached, the solution is also near at hand. There ensues a highly successful and impressive *péripétie*, a sudden turn of fortune, and all difficulties, though seemingly impossible, that stand in the way of a desirable conclusion, are continually and completely overcome as chapter succeeds chapter. The first chapter gives us the introduction to the whole, and the last gives us a supplement. Of the eight main chapters, the first four are devoted to the *tying*, and the last four to the *untying* of the knot. Two out of these eight regularly belong together in the first part, because of the relation of the plot to the counterplot; in the second part, because they refer to the removal of an identical difficulty.

Ahasuerus (Achashverosh), the powerful king of Persia, who has dominion from India to Æthiopia, *i. e.*, over one hundred and twenty-seven provinces, in the third year of his reign prepares a feast for the magnates of his kingdom, which lasts a half year. In this feast he exhibits to his subjects—and thus to the readers of the book likewise—the wealth and magnificence of his kingdom. The reader might readily anticipate the significance of the enmity or friendship of such a ruler with respect to the Jews and the honor accruing to Esther when he selects her as his consort. Neither are we likely to lose sight of the distinction that Mordecai receives by being made his all-powerful representative. When finally the king would parade the beauty of his wife Vashti (Vashthi), she declines to appear before him and his guests, and the consequence is that, by the advice of his seven counsellors he repudiates her. This is the substance of the first chapter; the real point of issue of the history is developed out of the second chapter. Ahasuerus prefers the Jewess Esther, who is to be a substitute for Vashti, before all other virgins. He solemnly elevates her to Vashti's position; at the same time Mordecai, her uncle, from whom her elevation removed her, remains near the court. She does not reveal her Jewish origin, and Mordecai makes the king his debtor by discovering a conspiracy against the life of Ahasuerus. One would think that now better days would dawn upon the Jews in all the lands of Persia (chap. ii.). The first elevation is followed by a second. Haman, who on account of his name and descent might be called a declared heathen and enemy to Judaism, is by Ahasuerus made his prime minister. Irritated by Mordecai's disrespectful attitude, he procures a decree which, so far as human foresight can predict, must inevitably result in the complete termination of the Jewish name. Haman loses no time in promulgating this decree in all the provinces (chap. iii.). In the fourth chapter we find in consequence that, in the entire Persian domain all who are called Jews are in deep distress, covered with sackcloth and ashes. Conspicuous among them is Mordecai in a mourning suit, standing with loud lamentation at some distance from the king's portal, so as to draw the attention of the female servants and eunuchs of queen Esther. By great exertions he finally succeeds in obtaining her promise that she will dare the utmost for the salvation of her people; and she is even ready to perish in the attempt. She induces him, together with all the Jews in Susa (the palace) to join her and her maids in preparation for the decisive event by a strict fast of three days' duration (chap. iv.). But she is graciously received by her consort, whom she approaches without previous permission; yet she deems it expedient to first invite the king to dine with her once or twice, and this in company with Haman, who is thus even by her highly honored and distinguished. Here although the reader begins to anticipate, that just this distinction will become, in the artfulness of fortune, the beginning of his end, nevertheless Haman himself does not yet perceive it, but puffs himself up, as those often do who are delivered over to the divine judgment, against his mortal enemy Mordecai. Just as he departs from the first of Esther's banquets, in order to go to his home, and by this manifest distinction having become of greater self-importance, and especially having already received a second invitation, it happens that he finds Mordecai again sitting in the gate of the king's palace and still refusing to give him the required homage. After he has taken counsel with his wife and friends, and finds that the only drawback to his great fortune is this disrespect of the hated Jew, he resolves, in order that he may enjoy the happiness and honor of the next banquet without alloy, to remove this proud Mordecai out of his way the very next morning. He causes a gallows fifty cubits high to be constructed, on which, in order that the punishment might be the more terrifying and disgraceful, he would have Mordecai hung. In short, while the Jews themselves are prostrated in mourning, fearing the very worst, nor yet hoping a more fortunate turn of affairs to be brought about by the intercession of Esther, their mortal enemy, purposely and in consequence of Esther's intercession carries his head especially high, thinking that his highest triumph is now near at hand, (chap. v.). But in the succeeding night sleep flees the pillow of the king. In consequence he calls his scribe to read to him from the annals of the kingdom. In these is recorded how Mordecai disclosed the conspiracy against him, thereby saving his life, and precisely this passage is read to him. This occasions the question, how Mordecai had been rewarded for having made himself so greatly deserving of his favor; or rather, since hitherto he had not been rewarded, how or what reward should now be given him? Hence, just as Haman enters in the early morning, with the design of obtaining permission for the execution of Mordecai, he has this question put to him, and an immediate answer is required. As the question is quite general and indefinite, namely, what should be done to a man whom the king would delight to honor; and as no doubt arises in the mind of the self-conceited Haman that his own preference is spoken of, it so happens as the point of culmination of this effective development that, in the same moment in which he expects to annihilate his mortal enemy, he both pronounces his own doom and elevates his enemy to the highest honor. The king forthwith instructs him to carry out his own sentence (chap. vi.). But upon this first blow, which of course naturally falls heavily upon him, and which even to his wife and friends presages his downfall, there follows in the seventh chapter the second. In the second banquet he is boldly confronted by Esther, and Ahasuerus, extremely incensed against him, has him hung on the same gallows which was erected for Mordecai. Thus in chapters vi. and vii. the originator of the danger that threatened the Jews is removed. Now the question remains, whether and how the special regal decree, which ordered the destruction of the Jews, can be made ineffective, in spite of the irrevocableness which it has as the king's decree. Chapter viii. relates how little Mordecai and Esther are content with that which they had gained in Haman's downfall, and how Esther now entreats the king for her people, and how Mordecai, to whom the king assigns the matter, adopts counter measures, by which the Jews are restored to their rights and protected. Mordecai gave them permission to assemble and defend themselves in the day in which they were to be attacked. Chapter ix. adds how fortunate the Jews were in consequence, as they averted the calamity from themselves and threw it upon their enemies. Indeed they succeeded so well that the day in which they apprehended their destruction, became a day of rejoicing; and Mordecai, as well as Esther, by means of letters and ordinances established this day to be celebrated annually as a day of joy, solemn reflection and memorial. With a view to indicating not only their deliverance, but likewise the elevation and honor, which both Mordecai and Judaism experienced, chapter x. is added as a supplement. There also it is stated how powerful was the sway of Ahasuerus over land and sea, and how Mordecai, still promoting the welfare of his people, was the second in the kingdom. If we briefly condense the whole matter, we have the following summary:—

PART FIRST. The origin and increase of danger to the Jews (chaps. i.—v.).

Introduction. The occasion of the history. The State-banquet of Ahasuerus and the rejection of his spouse Vashti (chap. i.).

First Section. The rise and meeting of the contrasts (chaps. ii., iii.).
Esther takes the place of Vashti, and Mordecai deserves well of Ahasuerus (chap. ii.).
Haman attains to consequence and power, and irritated by Mordecai, resolves and decrees the destruction of the Jews (chap. iii.).

Second Section. The conflict between the contrasts, (chaps. iv., v.).
Mordecai, deeply mourning for his people, urges upon Esther to beseech the king for mercy, and obtains her consent (chap. iv.).
Esther is graciously received by the king. Haman, highly honored by the queen, resolves to have Mordecai hung (chap. v.).

PART SECOND. The removal of the danger (chaps. vi.—x.).

First Section. Haman's downfall (chaps. vi., vii.).
Haman, while expecting the highest distinction for himself, is deeply humiliated, in the very act of seeking the destruction of Mordecai, his mortal enemy, by being obliged by his own judgment to concede, and even with his own hand to impart to him the greatest distinction (chap. vi.).
Accused by Esther, he is hung on the same tree which he had erected for Mordecai (chap. vii.).

Second Section. The removal of the danger which threatened the Jews in consequence of the decree of annihilation issued against them (chaps. viii., ix.).
Esther and Mordecai obtain permission for their people to defend themselves, (ch. viii.).
The Jews rid themselves of their enemies and resolve, by the advice of Mordecai and Esther, annually to celebrate the day of their deliverance, as the feast of Purim (chap. ix.).

ADDENDA. Authority, consequence and power of Mordecai the Jew in the powerful Persian world-monarchy (chap. x.).

§ 2. AIM AND HISTORICAL CHARACTER OF THE BOOK.

Could authentic evidence be brought to show that there was a custom, in order to enhance the attractiveness of the annual celebrations, of publicly reading a festival-book (such as in the last *Mazzoth* day, Solomon's Song; on the second of the Feast of Weeks, the book of Ruth; on the 9th of Ab, as being the day of the destruction of Jerusalem, the Lamentations of Jeremiah; on the third day of the Feast of Tabernacles, Ecclesiastes), and could this be traced back to the time of the authorship of our book, then we should be apt to suppose that the book of Esther was written for the express purpose which it afterward served, *viz.* as the festival-book (the *Megillah* or volume) of the feast of Purim.

It is manifestly the intention of the author to exhibit the reason for the feast of Purim, *i. e.* to narrate the remarkable events to which that feast had reference. He is so engrossed with this festival of Purim, that he declares to us in the ninth chapter how it came that no only the 14th, but even the 15th, of Adar was celebrated as a festival; and in vers. 24 sqq. he again briefly condenses the chief facts of the history, in order to give them in a definite and comprehensive manner as the ground of the feast; and finally he makes the name *Purim* conspicuous as having special reference to these events. Of course, the occasion of the feast receives from him particular attention, because it is of such moment to the history as well as faith of the Jews, and in order to show that there is in the government of the world a justice which protects Judaism and preserves it amid the greatest dangers.

It is a manifest design of the book to promote a revival of the Jewish faith, for the strengthening of which this feast of Purim was designed, and to demonstrate that the heathen enemies fall themselves into the pit which they dug for Judaism, and that the Jewish people have an easy rise to the surface though they may have fallen for a time into abjectness and dependence.

Now the question arises, whether, in order to attain this object, the author has treated his theme historically or poetico-didactically; and if the latter be true, whether he has employed a free poetic style or merely given to historic facts a poetic adornment. The historic treatment has tradition on its side. This view obtains not only with the Rabbins, but universally in the Christian Church also. In its defence even CLERICUS (in his *Dissert. de scriptoribus librorum hist.*, § 10) says: "It is a truly wonderful and paradoxical history (who will deny it?); but many wonderful things and foreign to our customs formerly obtained among orientals as also among many other peoples." The first attacks upon its credibility were made by SEMLER (*Apparatus ad liberaliorem V. Test. interpret.*, p. 152 sq.), by OEDER (*Untersuchungen über einige Bücher des Alten Testaments*, p. 12 sqq.), and CORRODI (*Beleuchtung des jüdischen und christlichen Bibel-Kanons* I., p. 64), and later by BERTHOLDT (*Einl.* V., p. 24 sq.), DE WETTE, GRAMBERG (*Gesch. der Religionsideen* I., p. 317), VATKE (*Bibl. Theol.* I., p. 580), and also by BLEEK (*Einl. zum Alten Testament*); but they were aimed against details, which are not definite; and they do not therefore much militate against a correct understanding of the plan and method of our book. Historical investigation, however, cannot reject such doubts because they seem to contradict the received opinions respecting the canon. The latter may possibly be corrected. Even conservative theology has been compelled to make the concession that the book of Job, indeed even its introduction and conclusion, although having the form of a historical statement, are nevertheless to be received as poetical works, and that the declarations of Solomon in Koheleth have a poetical garb. It has been conceded that the book of Jonah has not so much value as a historical book, but rather as a book of doctrine, since otherwise it would not stand in the same category with the prophetical books.*

We must, therefore, not pass too hastily the question, whether in the later periods of canonical literature there had not a new branch of literary activity developed itself, which might be termed, in some sense at least, as that of *religious romance*. In the Greek-Alexandrian period as is shown by our *Apocrypha*, this was very rife. It might also occasion the thought, that in all public readings on festival days, only those writings were selected to be read which belonged fully to poetry, such as Canticles and Lamentations, or which at least in a certain sense pass over into poetry, as the books of Ruth and Ecclesiastes.

One circumstance especially and primarily caused doubts as to the strictly historical character of this book, namely, that, in the real turning-point of the whole story, as if in order to raise the interest of the reader to a high pitch, and also to make a satisfactory conclusion as regards Mordecai and the Jews, the timely and fitting nature of many of the incidents seems to translate the reader involuntarily from the world of reality to that of ideality. Haman must take revenge upon Mordecai in the very moment of his anger, and cause the gallows upon which he himself should be hung in the morning to be erected over night. But in this very night, when Mordecai has so much at stake, the king is made to

* [The author has made this admission too vaguely and unguardedly. The result of modern criticism has been not to overthrow the historical basis of the books referred to, but only to confirm the opinion early broached, and not unfrequently entertained, that their *dress* and language is poetical.—TR.]

have a disturbed sleep, and thereupon cause the state documents (chronicles) to be read to him, by the means of which he is reminded of the desert of Mordecai. The question of the king, which is quite indefinite, is accordingly misunderstood by Haman, and thus misleads him, so that he applies it to himself, and in consequence of this self-deception, awards to his mortal enemy the highest distinction, and that too in the very moment when he is intent on his destruction In order to explain such facts one must have recurrence to the special divine Providence, which rules over Mordecai and over the Jewish nation in general.

However intent God may be in a plan where the salvation or protection of His own people depends upon it; and though at times He may bring about occurrences in their favor, which are so wonderful as to make His special interference manifest to the believer, nevertheless the facts are not usually so artistically arranged by Him, as appears here. Besides, it is remarkable that Mordecai should not ere this have received some suitable reward for his meritorious act; so likewise that Esther did not at the first feast bring her particular request before the king. It would really seem as if Esther had been enjoined to wait, at least until Haman should gain time to determine the execution of Mordecai. Above all, semblance is given to the thought that Mordecai's reward is purposely postponed, in order that it might be accorded to him in the supreme and decisive moment of the whole proceeding.

But if we must acknowledge the influence of a transformative and embellishing imagery in this chief stage of the drama, this would be inconsistent if it were not possible to hold the same in other places, where it comes within the didactic purpose of the author, and where by a change in form of the transmitted material the intended impression could be more seriously brought about.

Possibly it may be assumed that Esther did not—at least permanently—occupy the position of first (chief) wife, but held only a subordinate one, as a preferred concubine before several others in Vashti's stead. Indeed, our book hints at such a fact; since even after Esther's elevation, there is mention in chap. ii. 19 of another collection of virgins, which appears to have had the same significance as the first one. It is well known that the profane writers are not only silent in reference to Esther, but they also relate several things as regards the chief wife of Xerxes, which have no application to Esther. They call the former *Amestris,* and say in reference to her, not only that she was a daughter of Otanes (HEROD. VII. 64), or of Onofas (CTESIAS, § 20), but also that Xerxes was married to her even previous to the expedition to Greece (HEROD. IX. 109). Further on it states that he married off Darius his oldest son by her, in the year 479, or immediately after the march to Greece (HEROD. IX. 108), while Esther, as we shall presently see, was raised to be queen after the Grecian expedition. To this may be added that, according to HERODOTUS III. 108, the real queens were selected only from the seven chief *Persian* families. Moreover, according to the Zend-Avesta (comp. KLEUKER, *Anhang.*, I. 78), marriage proper with women of any other tribe was, to the Persians, strictly forbidden.

Perhaps it may further be stated, indeed one might safely affirm that, Haman was not really an Agagite, *i. e.,* a descendant of the Amalekite king Agag, but that this designation was only given in a symbolical way. Hence, according to his whole manner, as is affirmed by the Targums *prius et posterius,* he would as the arch-enemy of Israel, hold a relation to Edom intrinsically identical, but varied in its outward expression, by being opposed to Mordecai, who had sprung from the family of Saul. Thus the name *Haman,* as well as that of his father (comp. on chap. iii. 1), might be of significance in this relation.

The remark, that Shushan, the city (not usually the Jews resident there, but the city itself), fell into consternation and alarm at the announcement of the first regal decree, which commanded the destruction of the Jews (comp. chap. iii. 15) may perhaps be somewhat exaggerated. So likewise at the publication of the second decree, in which the Jews were permitted to defend themselves, the assertion that the city rejoiced exceedingly (comp. chap. viii. 15) is not to be accepted as strictly true. This remark, perhaps, has its ground in the intention of the author, to bring into prominence the cruelty of the first decree, and the justice of the second, as also the greatness both of the threatened misfortune and of the following good fortune. Finally, the statement given in chap. ix. that, on that decisive day seventy-five thousand persons perished at the hands of the Jews, doubtless does not rest upon an actual count; but it is rather the design of the author to represent the victory of the Jews as grand and extensive. Of course in all these points we are necessitated to content ourselves with a bare "possibility," or even "probability." Yet we must not forget that a judgment may in such things be rendered merely from a subjective and individual point of view, and that we lack objective criteria. Finally, the conditions and circumstances of the case are to be regarded, of which we now have not sufficient knowledge.

The anti-traditional view, as held by SEMLER, OEDER, CORRODI, and among later critics HITZIG (*Gesch. Isr.* I. p. 280), and ZUNZ (*Zeitschrift d. D. M. G.* XXVII. 4, p. 684), which is that the history of our book is in several places not only poetically adorned, but really invented as a whole, in order to represent naturally a truth that seems to require statement in a historical form—is a view which would incline us to accept the theory of an apologetical tendency in reference to our book, could we thus be enabled to look upon it as actual, if not in all respects, yet at least in the cardinal points, especially as regards the persons treated of, in their manner, their destiny, or even in their names, intentions, and thoughts. Under that view Esther, who had grown great in lowly circumstances, herself poor but amiable, might represent the later Jewish nation growing up in exile, and not distinguished from other peoples by its external greatness, but rather by its internal importance and effectiveness. Esther's name is really *Hadassah*, or "Myrtle." In Zech. i. 8 the post-exilian nation is compared to the myrtles on the shore of the roaring sea, a symbol of the moving masses of humanity. Her assumed name *Esther* (*aster*, "a star"), on the other hand, might point to the reflection of light, which flows from the fulness of salvation as from the Lord, notwithstanding the tribulation inflicted upon her nation. Or she might have simply pointed to the hope which the older generation, in the midst of the night of the tribulation of their exile, placed in the younger. This nation stands under the lead and care of the old and serious Mordecai, who perhaps derived his name from the Chaldee god *Merodach*. But even he desires to conduct himself according to the Jewish laws in the midst of Chaldæa and Persia, though it be at the risk of his life, defying the power of the heathen potentate. Thus as an exile, carried to Chaldæa, he might represent a type of the old generation, which, as it were, had fallen a prey to Merodach, and yet, even in this heathen land, maintained a strong repugnance against heathen morals and laws, and opposed them with an unbending inflexibility. Esther's father, *Abihail*, *i. q.*, "the man of power and skill," had long since departed. Thus the fathers, to whose freedom and dignity the younger or rising generation would gladly have aspired, was gone. But the real fathers still remained, to whose covenant rights and inheritance a claim might still be laid. Or, if we would be guided by certain analogies in the book of Daniel, we might regard Esther as the image of a *guardian angel*, who, where the destinies of nations are decided, makes intercession for Israel (comp. Dan. x. 13, 20). Mordecai would then certainly represent the Jews who, above all others, are loyal and trustworthy; and he accordingly shows his loyalty to Ahasuerus, by opposing the scheme to take away the life of that ruler. Haman, on the other hand, *i. q.*, "the one sacrificing to Somao," the son of Hamadatha, as "belonging to the moon," *i. e.*, the chief heathen deity, the Agagite and the Amalekite, would be a type of the principal heathen potentates who hate and seek to destroy the people of God. Vashti's rejection and Esther's acceptance in preference to many others, rather would signify that Israel has long been preferred before other peoples, though this has as yet been a secret to the world. But that Haman comes to power and forthwith designs the destruction of the Jews, would indicate that in spite of the election of Israel the world is still the principal enemy to the kingdom of God. Indeed, this, which might be called, as in the N. T., the anti-Christian world, has dominion over the people of the covenant, as is strikingly evinced in the Jewish exile in contrast with the theocracy. What is stated of Ahasuerus, as being the Lord of the then known world, would remind us of the mode in which Providence seems to govern the world, leaving full liberty to the rulers inimical to God. This ruler is found to be indifferent to the distress of the oppressed and threatened people (comp. chap. iii. 15), indeed he is bound by an irrevocable edict of persecution against the people of God. The troubles of this exile had been inflicted by divine justice and now the question remained how grace could have scope again (comp. Isa. xlix. 24). But grace ever active, makes itself known, and remembers those who are recorded in the great book of life as God's faithful ones. The fall of Haman would then picture forth the removal of Anti-Christ. The destruction of the remaining enemies would shadow forth the overthrow of those who are not actively hostile, but simply not receptive of the kingdom of God. Both would foreshadow the judgment of God in its negative aspect. The conversion of many in Persia (chap. viii. 17) would indicate the conversion of heathen people as the positive side of the divine judgment upon the world. In short the whole would be an allegory, which would teach those who in later times are oppressed, that a higher Power is fighting for Israel; that its bitterest enemies are, by reason of their hostile machinations, the cause of their own destruction; that the faithful ones will yet get the victory, in spite of all their tribulations. This would be a vivid representation of what would come to pass after the sufferings of the exile, by way of contrast, and especially the judgment to be brought about by the coming of the Messiah, and even that which shall yet come at the end of time. Hence many things, which according to the letter of our history, seem low and worldly, indeed repulsive, would, if viewed in this aspect, contain a high religious truth, and our book would be regarded with far greater favor than has hitherto been given it. Every one feels that Esther, Mordecai and Haman have in fact a higher and more general signification. There are, however, many positive traits, which cannot be explained by this allegorical theory. Especially noteworthy is the circumstance that our book at its close (chap. ix. 16), in relating the inauguration of the Feast of Purim, explicitly claims to give real facts. The occurrences which lie at the basis of the story have been apprehended by the author much more clearly than he could have done the future history of the Jews, and yet in such a light as to make them the mirror of grander developments thereafter. The chief persons, of whom he speaks, have as it were gained representative positions, so that at their mention we think also of other persons. But these are not mere pictures, and the material employed is not to be regarded as poetically invented, but as historically given.

Should we even regard the substantial part of the history of Esther as unhistorical, still the question would necessarily arise, how to account for the history of the Feast of Purim. According to 1 Macc. vii. 40 sqq. Judas Maccabæus defeated the Syrian general Nicanor on the 13th Adar, a day before the Feast of Purim, near a place called *Adasa*, which might possibly be interpreted as *Hadassah*, "the myrtle." As a memorial of this victory the 13th of the month Adar was to be celebrated annually as a national holiday. The fact that on this occasion the Feast of Purim was not mentioned, has been taken as a proof by J. D. MICHAELIS, that the author of the 1 Maccabees had no knowledge as yet of the Feast of Purim. One might even go farther and assume that the Feast of Purim took its rise from the day of the defeat of Nicanor. The author of the apocryphal additions of our book designates Haman as a *Macedonian* (comp. § 4), in which case a relation to Nicanor might be established. Certain it is that the day of Nicanor's defeat gradually went over into that of the Feast of Purim.

Although the former is still mentioned in the Mishnic tract *Taanith* (ch. xii.), also in the *Babyl. Talmud* (*Tannit*, seq. 18 *b*), and in *Massachet Sophrim* (ch. xvii. 4), yet, according to GRIMM (on 1 Macc. vii. 49), it has not been celebrated as a memorial of Nicanor for at least one thousand years back. For the so-called Feast of Little Purim has nothing at all to do with it; but the latter is merely the usual Feast of Purim, occurring on the 14th and 15th days of the 12th month in a leap year, when the Feast of Great Purim falls on the same days of the 13th month. Still there was required more time for such a metamorphosis, by which a Nicanor was transformed into a Haman, than is thus allowed. Even the author of 2 Macc., according to ch. xv. 36, recognizes Purim as the Μαρδοχαικὴ ἡμέρα, and he then distinguishes the Feast of Nicanor as quite another. In agreement with him Josephus, in his *Ant.* xi. 6, 13, also affirms that Purim was celebrated by the Jews of the whole world as a remembrance of the occurrences detailed in our book. Indeed he himself is fully convinced that it was so celebrated since the time of Persia. Haman and Nicanor are entirely different persons, and the deliverances which the Jews enjoyed with respect to them are too different in nature to favor the idea of a transformation of the one into the other.

HITZIG (*Gesch. Israels* I., p. 280) supposes that Purim had been originally the New Year's Feast of the Persians. They began their year in the Spring, when Purim was celebrated; and in Arabic the New Year is still called *Pur*. Hence he also takes into account the Persian *Purdeghan* (Leap-year), to which HAMMER had already referred as being a foundation for the Jewish festival. ZUNZ also (*l. c.*) thinks that the Jews had appropriated to themselves the Persian Spring-festival which corresponds to the German Christmas festivities. The authorities, not able to abolish this feast, or perhaps unwilling to do so, took care to legitimize it as a day of rejoicing, and hence gave it a Jewish origin and import. HITZIG also assumes further that a fact of the Parthian period first gave the significance of Purim as being that of *lot* ("loose"); the Parthians of Scythian origin probably had such words as *Pur*, lot (loose), and *Agha* whence Haman probably derived his epithet of Agagite (ch. iii. 1); for even they also without a doubt had a Kislar-Agha (comp. ch. ii. 3). But that the custom of celebrating a day of rejoicing in the month of Adar had not only crept in here and there from heathen surroundings, but that it should also have attained to recognition by those who were strict in their national observances, and even with the authorities themselves, is not to be conceived of as possible under the then existing circumstances, unless it took its rise in a historical occasion adequate to account for its adoption into Judaism. Hence the necessity of recognizing the fact which our book relates, as the real foundation, in any case. To suppose that the festival could everywhere have gained currency independently of this basis, would be to confound those ancient times, in which an inflexible opposition to Judaism was predominant, with our modern age, in which this has to a great degree ceased. Besides, the festival of *Purdeghan* has but little resemblance to that of Purim. The former lasted ten days. The first five were devoted to the memory of the dead, and hence were a season of mourning (comp. HERZFELD, *Gesch. Israels*, II. 1, p. 183). If HITZIG finds it improbable that the feast of Purim took its name from the casting of lots over Haman, on the ground that the latter retreats out of sight in the history, on the other hand we should consider that the lot of Haman was the voice of God. The day selected for the casting of the lot, if it had brought the destruction of the Jews, would have been the day of the victory of heathen gods over the God of Israel. But since that event did not occur, it became a day of the refutation of the heathen deities, *i. e.*, of the victory and triumph both of Judaism and the Jewish law and God over them.

That such a history is basal to the Feast of Purim, as our book relates it, will always remain by far the most probable view, and hence is maintained in more modern times by such men as BAUMGARTEN (*De fide libri Estheræ*, 1839), after HAEVERNICK; also by KEIL and J. A. NICKES (*De Estheræ libro et ad eum quæ pertinent vaticiniis et Psalmis libri tres*, Romæ, 1856). These defend the historical character of our book in its strictness, and are reinforced by STAEHELIN (*Spec. Einl. in d. Kan. Büchern. d. A. T.*), BERTHEAU, and especially by EWALD (*Gesch. Israels*, IV., p. 296), who hold our book to be substantially historical.

Several things, which in our present condition seem to us very improbable, could perhaps be easily explained by reference to the peculiar circumstances, customs and usages of the ancient Persian empire, especially from the characteristic traits of Ahasuerus (Xerxes). We do not propose to enter upon this subject, so much for the purpose of directly corroborating the historical character of the book as in order to show that the attacks made against it are very doubtful. If DE WETTE thinks he finds a marked weakness in the narrative in the circumstance that Esther is represented as keeping secret her Jewish descent, not only at ch. ii. 20, where she is chosen queen by the king, but up to the very time of the catastrophe, and that even Haman does not suspect her relation to Mordecai, while the king himself is surprised at her request to be saved (comp. vii. 5); on the other hand we may consider that a great king, such as Xerxes, doubtless was too highly elevated to concern himself about the personal circumstances of his female favorites, and that Haman, in his official relation, had nothing to do with the harem of the king.

But the main fact that Ahasuerus at Haman's request resolved to issue an edict which ordered the destruction of all the Jews in the entire Persian empire, is not without analogy. Mithridates, king of Pontus, in his war against Rome, issued secret orders to all the satraps and chief local authorities of his kingdom, to murder on a certain day all Romans without distinction of sex or age, whereby eighty thousand, or as some estimate, one hundred and fifty thousand persons lost their lives. Mehmed, a pasha of Zaid, in the sixteenth century, surprised the entire nation of the Druses, and caused all that were met with to be killed (ARVIEUX, *Merkw. Nachr.*, I., p. 391). A similar thing occurred also in Europe. At the time of "the Sicilian vespers" there fell eight thousand Frenchmen in Catanea alone. Ferdinand the Catholic drove out of Spain over three hundred thousand Jews, and Louis XIV. drove out of France several hundred thousands of Protestants, after causing thousands more to be murdered (comp. ROSENMUELLER, *Bibl. Alterth.*, I., p. 379). The Parisian massacre of St. Bartholomew's night is another specially analogous case. KEIL very justly makes prominent the point in reference to these facts, that Greek and Roman authors are unanimous in their portrait of Xerxes, and paint him as a very riotous, licentious monarch, and an extremely cruel tyrant. The commentator last cited goes on to say: "Xerxes was the despot who, after the wealthy Lydian Pythius had most richly entertained the Persian army in its march against Greece, and offered an immense sum of money as a contribution to the costs of the war, on his making a petition to have the oldest of his five sons then in the army given to him as a solace for his old age, became so enraged that he caused the son asked for to be cut in pieces, and laid the pieces on both sides of the way, and ordered his army to march through between them (HEROD. VII. 37–39; SENECA, *De ira* VII. 17); the tyrant, who caused the heads of those to be cut off who built the pontoon bridge over the Hellespont, because a storm had destroyed the bridge, and who ordered the sea to be lashed with whips and bound with chains sunk under the waves (HEROD. VII. 35); the debauchee, who after his return from Greece, sought to drown the vexation of his shameful defeat by means of sensuality and revelry (HEROD. IX. 108, 599). Such a frantic tyrant was he as to be capable of all that is related in our book of Ahasuerus." SPIEGEL, in his *Eranischen Alterthumskunde* (II., p. 402), gives a very mild judgment concerning Xerxes, yet even he says: "There is no question that he fell far behind his predecessors in regard to energy and other capabilities; he seems to have been of a sanguine nature;" and the same writer also proves the great thoughtlessness of that king, especially in his relations to his uncle Artabanus (HEROD. VII. 10, 11, 48, 49), and in regard to Demaratus (HEROD. VII. 101–104).

Haman's publishing of the decree of extermination eleven months previous to the day appointed for the butchery was perhaps less foolish than it would appear to us in our circumstances. Besides it is very questionable whether so short a time as a month would have been sufficient to carry the edict to the remotest parts of the empire, as BERTHEAU seems to suppose. Mordecai, who issued the counter-edict three months later, urged (as is expressly stated in chap. viii. 10–14) the greatest speed. This was done not only to remove the terror of the Jews as soon as possible, but also to prevent any acts of oppression. To us of to-day it would indeed appear as if Haman would have made the destruction of the Jews only the more difficult, if not impossible, by what might seem to us an untimely and hasty publication of his decree. But to a Persian despot his subjects were never out of reach. The Jews might here and there have made an attempt at flight. But this might not have been very unwelcome to Haman, since the goods of the fugitives could have easily been confiscated. To Haman it was a matter of great importance to cause the decree of the king to become very early a fixed irrevocable law; and this doubtless would be attained most certainly by its publication. Besides, it was a gratification to himself to torment those detested Jews long before the blow was to be struck, and especially to let them see that their enemies were deliberate and easy in their preparation for the final blow.

The success of the orders issued by Mordecai, which appears from the statement that, in the various parts of the Persian dominion 75,000 persons perished in their attack on the Jews, will seem less doubtful than it might at first, if we consider the great extent of Persia, reaching from India to Æthiopia. The aggressors might very easily have overestimated the sympathy which they received from their own people and religious associates; and the power of resistance on the part of the Jews might easily have been underestimated. Hence it is not to be wondered at if the former were badly vanquished and perished. The number seventy-five thousand can, of course, be only assumed as an approximation, and the intention of the author may have been influenced to its acceptance by reason of the facts above stated.

The circumstance that Ahasuerus granted a new edict at the request of Esther, in which the Jews resident in Shushan were permitted to continue the massacre on the following day also, even when no new attack was attempted upon them, might be explained by the assumption that, in such a large city there was a great rabble element which had fallen upon the Jews the first day, and which would recommence the conflict after they had come forth from their temporary hiding-places. To such as had begun the conflict, and regarding whom the Jews were on the defensive, this second decree had equal reference. It only permitted them to fulfil what the first edict ordered, (chap. ix. 13).

A favorable opinion is created with regard to the historical veracity of the author, in that he correctly knows and vividly describes the customs and arrangement at the Persian court, in so far as they have interest for him; and that he calls by name those persons who enter into the history portrayed by him, such as courtiers (chapter i. 10), the seven Persian princes (chap. i. 14), the keepers of the women's houses (seraglios) (chap. ii. 8, 14), the chamberlain whom Esther sent out to Mordecai (chap. iv. 5), the wife and ten sons of Haman (chapters vi. 13; ix. 7–9). Further, he makes reference to the annual records of the Medo-Persians, as to the source in which were described, not only the deeds of Ahasuerus, but also Mordecai's greatness and power (chap. x. 2). Of course, a poet should correctly represent the manners and conditions which he would portray; and our author might very properly have been in possession of sufficient learning, or he may have written in a time and place where one could easily and almost intuitively learn about Persian matters. On this account we would naturally expect the absence of vulgar mistakes. Still it was not the habit with the Jewish authors of the last centuries B. C. to distinguish themselves by correct historical knowledge, or by an accurate apprehension of those far-off times. The contrary was of such common occurrence and fault that our book, in this regard, is entitled to the more distinction. It has been asserted that the office of Grand Vizier, such as was held by Haman, and afterwards by Mordecai, was not properly Persian. But ENGER (*Zeitschr. d. D. M.* 1859, p. 239 ff.) has conclusively shown that the office of vizier really originated and had its development in Persia. To resign the proper functions of government to a favorite, must have been a chief concern to a weakling like Xerxes, who lived only for sensual pleasures. Thus also the Merovingians had their *major domus* who finally usurped the government and power of the kingdom.

It is especially remarkable that the events related in the narrative can, according to their historical dates, which the author gives, be very appropriately inserted in the rest of the history of Xerxes as given by Greek historians. This is of the greater importance, since the author does not at all refer to previous history. It was in the third year of his reign that Ahasuerus gave the great feast in Shushan, which lasted one hundred and eighty days (one half of a Persian year). According to Herod. vii. 8, Xerxes proclaimed an edict in the third year of his reign, after the termination of his war against Egypt; and in that edict he convoked all the princes of his empire to Shushan, in order to plan the campaign against Greece. Such deliberations were generally accompanied with festivities by the Persian kings (comp. WINER, *Realwörterbuch*, II., p. 229, and BAUMGARTEN, I., p. 139). Vashti's rejection, there fore, occurred in the third year of Ahasuerus, and soon afterwards the choice of a new queen was made. Yet Esther, according to chap. ii. 16, was chosen near the close of the seventh year; and, according to chap. ii. 19, another assembly of virgins was ordered, from which a further selection was to be made to take the place of Vashti. This remarkable postponement may be explained by the fact that between Ahasuerus' third year and his seventh the time of preparation and the war against Greece intervened. Xerxes returned to Persia in the Spring of his seventh year. Thus his special history becomes, as it were, a commentary for our book.

§ 3. CANONICAL DIGNITY.

It seems as if the canonicity of our book had at first been doubted among the Jews. In the Jerusalem Talmud (*Megilloth*, lxx. 4) and in the Midrash (*Ruth*, 45 *c.*) we find the statement that eighty-five elders, among whom were thirty or more prophets, combated the introduction of the Feast of Purim, though they finally gave it their sanction. It is also intimated that these men were contemporaries of Mordecai. This remark has really nothing to do with the book of Esther as such, but has only reference to the precepts in regard to the fasts, which were ordered by both Esther and Mordecai, (chap. ix. 29–32). Still, to combat the latter would be to indirectly attack the genuineness of our book. Such an opposition to the institution of Purim, however, does not well harmonize with the reverence paid to the book as belonging to the Canon. The opinion of HERZFELD (II. 1, p. 358), that this tradition was a conclusion derived from the statement of chap. ix. 29 merely, from which it was inferred that Mordecai and Esther had written a second time in reference to the introduction of the feast of Purim, is very improbable, as is also his supposition that the number of the elders was taken by mistake from Nehem. viii.—x. grouped together. There are no other oppositions found among the Jews in this regard. Even JOSEPHUS reckoned our book as certainly belonging to the Canon (comp. *c. Ap.* I. 8); otherwise he would not have made the remark that the history therein described reached down to Artaxerxes, who to him was none other than the Ahasuerus of our book. But the later transactions which took place with reference to the Canon, namely, at the Synod of Jerusalem, A. D. 65, where a determination was called for between the Hillelites and the Shammaites, and also at the Synod at Jamnia, A. D. 90, had reference more especially to Ecclesiastes, and next to the Canticles, and lastly to the book of Ezekiel, which some would have withdrawn from public use, because it seemed to diverge in its legal requirements from those of the Pentateuch. (גנז). Moreover, our book has been very highly esteemed among the Jews (comp. GRAETZ on *Koheleth*, Appendix I.), which may easily be seen by its designation as "the Megillah" by eminence. Indeed it has been preferred to the "Kethubim," and even to the "Nebiim," and has finally been placed by the immediate side of the "Torah" itself. MOSES MAIMONIDES thought that in the days of the Messiah all the Nebiim and Kethubim would be abolished; and that only the book of Esther and the Torah, together with the oral law, would be perpetual (comp. CARPZOV, *Introd.*, I., p. 366). This special regard, however, was simply owing to the mournful circumstances under which the Jews learned to value the consolation derived from Haman's destruction and their own victory over their opponents, events to them at the time important and precious. In our book, accordingly, these incidents are given from a nationally limited point of view.

As regards the ancient Christian teachers, MELITO, bishop of Sardes (about 172) does not give the book of Esther in his list of the canonical books. Neither are the Apocrypha nor Pseudo-apocrypha mentioned by him. He was importuned by his Christian brother Onesimus to give him a more specific and correct statement with regard to the number and order of the O. T. books, since he had made researches respecting them in his journey to Palestine. The book of Nehemiah, concerning which he is also silent, he doubtless includes in Esther. But that he should thus have embraced the book of Esther likewise, as belonging to that of Ezra, although he himself never included the one in the other, as was the case with Nehemiah, is not, with EICHHORN, HAEVERNICK, and others, to be supposed (comp. EUSEBIUS, *Hist. Eccl.*, VI. 25). EPIPHANES (died about 402) (in his *De mens. et ponder. c.* 22, 23), HILARY (in *Prol. in Psalm.*) and JEROME (in *Prol. Gal.*) all include Esther in the Canon, but place it at the end. ORIGEN places it after the prophets and Job, which he brings in as the last. EPIPHANIUS places it after the prophets and i. and ii. Ezra. JEROME places it after the other Kethubim, especially after Chronicles and Ezra. HILARY places it after the prophets and Job. ATHANASIUS in his *Epist. Test.* omits it from the list of the canonical books, and assigns it to the ἀναγιγνωσκόμενα, *i. e.*, the books to be read before the congregation, which, with him, form a middle class between the canonical and apocryphal books. In the *Iambi ad Seleneum* written between 350 and 400, it is also omitted; yet the remark is made at the end, "Some add the book of Esther to these." True, the *Synopsis* (probably by the Alexandrian church and after to ATHANASIUS) remarks that some say that Esther was regarded by the Hebrews as belonging to the Canon; but this also proves that it did not have canonical authority in the Christian church, at least not in that of Alexandria. Still more, JUNILIUS (*De partibus legis div., c.* 3) writes that in his time (in the sixth century) it was very much doubted whether the book of Esther belonged to the Canon. It was, of course, not the former vacillating treatment of this book by the Jews that caused the opposition of Christians to its reception, but rather its high estimation with the later Jews. Its contents might very easily be objectionable to Christian views and sentiments. This is evinced by LUTHER, if indeed we can justly apply his harsh judgment to the Hebrew book* of Esther. As the passage referred to is somewhat ambiguous, we quote it in the original Latin: "*Licet recusare possim jure hunc liberum (Ecclesiasticum), tamen interim recipio, ne cum jactura temporis me involvam disputationi de receptis libris in canone Ebrœorum, quem tu non nihil mordes ac rides, dum Proverbia Solomonis et Canticum (ut scommate ambiguo vocas) amatorium comparas cum libris duobus Esræ, Judith, historia Susannæ et Draconis, Esther, quamvis hunc habeant in canone, dignior omnibus, me judice, qui extra canonem haberetur.*" [We translate as follows: "Although I might justly reject this book (Ecclesiasticus), yet for the present I admit it, lest with a loss of time I involve myself in the dispute concerning the books received in the canon of the Hebrews, which you not a little attack and deride, while the Proverbs of Solomon and the amatory canticles (as by an ambiguous sneer you call them) you compare with the two books of Ezra, Judith, the history of Susanna and the Dragon, and Esther; though this last they have in their canon, yet it is, in my judgment, more worthy than all the others to be kept out of the canon"]. In his *Tischreden* (ed. Walch, xxii., p. 268) Luther had also to do with the apocryphal books. He undertook to correct the second book of Maccabees, and he then uttered these words: "I am," said he, "so inimical to this and the book of Esther, that I could wish they did not at all exist; for they are excessively Jewish, and contain many disreputable heathen practices." It is, therefore, not at all improbable that he had reference not so much to the Hebrew, but rather to the Greek book of Esther, which was so greatly corrupted by other additions. Besides, he had just made the remark, "The third book of Esther I will throw into the Elbe. In the fourth book, in which are noted what Esther dreamed, there are many pretty and otherwise very good jests, such as: Wine is strong, the king stronger, women still stronger, but truth is the most powerful of all." Here he doubtless clearly mistook Ezra for Esther, and the fourth book of Ezra for the third (comp. p. 13). It is clear, also, that the apocryphal books were in his mind. The remark that his objection had its ground in the contents of the Hebrew book of Esther, instead of the comparatively innocent apocryphal additions, is opposed by the fact that the second book of Macc., of which he had just spoken, is placed before it. His objection to it seems to have consisted more in the fabulous than in the morally objectionable elements of both books.

What makes us especially suspicious with regard to the canonical dignity of this book is the fact that there is wanting in it the religious patriotic spirit which we find in the other Old Testament historical books. The author makes prominent the attractions of Esther in the eyes of Ahasuerus over all other virgins, and thus she became the guardian genius of her people. If he had written his book after the manner of the older canonical books, we might have reasonably expected that he would first of all speak of her piety. Indeed we should have looked that he would treat of it as the reason why God gave her favor in the king's sight, and that he would regard it as the source of her gracefulness and loveliness. But we find no trace of this. Least of all is there a reference to a joyful confession on her

* In his *De servo arb.* (ed. Jen. III., p. 182; ed. Erlang. XII., p. 194) LUTHER censures ERASMUS for regarding the book of Ecclesiasticus (Jesus Sirach) as authoritative (canonical), and for placing it on the same level with the book of Proverbs, in contrast with both books of Ezra (doubtless the third and fourth), Judith, the history of Susanna and the Dragon. Hence he fought against degrading the books handed down in the Hebrew Bible as canonical, and placing them on a level with those contained in the Greek Bible, which he afterward cast out as apocryphal. When he furthermore states that in his opinion the book of Esther deserved to be thrown out of the Canon, by this, as CARPZOV remarked (*Introd.* I., p. 370 sq.), he does not mean the *Hebrew* but the *Greek* book of Esther. In other words, he objected to JEROME's apocryphal additions to the book.

part to Jehovah. But we rather discover that Mordecai shrewdly advises her to keep secret her Judaistic descent from Ahasuerus. And she faithfully follows this injunction. Nor does she point to the Lord as being the Almighty Protector and Avenger of those who do him homage, even when she is compelled, in order to save her people, to declare her Jewish origin to the king. She seems rather to aid her nation, not because it is God's people, but because it is *her* people.

So also, according to our author, Mordecai refuses to bow the knee to Haman. A more ancient author would no doubt have faithfully given a clear and definite religious reason for his conduct. But our author gives it so little space, that most interpreters have misunderstood him. He rather permits us to guess the reason, so to speak, by designating Haman as an Agagite. And of Mordecai he testifies that he braced himself by his Judaism in his conduct. Hence that fact which would, we might imagine, have added the proper interest to the book, and should really have been the soul of it, and would have given it the best dedication—the truth that reverence for man does not militate against the honor due to God, and yet should not be given to those condemned and rejected by God—does not very clearly appear, and indeed might easily be wholly overlooked. The entire proceeding almost assumes the appearance of a common court-intrigue, in which Mordecai would hardly rank higher than his opponent.

As regards the measures taken by Mordecai and Esther for the deliverance of their people, we should naturally have judged that our author ought to have made their necessity more apparent, in order not to be misunderstood in a moral aspect. He should have called especial attention to their necessity for the maintenance of true religion. The first edict of the king against the Jews was irrevocable. Hence the authorities could not be called on for their protection. There remained, therefore, only the one way, namely, for the Jews to assemble and stand for their lives in a common self-defence. This was virtually a war in the time of peace. Still it was forced upon the Jews, and although thus premeditated and organized, it was, under the circumstances, their only available mode of defence. But instead of making prominent the fact that this deplorable conflict could not be avoided, and instead of showing that upon it depended the defence of law and religion, the author speaks only of the honor which Mordecai attained by adopting these measures with the king's sanction. He states that Mordecai passed out from the regal palace dressed in royal apparel, having a large golden crown upon his head, and that the whole city of Shushan, especially the Jews throughout the empire, rejoiced exceedingly (ch. viii. 15–17). Indeed, instead of telling us definitely that only a common defence was intended and permitted against anticipated hostile attacks, he employs the same expressions as when speaking of Haman's edict in ch. iii. 13, namely, the *jus talionis*. In this edict it was permitted the Jews to destroy, to kill and plunder the whole of the people and country, or whoever should attack them; and they were not even to exempt women and children. The measures thus have the appearance of having been adopted, not as being the only ones at hand, but because they were most agreeable to the Jews. Nor does it appear as if the author had in any wise regretted or disapproved of them, but rather that the joy of Mordecai and of the Jews was shared also by him. He is equally liable to misconstruction as regards the petition of Esther by virtue of which the Jews were permitted to repeat also on the second day the same self-vindication exercised on the first. He contents himself with the satisfaction experienced from the great success which attended the measures of Esther and Mordecai on the first and second day, namely, that in Shushan five hundred fell on the first day, and three hundred on the second (ch. ix. 11–15).

One thing, however, he repeatedly and pointedly makes reference to, namely, that the Jews did not lay hands on the spoil of their enemies (ch. ix. 10, 15, 16). This trait nevertheless can only be regarded as redounding to their honor if all the other transactions had a higher religious import. But if these are to be understood as having merely a common national meaning, they exclude indeed a base covetousness, but do not negative a passionate eagerness and vindictiveness which are but little removed above the desire of gain.

That the Jews should also slay defenceless women and children while attacking the men, and that they did actually kill such a great number as seventy-five thousand persons (ch. ix. 16), was too common a characteristic of ancient warfare, to deserve a specially severe censure. But the author had quite other intentions than to regard the war as being conducted in the interest of higher principles, and as absolutely necessary; indeed he has expressed himself in terms which lead to quite a different conclusion. (Comp. ch. ix. 5: "Thus the Jews smote all their enemies with the stroke of the sword, and slaughter, and destruction, and did what they would unto those that hated them.") His narrative creates quite a different impression and gives greater offence than if he had stated that the Lord had given a great victory to His people, in the course of which seventy-five thousand perished. This might easily have been done in a way and by a connection in which the greatness of the danger and the persecutions of the people of Jehovah would have been strongly manifested.

The satisfaction which the author, together with Mordecai and the Jews, felt we can easily enough excuse, because of the greatness of the defeat of the attacking enemies, inasmuch as they suffered great insults and injuries, of which their heathen enemies were by no means sparing. It was in fact only the natural instinct of a worm, when in danger of having its life trodden out under the march of the peoples of the world, and therefore only escaping with life when its destroyers were themselves destroyed. But the author would have given us a much more satisfactory justification of these things had he designated his own people as the people of Jehovah, in opposition to the heathen as such, instead of terming them Jews merely, of whom one does not anticipate a higher task or even a higher principle.

But with all the foregoing criticisms we have not yet looked at the chief point of the discussion. It is remarkable that we do not even once find mention made of the name of God, much less of Jehovah. If under other circumstances, this would perhaps be something external or accidental; here it is closely connected with the general view of things.*

There seems to obtain another kind of historical portraiture in this book from that of those of the more ancient histories. The latter are very properly called *sacred history*, because their purpose was to derive the incidents which they describe from God, or from His justice, or yet from His gracious intentions towards man. They also seek to show the bearing of that which has been attained upon the ultimate honor of God. But our book appears to give us a different mode of historical description, in that it takes up the lower facts and things lying nearer, be they causes or aims. We find it nowhere distinctly stated that at the very beginning a higher Power was at play, which finally placed Esther in her high position. In this position she could become the intercessor for her people. This power was likewise manifest later in causing Ahasuerus at the proper time to remember Mordecai, and to reward him. Thus also the great and threatening danger to the Jews was averted, and victory leaned to the side of the people of God in their conflict with their enemies. Nowhere do we discover expressions of religious feelings or thoughts in the persons of whom the author speaks. Even in Mordecai these are not manifest, since he is not a representative of Jehovah-worship; nor yet do those principles appear to have actuated him which his religion would have enjoined him to observe. On the contrary his motives and sentiments are indefinite and scarcely national. It is simply because of his Judaism that he refuses to do reverence to Haman. Neither are any such feelings or thoughts as we might have presumed perceptible in Esther, who, in common with Mordecai, instead of employing the office of prayer for the removal of the danger, brings into requisition the Jewish custom of fasting. Certainly Mordecai expresses a firm assurance that help would come to the Jews from some source; but it would hardly do to suppose that he thought of God, when in ch. iv. 14 he expects deliverance even if Esther should not venture to petition the king. He might easily have meant another human person instead of Esther, who would have taken her place. There is never a mention made of prayer, pressing as were the occasion and circumstances that justify our expectation of its employment.

* Even the rabbins took notice of this fact, and sought an explanation for it. Comp. what August Pfeiffer has written with reference to the canonicity of the book of Esther and its programme. Aben Ezra held that Mordecai, being the author of the book, had purposely expunged the names of God in it, in order that they might not be desecrated by the Persians, if they made use of them.

Now it is very necessary for a correct estimation of our book to place the above-cited phenomena in their proper light. Without doubt we would do great injustice to the author if we were to hold him to be religiously indifferent or entirely irreligious because of his non-religious mode of statement. To a man enthusiastic for Judaism and Judaistic law, irreligious feelings are hardly possible. Even if his enthusiasm had been pre-eminently national, so that in his eyes Esther, Mordecai and the Jewish nation, in short all that was Jewish, deserved, as such, preference and distinction, it would still have shown some religious side. This would have been nationally religious, since it would have based itself on the preference of Israel on the part of God. Even though it would have led to a certain religious externality, in which a more intimate relation to God would not have been possible, this would not exclude the fact that the name of God would have received mention now and then. The reason why our book is silent with respect to God demands another explanation. The subject of which the author treats points to the preference or choice of Israel on the part of God. The fact of his belief in the continuance of Israel, as it is expressed by Mordecai, is proved too plainly and definitely for him to have placed no meaning or merit in it. We may add to this, that the rule of a higher providential Power, although nowhere noticed particularly as such, is nevertheless sufficiently expressed, both in the entire plan of the book and in the facts themselves.

If we regard Haman as representing the enemies of the people of God and thus as carrying out their plans of destruction against Israel; if in Mordecai and the Jews the people of true religion as such suffered; if in Ahasuerus the higher government of the world was awake, and if in Esther the good Spirit, which ever watched over Israel, brought his petitions before the throne of the highest decisive tribunal; if the battle of the Jews against the Persians is the conflict of the oppressed and deeply humiliated kingdom of God against heathendom, and if the destruction of these enemies is the removal of all that is unimpressible, and past improvement, and is the means by which the true happiness of mankind is to be prepared,—in short, if the author intended to speak in such far-reaching pictures rather than to write history, then a sufficient explanation is discovered of his seemingly irreligious tendency and of this parabolic method. What would otherwise appear as having no reference to religion, would then be full of the religious element. It would be like a N. T. parable, where there is no express reference to God and His kingdom, since the higher is the lower. We may, indeed, be compelled to admit that the intention of the author is not clear; nor do we plainly see how far the author has sought to employ this parabolic mode of statement. Whether or not he intended to make these representative persons transparently illuminated types, cannot be certainly known. But this much may possibly be affirmed, indeed it can be proved, that he is in this religious aspect reticent, because he desires to call in the attention of the reader,—to point out, as from afar, what was yet to come—and also to bring into requisition the expanding, even advisory activity of the reader, since he seems to have thought he could thus write the more appropriately and advantageously.

A similar phenomenon, and one which is entirely appropriate as yielding the proper explanation, is found in the first Book of Maccabees. In it the mode of writing history is not that of the more ancient authors, any more th in in our book. "One nowhere reads how God had awakened or directed the hearts and minds in this sacred warfare for the faith, as one can still find in the books of Ezra or Nehemiah (Ezra viii. 31; Neh. ii. 8, 12, 20; iv. 9; vii. 5). Of none of the heroes arising in this war is it said that he was inspired by the Spirit of God. According to chap. xiii. 7 the spirit of the people again revived, but the people was not influenced by the Spirit of God. It would almost seem as if the author had lost sight of the fact that the immediate indwelling and governing presence of Jehovah in and among His peculiar people, was essential to the Hebraistic conception." (GRIMM *on* 1 *Macc.*, p. xviii.). As in the books of Ezra and Nehemiah we miss that theocratic pragmatism which throws a supernatural illumination over the events transpiring, the same can be much more truly affirmed of the first book of Maccabees. In like manner with the author of our book, the writer of that history also avoids the mention of the name of God, and it is not found even once, whether by the term θεός or κύριος. Those passages of several of the editions of the

Alexandrian text, which have θεός, (chap. iii. 18; iv. 24; vii. 37, 41), are, as GRIMM also holds, critically more than doubtful (comp. ROSENTHAL, *Das 1 Mack.-Buch, eine historische und sprachlich-Kritische Studie*, Leip. 1867). Still the religious spirit, though it be peculiar, is present in that book. It is also clear that it is more than mere enthusiasm for the law and legal sentiment as to the mode of worship, *etc.* The faith is just as important to the author as is the faithfulness to law. In him, too, we find the designation of the people as the people of the faith (Macc. iii. 13; ii. 59, 61, *etc.*). In distinction from our author, however, he frequently reveals to us the fact that his heroes pray. His reference to God is at times so manifest that Luther did not hesitate to add the name of God, even where the author speaks very indefinitely of the law, or covenant, or of a will in heaven; and where it is unquestionable that *God's* law, covenant or will is meant (1 Macc. ii. 21, 54; iii. 60).

This spirit is further seen in the apocryphal book in question not only in such expressions as: *ἵλεως ἡμῖν καταλιπεῖν, etc.* ("God forbid that we should forsake," chap. ii. 21), but also when the author says that they cried (to God) in prayer (chap. v. 33, *etc.*). This is especially true of the language and prayers of his heroes, who, though zealous for the law and the faith, are still prevented from calling God by name. Judas says: "Victory (strength) cometh from heaven" (chap. iii. 19). And still speaking of heaven he says: "He (αὐτός), (the Lord) Himself will overthrow them" (chap. iii. 22). Again: "Let us cry to heaven" (chap. iv. 10), "if peradventure He (the (Lord) will have mercy upon us." Of their victories it is even said that, "they turned back and praised (the Lord) heaven that He (the Lord) had been good, and His mercy endureth for ever" (chap. iv. 24).

From this comparison of the books of Maccabees we arrive at the following explanation with reference to the matter in question: The *naive* and direct piety of former times, being devoid of reflection, gradually give way to a different state during the exile. The Jews were in that age very sensitive not to manifest their innermost and holiest thoughts to the gaze of day, after the manner of their forefathers. It was a great satisfaction to the Jewish national feeling, groaning under oppression and opposed to heathenism, to know that the secrets of their faith and law were well known and understood by themselves without having to enter expressly upon a declaration of them; and also that these were unknown and unattainable by the heathen. The more general the fidelity to the law and the faith of the fathers became, at least externally, the more they took courage. The more apparent the contrast became between heathenism and Judaism,—which was however gradually lost by their political dependence, their political character, also being thus effaced,—the more the characteristics of their religion shone forth. Indeed, the Jews were henceforth persecuted only because of their laws and faith, in a word, their being different from their captors. Hence it was quite natural that the Jews, as such, should feel themselves to be the people of the true God, before all others. So it was also with the author, who represented them as being in this exalted relation, without even distinctly so expressing himself. To all this was added the progressive spiritualizing of God, which had previously reached a high stage in the prophetical times. This was now carried to a still higher pitch of development. Hence, those modes of anthropomorphism and anthropopathism, which before were a necessity of the more vital piety, were now avoided. Thus in bringing out the exalted character of God, as being above the creature, His transcendental character was brought into greater prominence, and His imminence was more and more kept out of sight. It is well known that the name Jehovah was entirely withdrawn from usage, as being too holy. We might very easily suppose that God Himself was held to be too holy and exalted to be much spoken of, even in divine worship. But once having entered upon this tendency of mind, a further step was not difficult of execution. Some, as our author, would not even mention in a general way the influence of a higher power, while others, as the author of 1 Maccabees, contented themselves with a little less reserve.

It is doubtless true that such a tendency had its great dangers. While the Old Testament theism, being faith in a living God, active in the development of the world and of mankind, held the proper middle ground between pantheism and deism, by believing in an ever-present real divine Spirit, it gradually and unmistakably leaned over to deism, in strong contrast with pantheistic heathendom. We thus have it exhibited to us in the Apocrypha. There, in place of the living immanent Spirit of God, we have the transcendental νοῦς or the abstract σοφία. Hence a childlike trust in God and a true moral fear of God, had no more a proper place. Indeed it went still farther and degenerated into an abstract one-sidedness. Of this we have an example in later Judaism as opposed to Christianity. This also characterizes Mohamedanism. By cherishing such a worldly and materialistic spirit which ignores God, is very apt to grow more and more inveterate, as was especially manifest in Israel in later times.

Still, we must not suppose that this tendency had in the time of the present author proceeded to such a length; it was as yet but the normal development of the people of Israel. In its proper limits, and proceeding from a good foundation, it had a worthy aim. This was first of all to bring to general recognition the religious element as something self-evident and elevated above all exposition. Our author does not really intend to lose out of sight the mysteries of the faith and law. He rather presupposes them as self-evident. This is apparently from the circumstance that he not only represents the history of which he treats as being decidedly providential in its development, but also from the manner in which he gives the reason why Mordecai refused to bow the knee. So also in respect to the time in which the edict of Haman was published, and which should prove so destructive to the Jews (it was during the time of their Paschal festival), he is very indefinite, simply indicating it. Again we may note how he causes Mordecai to speak so indefinitely and yet in a manner so easily understood with reference to the help that would certainly come to the Jews. So also Esther is urged to take refuge in fasting which is almost inseparable from prayer, instead of praying at once as the nearest remedy at hand. The feeling arises in us on reading these passages, that he thought far more than he said, and that his silence has its ground in something quite different from infidelity.

Besides, the style of our book is most appropriate to its contents. Indeed we can readily recognize a divine providence in the fact, that just such a style and not a more religious one should have been employed. The deliverance of the Jewish people within the Persian dominions, which forms its subject was, of course, in itself a great and important event. But this was not brought about by a divinely-inspired hero, nor yet by the faithful valor of the people, but through the influence which a woman exerted over the king. In how different a manner will the soldiers (combatants) of the kingdom of God gain the victory in the future time of decision! Not through the charms of flesh, but by the Spirit and living energy of the Lord. Not by means of a forcible uniting and a bloody massacre, but by a willing submission. Instead of destroying others, they rather endure the utmost injury. It is in this succumbing that the highest power and glory is revealed; not in persecuting but in blessing! The plot is wrought out according to a human method. To have regarded the representative character of the persons and events described as being after the earthly type, and yet to have exalted them to a higher and holier tone, by which they would be brought into an immediate relation to God, would have created a discord. This would hardly have satisfied or edified the religious sentiment, but rather would have been a cause of irritation.

Certain it is, that although our book does not expressly take notice of and cultivate religion as such, still it forms a very essential part of the religious history of the kingdom of God. We were early reminded, in the introduction to the books of Ezra and Nehemiah, § 1, that the Diaspora remaining in heathen countries was by no means a rejected branch of the people of the covenant, but rather that it had a very important purpose to fulfil as regards the final accomplishment of the mission of Israel. This was clearly seen in the apostolic-Christian period. Hence the preservation of the despised Jews might very easily have become just as important as was the new founding of the people in Judæa and Jerusalem. Our book has to do with the preservation of this Diaspora, which, conditioned by peculiar circumstances, had taken on a low form, because living in a heathen world. But this in its deeper aspect still continued to be a part of the history of God's kingdom. It was an act of God by which He confessed Himself to this people as to His own peculiar people, and drew it up to Himself as its God. In addition to this the book is not only evidence that there is a just government of the world—that he who digs a pit for another will fall into it himself—that the enemies of the elect people are destroyed because of their enmity; but it also teaches, if we rightly understand it, the very simple and yet difficult duty of placing God's honor above that of man, and God's cause above the interest of man. At least it encourages us so to do. It represents to us the conflict into which the God-fearing man, as also the whole people (or church) may be plunged, in the execution of that duty. When the State is no more guided by divine principles, and as such is no more either theocratic or Christian, but purely human and heathen, this book points to the victory which the true people will in some way cr other continue to obtain.

If we place this book, having such an important message, by the side of both the other post-exilian books as regards Judaism, namely Ezra and Nehemiah, it clearly testifies, as do also those, that the people of God, conceived as a religious society, can exist without having political independence, and fulfil their final destiny. But it shows also that they could maintain their integrity, even if separated and scattered. This is a truth which nowhere else finds such definite expression, but yet it forms the basis of existence for the most of the Israelites during all the following periods of time. Hence, also, the peculiar reverence paid to our book in preference to others by later Judaism. And this is not from any pathologically unsound cause. It rests not upon a passion aroused by the inimical and oppressive acts of other people, but it can be justified by a genuine religious reason. In so far as it celebrates the victory of the divine law over the world, and reveals its inviolableness in this new and distinct method, thus becoming an indispensable support of the Torah, it justifies the remarkable manner of its statement, as MAIMONIDES and later writers have fully shown. In so far as it teaches that the glory of God is pre-eminent over that of man, that those who refuse to honor man lest they deprive God of His due regard will not fail to receive their reward from God; in so far must Esther be to us indeed a *star* which leads us to battle on faithfully and courageously, should the State seek to put forth its power and endeavor to enter the religious domain in too absolute a manner.

If the canonical merit of the Old-Testament books consists to a great extent in the fact of their passing beyond the bounds of their own nation; if they have a more general relation, on account of which they are closely related to the cosmopolitan New Testament, still we must not forget that the national tendency of our author had not yet reached this point. He had not attained to that sense of superiority and contrast which ultimately made the Jews jealous of the communication that was given to them for transmission to other nations. He was at least indifferent to the weal or salvation of others, and even sought to obtain advantage over them, and to injure them. He does not reveal any timidity, such as we find in the book of Judith, where Nebuchadnezzar is degraded far below Ahasuerus. There, however, the Jews appear in a far more ideal light.

Thus in ch. viii. 17 he gives prominence to the fact that many of the people of the land—even though incited by fear—were converted over to Judaism; and he thereby indicates that, in addition to the negative effect, which for the purpose in hand he is necessitated to notice, this judgment of God over the world had also a decidedly positive result, namely, the reception among His people of heathen subject to His influence. The writer also recognizes in the great ruler noticed in this book a capacity to appreciate Judaism and its representatives to some extent at least. So also among the majority of the heathen populace he indicates a sense of justice and humanity which did not suffer them to rejoice at the promulgation of the first unrighteous decree for the extermination of the Jews, but on the contrary he shows that they were exceedingly glad because of the second favorable edict. He seems to be impressed with the fact that they have both the inclination and the capacity at some time to arrive at a knowledge of the true God, and for his part he would gladly leave the door open for them.

[Excursus on the Liturgical Use of the Book of Esther.]

[BY THE AMERICAN REVISER.]

[It is well known that this book is a favorite with the Jews, by whom it is often entitled הַמְּגִלָּה, *the Roll*, by way of distinction from all others; and it is more frequently used in a separate form than any other of the sacred books. The extravagant estimate of the Rabbins is well represented by the saying of MAIMONIDES, above alluded to, that in the days of the Messiah all the books of the Old Testament will pass away, except the Pentateuch and Esther. This fondness for the book in question has doubtless arisen from the fact that it so highly gratifies the Jewish national pride.

The Feast of Purim (פּוּרִים, *lots*, so called from the fact stated in chap. ix. 26–32) is a standing memorial of the historical character of this book. As we have seen, it has been commemorated even since the days of the writer of the second book of Maccabees (xv. 36—the "Mordecai's day"—ἡ Μορδοχαϊκὴ ἡμέρα). The festival was so popular in the time of JOSEPHUS that he tells us: "Even now all the Jews that are in the habitable earth keep these days festivals, and send portions to one another" (*Antiq.* XI. 6, 13). That popularity has not diminished since. It has even been maintained by many (PETAVIUS, OLSHAUSEN, STIER, WIESELER, WINER, ANGER, ALFORD, ELLICOTT, *etc.*, after a suggestion by KEPLER) that our Lord observed this festival (ἑορτὴ τῶν Ἰουδαίων, John v. 1); but the absence of the Greek article there is not at all decisive (as WINER himself admits, *Gramm. of N. T. Idioms*, MAYER'S Ed., p. 125), and there are very great objections to the identification of the "feast" in question with that of Purim, especially the fact that the parallel gospels show that the one which our Lord at that time attended was during the harvest-season (Matt. xii. 1; Mark ii. 22; Luke vi. 1).

Among the modern Jews the festival of Purim is regularly held on two days, the 14th and 15th of Adar, the last month of the year, corresponding to our March in general. In intercalary years it is repeated in full on the same days of the 13th month, Ve-adar. A preliminary fast, called "the fast of Esther," is appointed to be observed on the 13th day, in accordance with the command of Esther (iv. 5, 6); and sundry prayers of repentance, humiliation, *etc.* (סליחות) are introduced into the regular ritual for that day. As on all the fast days, the lesson from the Law consists of Exod. xxxii. 11–14; xxxiv. 1–11; and that from the Prophets of Isa. lv. 6—lvi. 9. If the 13th of Adar falls on a Sabbath, the fast takes place on the Thursday preceding, as no fasting is allowed on that sacred day, and it could not be held on Friday, because those engaged in preparing food for the Sabbath would necessarily have to taste the dishes to try them, or at least would be occupied in the labor connected with that preparatory day. If the 14th happened to fall on a Sabbath, or on Monday, or Wednesday, the commencement of the festival is deferred for similar reasons of convenience till the next day. On the evening closing the 13th and beginning the 14th, as soon as the stars appear, candles are lighted in token of rejoicing, and the people assemble in the synagogues. After the usual evening service, consisting of prayer and thanksgiving, the entire book of Esther is read through by the prælector from a roll written separately in Hebrew characters on good parchment with ink (Mishna, *Megillah*, II. 2). Any one is qualified to read it, except deaf people, fools and minors (*ibid.* II. 4), and it is lawful to read it in a foreign language to those who can only so understand it (*ibid.* II. 1). The prælector reads it in a histrionic manner, suiting his tones and gestures to the changes in the subject matter. Whenever he comes to the name of Haman, the congregation stamp on the floor and cry out: "Let his name be blotted out! The name of the wicked shall rot!" At the same time, in some places, the boys who are present make a great noise with their hands, with mallets, with rattles, and with pieces of wood and stone, on which they had written the name of Haman, and which they rubbed together so as to obliterate the writing. The passage in which the names of Haman's ten sons occur (ix. 7–9) is read very rapidly, and, if possible, in one breath, to signify that they were all hung at the same time. For this reason that passage is written in larger letters, and the names are arranged under one another. The tradition is that the names are written in three perpendicular columns to represent the hanging of Haman and his sons upon three parallel cords, three upon each cord, one above another (STAEHELIN, *Rabbini. Literat.*, II. 349). The Targum on Esth. in WALTON'S *Polyglott* (*ad loc.*), however, states that they all hung on the gallows in one line, Haman at the top, and his ten sons at intervals of half a cubit under him. It is added that Zeresh and Haman's seventy surviving sons fled, and begged their bread from door to door (in evident allusion to Psalm cix. 9, 10). After the roll is finished, the reader dismisses the congregation with a short benediction. All go home and partake of a repast said to consist of milk and eggs.

On the morning of the 14th, the proper feast-day, the Jews again attend the synagogue, where several appointed prayers are added to the usual daily ritual, and instead of the regular lesson, the passage is read from the law (Exod. xvii. 8–16) which relates the destruction of the Amalekites, the people of Agag (1 Sam. xv. 8), the supposed ancestors of Haman (Esth. iii. 1). This is read by three persons—a priest, a Levite, and an Israelite. After this the roll of Esther is read through again in the same manner, and with the same responses as on the preceding evening. All who possibly can are bound to hear it read—men, women, children, cripples, invalids, and even idiots—though they may, if they please, listen to it outside the synagogue (Mishna, *Rosh ha-Shanah*, III. 7). When the service in the synagogue is over, all give themselves up to merry-making. Games of all sorts, with dancing and music, begin. The rest of the day is spent in feasting and rejoicing. Open house is kept; poor and rich, young and old, have free access to come and enjoy themselves. In the evening a quaint dramatic entertainment is often held, the subject of which is connected with the occasion. The men sometimes put on female apparel, declaring that the feast of Purim (Esth. ix. 22) suspends the rule in Deut. xxii. 5. A dainty meal then follows, sometimes with a free indulgence of wine, which the Rabbins allow on this occasion to the extent of absolute intoxication (Gemara on *Megillah*, VII. 2).

On the 15th day of Adar the rejoicing is continued, and gifts consisting chiefly of sweetmeats and other eatables are interchanged. Offerings for the poor are also made by all who can afford to do so (Esth. ix. 19, 22). See GINSBURG, in KITTO'S *Cyclopædia*, *s. v.* Purim; CLARK, in SMITH'S *Dictionary of the Bible*, *s. v.* Purim; SHICKART, in the *Critici Sacri*, III., 1184; MILLS, *British Jews*, p. 188; ESKUCHE, *De festo Judæorum Purim*, Marburg (1734, 4to.); AXENFELD, על פורים *Betrachtung, etc.* (Erlang., 1807).]

§ 4. COMPOSITION, TIME OF ORIGIN AND INTEGRITY.

The discussion respecting the *author* of this book had to be reserved until after the preceding questions had been determined, inasmuch as an answer to it would otherwise have been only of the most uncertain kind. Nor could we have hoped, by the solution of this point, to throw much light on the historical character of the book, or its canonical dignity. In chap. ix. 20 it is stated that: "Mordecai wrote these things, and sent letters unto all the Jews;" in verse 23, "The Jews undertook to do . . . as Mordecai had written to them;" and in verse 26, "Therefore for all the words of this letter." We are not, hence, to conclude that our book was written by Mordecai, nor that it is so claimed, but that the author had knowledge of such writings referable to Mordecai himself, with respect to Purim, and also that he made use of them. In the rest of the book we are at a loss for even a hint in regard to the person of our author. Even as relates to the locality where it was written we are in great uncertainty. Still the unusual familiarity which it evinces with Persian matters, which is in strong and remarkable contrast with the ignorance of later apocryphal books, and especially its total lack of allusion to Judæa or Jerusalem, makes it very probable that the author did not belong to the parent body in Palestine, but to the Diaspora in Asia. According to the Talmud (*Baba Bathra*, p. 15, c. 1), the book of Esther belonged to those (Ezekiel, the twelve lesser prophets, Daniel and Esther) which were written by the scribes of the Great Synagogue. But it is evident that this tradition has reference not so much to its composition as to its authoritativeness, a final editorial supervision. In the same sense the Talmud speaks of Hezekiah and his college, that they wrote Isaiah, Proverbs, Canticles, and Ecclesiastes.

As regards the *time of the origin* of our book, we are told by ZUNZ (*Zeitschr. d. D. M. G.*, 1873, p. 687) that among other results obtained, he not only finds in it Persian and later Hebrew expressions, but also some terms derived from the Mishna. He assumes that the composition of Esther belongs to the post-Maccabæan period, in which the knowledge of the persecutions in Palestine had reached the Eastern countries. But he has cited only a very few expressions "which remind us of the linguistic usage of the Mishna," *viz.*: עָבַר with and without מִצְוַת, in the sense of "transgressing" from (chap. iii. 3; ix. 27, 28), עָשָׂה יוֹם טוֹב (chap. ix. 19) and וּמָה רָאוּ (chap. ix. 26), expressions which equally belong to the ante-Maccabæan period, and to the later age. Certain it is that our book belongs to the last written (youngest) in the Canon. In its language it stands nearest to Ecclesiastes, after that to Ezra, Nehemiah, and the book of Daniel. It has three later words, in common with Ecclesiastes, (זמן, בקשה, בירה) as well as with Ezra, Nehemiah, and 1 Chron., and שלט in common with Ecclesiastes and also with Nehemiah and the 119th Psalm. Five expressions are in common with Eccles. only (כשר, יותר ממני, זע, ובכן, אִלּוּ). The entire method or style, so far as it deviates from the mode of old and sacred historical composition, and approaches that of the 1

Book of Macc., and especially where the author endeavors to preserve an artistic and fascinating mode of development, would clearly show that he had already past one æra of progress, such as had not yet shown itself in the time of Ezra or Nehemiah, or at least first began in the age of those writers to break a way for itself. This fact also appears from the manner in which the author treats or rather neglects to treat of the relation which Judaism bears to heathenism, namely, its religious element, and more particularly in his non-reference to God and the divine government. Perhaps, in the period in which he wrote, the Greek age was near at hand or had already come. This would agree with the reference of Ahasuerus to Xerxes, whose position in ancient history is well defined. Still we must not insist too much on this feature, lest we come into conflict with the authorship of the Greek manuscripts and the consequent age of the Greek translation of the book.

The subscription to these Greek copies, which may have been added later, and has the air of being based upon an invention or supposition, relates that a certain Dositheus had brought to Egypt, in the fourth year of the reign of Ptolemy and Cleopatra, a translation of this epistle of Purim (*i. e.*, of our book of Esther, perhaps without the apocryphal additions), prepared by Lysimachus in Jerusalem. Among the four kings of the name of Ptolemy, who had queens named Cleopatra (B. C. 204–81), the one above-mentioned was probably Ptolemy Philometor, in whose reign, which was so friendly to the Jews (B. C. 181–145), the feast of Purim, and therefore also our book, might most readily find entrance into Egypt (comp. FRITZSCHE, *Exeg. Handbuch zu den Apokr.*, I., p. 72 sq.). It also says that there was a translation of Esther as early as the first half of the second century before Christ. Were we to conclude from 1 Macc. vii. 49, where the festival of Purim is not mentioned on the occasion of the celebration of the day of Nicanor the day previous, that the festival of Purim and the book of Purim had not found an earlier and more general recognition in Palestine than it did in Egypt so that at the time of the Maccabees it was not even known, still there would be nothing strange or contradictory in such an assumption. Nevertheless we could not reach any conclusion from this with respect to the time of the origin of our book. The Jews *in Palestine* were not threatened by the occurrences related in Esther, nor did the danger to the Jews there mentioned, or the defeat they brought upon their enemies, have much to do with their existence in that country. No inimical heathen people lived among the Palestinian Jews, to rise against them, or cause them to perish. Neighboring nations could only have shown their enmity by means of an invasion, which would not have differed greatly from an ordinary war (comp. HERZFELD, *Gesch. Israels*, II. 1, p. 8). Hence there was no immediate occasion for a festival of Purim for them. At all events such a conclusion as a mere *argumentum e silentio* would be very hazardous. It may not be improbable, indeed, that the day of the defeat of Nicanor, so far as we know concerning it (comp. § 2), might have been similar to our more modern days of battles and victories; and although at first there was a purpose of celebrating it annually, as a festival day, yet after several times, at last its memory became obliterated and it was forgotten by the majority. Hence the author of the 1st book of Maccabees had no real occasion to bring it into any relation to the day of Purim which came a day after.

Finally, we come to the question of the *integrity* of our book. If we hold fast to the Hebrew text, we will find that, as we have seen above (comp. chap. i. 9, 19; x.), it forms a beautifully arranged and greatly progressive whole, in which every individual part furnishes an integral and indispensable portion, and in which nothing essential is found wanting. But the case is very different in the second half of chapter ix. J. D. MICHAELIS asserts the beginning of this latter section to be the seventeenth verse, but BERTHEAU holds it to begin at vers. 20-32, in which reference is made to a letter by Mordecai to the Jews, and some of its contents are brought to light. Even the style of expression of this part is in unmistakable contrast with the rest of the book. קִיֵּם, in the sense of "establishing ordinances" or "making them authoritative," in verses 21, 27, 29, 31, and 32 (elsewhere only in Ruth iv. 7; Ezek. xiii. 6; Psa. cxix. 28, 106); the singular immediately preceding the plural of the subject, as in ver. 23 (וְקִבֵּל הַיְּהוּדִים); the fem. substantive in a neuter sense, as in ver. 25 (וּבְבֹאָהּ); further the mode of speech עִם־הַסֵּפֶר (ver. 25), וּמָה־רָאוּ (ver. 26), *etc.*, all this does not again occur in the rest of the book. To this we are also to add matters of fact. The short report which is given in vers. 24-26 concerning the occasion and significance of the festival of Purim, sounds quite different from what we would be led to expect from the previously given history. It is especially remarkable that no mention is made of Esther's interference. But it rather seems according to ver. 25 ("and when it came before the king he commanded by letters") as if the king had before been ignorant of the intention of Haman, at least with its real import, and only needed to be more fully informed with regard to it; and that he then at once proceeded against Haman. One would think that the author would have apprehended the chief facts at issue quite differently, if he himself there gave their *resumé*. This *resumé* seems to be based upon a mode of statement by which many things that appear essential and important, are treated as of less significance, or are entirely omitted. Now we would not venture to assert, as does BERTHEAU, that the method of statement, lying at the basis, was in such flat contradiction to the substance of our book. We can easily conceive that the author may have differently presented the leading events in different parts of his work. Certainly the *resumé* of vers. 24–26 falls far short of proving the contrary. Again between verses 15-19 on the one hand, in which a part of the Jews celebrate the 15th of Adar on the 14th, even in the author's time; and vers. 20 sqq., on the other hand, where the celebration of *both* days is introduced through the writings of Mordecai, a contradiction is very unjustly urged by BERTHEAU (comp. chap. ix. 19).

We may presume from the peculiarities found in the section verses 20–32 there is contained in it an element more fundamental than elsewhere. Yet we have no right to argue from the absence of all real contradictions that the author had himself expunged them.—According to verse 20 there did exist a book of Purim referable to Mordecai. Perhaps the same one is meant in verse 32, by the writing in which the orders of Esther were recorded. It is quite possible that from it our author should have taken this section extending from vers. 20 to 32.

But next to the original text we must have regard to the older versions. In the Septuagint version there are several additions, which Luther threw out as being "apocryphal parts in Esther." But these are so interwoven into the text of the Greek Bible that they could easily be held to be integral parts of the book. Thus, to begin with, there is in chap. i. a dream of Mordecai, in which are indicated the most important phases of the subsequent history. In chap. iii. we find an edict by Ahasuerus ordering the extermination of the Jews. In chap. iv. there is a prayer by Mordecai, and also one by Esther, which they offered in their distress. Chap. v. has an explicit description of the appearance of Esther before Ahasuerus. Finally in chap. viii. 13 we find the new edict, issued by Mordecai, favoring the Jews, and as a conclusion of the whole an interpretation of the dream that had been indicated in chap. i.

Now the question is, What are we to think of these expansions? The assumption of BELLARMINE (*De verbo Dei*, chap. vii., § 10) and of DE ROSSI (*Specimen variarum lectionum s. textus et Chaldaica Esteris additamenta*, Romæ, 1782), to whom SCHOLZ may also be added (*Introd.*, II., p. 538 sqq.), is that, originally, there were two books of Esther in existence; a larger one, from which these additions of the Greek version were taken, and a smaller, which was perhaps only an extract of the former. That the latter, however, should be regarded as our present Hebrew book, is not to-day held by any one. Equally untenable is the position taken by JOS. LANGEN, that the passages referred to were taken from Mordecai's "memoirs" (comp. ch. ix. 29 sqq.), or even from the annals of the king of Persia (comp. chap. ii. 23; vi. 1). See LANGEN, *Die deuterocanonischen Stücke des Buches Esther*, Freiburg, 1862). The hypotheses in question were only originated to defend the canonicity of these additions decreed by the Council of Trent. A second, more enlarged book of Esther, whose expansion has been gratuitously assumed, but which was not regarded worthy of preservation, is nothing more than a wilful and highly improbable fiction, as indeed is virtually conceded by LANGEN. But as to these additions themselves, which according to LANGEN still have documentary value, we would call attention to the following considerations:

(1) The dream of Mordecai stands in such a slight connection with the rest of the history

that its very presence declares it a useless and unessential work. In order that it might not appear too isolated, its author has connected it with the discovery of the conspiracy of the two court officials, as if this were the first and the chief point of the general history, especially of the enmity of Haman against Mordecai. But thereby he becomes involved in contradictions with the original book, as is evident in departures from the latter traceable in the additions. For example, it is stated that Mordecai had his dream in the second year of the reign of Artaxerxes (Achashverosh). Consequently he must then also have discovered the conspiracy. But according to chap. ii. 21 sqq. these court officers entered into a conspiracy after the elevation of Esther. It must, therefore, have been in the seventh year of the reign of the king. Again Mordecai is represented as having already received some presents, by which the jealousy of Haman was intensified; whereas in chap. vi. 3 it is stated that he had not yet been rewarded. But what makes the whole account very suspicious is that the contents of our book would be materially altered and weakened by this incentive to the hostility of Haman towards Mordecai. The conflict between heathenism and Judaism, as such, would be transformed into an ordinary contest between two rival aspirants.

(2) These additions contrast so strongly in their spirit and tone with the genuine book of Esther, that we are obliged to look for their origin elsewhere. The religious element, which in the real book of Esther is so rarely manifested, is in them very decidedly, we might say extravagantly, expressed—so much so that we could properly accuse them of a species of hypocrisy.

(3) Even the diction makes it clearly probable that the passages referred to were originally written in Greek. Thus the circumstance speaks against them, that where the conference between Esther and the king is related, they have a strong Græcizing, and even an Alexandrine romantic character; which, according to EWALD, reminds us very forcibly of the 2d book of Maccabees. So also the notorious fact, that for a long time they were accepted by the Jews who spoke Greek, but not by the others, at least not by the authors of the Targums. In keeping with their Greek-Alexandrine origin, is the peculiarity that the author of these additions in several places designates Haman as being a *Macedonian* (Μακεδών) instead of an Agagite. This is done, doubtless, to make the epithet intelligible to his own vicinity and age, as that of an enemy of the Jewish people (in accordance with the text yet to be referred to, but which is rarely found at the end of the first addition; and also according to the edict interpolated at chap. viii. 13, as well as chap. ix. 24, where no tampering hand would be likely to be traced).

Doubtless we here have only embellishments, which some one has permitted himself to add, on the ground of tradition, or through his own poetic fancy. The comfort which the book gave was too desirable for it to wait long to become a favorite book with the people. They might indeed, perhaps, have felt the absence of the religious element. But, as has already been remarked, the Jewish community did not stand in such a receptive attitude towards those books written later, as towards the older sacred writings, which for some time previous had received a closed form. Yet they infallibly detected these suspicious passages by the interrupting of the general scope of the work by the conjectures thereby made by the mention of edicts that were decreed, as if those missing things should be added to complete the narrative. Indeed some one had evidently felt called upon, at these interesting points of detail, to expand the narrative occasionally. But how and when were enlarging or finishing touches given? That these additions had their origin in the reason just mentioned was held by Jerome, who in the preface to Esther remarks: "The Vulgate edition draws this book hither and thither by redundant coves (*laciniosis sinibus*) of words, adding whatever could on the occasion be said or heard; as is the custom in school exercises, after taking a theme to think out what words he can use who has sustained an injury, or he who has done an injury."

We may also observe the presumed progress of this tradition in the history of the book of Esther. In an earlier text of the Septuagint version (in Cod. 19, 93 and 1086 first published by JAMES USSHER in his *Syntagma de Græca LXX. interpretum versione*, Lond., 1655; next by FRITZSCHE in his 'ΕΣΘΗΡ, *duplicem libri textum*, ed. Turici, 1848), we find a special mode of treatment, which, of course, is but a remodelling of the original text. This text changed what was unintelligible and objectionable, and contracted what was too broadly asserted; thereby removing contradictions. But it also added other emendations (comp. FRITZSCHE, *Exeg. Handbuch zu den Apokr.*, p. 70 sq.). JOSEPHUS, on his part, holds unreservedly to the Septuagint version, especially following the more ancient text. But he omits Mordecai's dream and its interpretation, and thus discloses a growing tradition by relating that a Jewish slave, Barnabazu, had revealed to Mordecai the conspiracy of the door-keepers spoken of in chap. ii. Even the old Latin translation, made prior to Jerome's time, used some free ornamentations (comp. FRITZSCHE, as above p. 74 sq.).

The Chaldee paraphrases or Targums are very important to the understanding of our book, chiefly because they have not adopted the Greek additions. If the latter had been at all genuine and authentic, they must have done very differently. A tradition would probably have arisen which, after the Talmudic period, would have asserted its authority. Still we must notice that some of them at least have embellishments. Among the earliest of the Chaldee versions we regard the Targum on Esther as now found in the Antwerp Polyglot Bible. This is nothing more than an exact translation of the Heb. book. But the so-called first Targum on Esther found in the London Polyglot (comp. *Targum prius et posterius in Estheram nunc primum in ling. Lat. transl.*, stud. et op. FRANC. TAILERI, Lond., 1665, 4to.; see also another edition by WOLF, *Bibl. Hebr.*, II., p. 1171 sqq.). This follows very closely the Hebrew book verse for verse. Hence it has no place for the dream of Mordecai. But in order to give our book a higher and wider relation, it designates Ahasuerus in ch. i. 1 as the one in whose time the building of the temple was at a stand-still, and looks upon Haman as the one to blame for that delay. It understands that the two courtiers in chapter ii. 21 entered into a conspiracy against the king, because they saw Mordecai sitting in the Sanhedrim, which had been built in the king's gate by Esther's orders, and they deemed themselves thereby crowded out of favor.—בְּיוֹמַיָא הָאִנּוּן מָרְדְּכַי יָתִיב בְּסַנְהֶדְרִין דְּתַקִּינַת לָהּ אֶסְתֵּר בִּתְרַע־מַלְכָּא. It has also discovered that Haman, who is poetically represented in the beginning of ch. iii. as having been promoted for the exaltation of the divine glory, is angry at Mordecai above all others, inasmuch as he himself wishes to make his own daughter queen in the place of Esther. It ignores the prayers which the Greek Bible puts into the mouth of Mordecai and Esther. Still it points out in ch. iv. 16 that Esther requested not only that a fast should be observed on her behalf, but also that they should pray day and night. Besides it puts a prayer in an altogether arbitrary manner into the mouth of Esther herself in ch. v., in which she does not, as is stated in the Greek Bible, have regard to her people first and chiefly, but to herself purely: "Lord of the universe, do not give me over into the hands of this uncircumcised man, and fulfil not the desire of this wicked Haman on me!" *etc.* The so-called second Targum which, especially in ch. i. 1, has a style at once homiletical and extravagantly rhetorical, but which in general is more simple and brief than the former one, knows just as little of Mordecai's dream.* But, on the other hand, in ch. iii. 3, Mordecai is made to declare that God alone is to be worshipped, and to show the baseness of man and the exalted character of God. In ch. iii. 8 Haman in a very round-about way exposes the customs and ordinances of the Jews. An edict of Ahasuerus, having for its object the destruction of the Jews, is here inserted though it is first properly supplemented in ch. iv. 1. But this is just as peculiar as the prayer of Esther referred to in ch. v. 1.

The book ascribed to JOSIPON BEN GORION contains the dream and prayer of Mordecai and also that of Esther in its ch. ii. 1–3. It has also very faithfully copied from the Greek Bible the statement of the appearance of Esther before the king; and it has formed the medium by which such passages might be transmitted to the Jews speaking or writing in Hebrew, in the Midrashim, *etc.* We find the prayer and dream of Mordecai, as given in JOSIPON's work carried over verbatim into the oldest Midrash on Esther (WOLF, *Bibl. Hebr.*, ii., p. 1332; and ZUNZ, as above, p. 264).

The Chaldaic section also, beginning with the superscription: "A prayer of Mordecai;

* It is an erroneous or indefinite mode of expression when ZUNZ, in his work (*Die gottesdienstlichen Vorträge der Juden*, p. 121), remarks: "The dream and prayers of Mordecai and Esther are found to vary very much from the Greek text, especially in the second book of the Targum of the Book of Esther," *etc.*

a prayer of Esther, and a dream of the former," and occurring in several not very ancient manuscripts of the Old Testament (comp. ZUNZ, p. 121), is really nothing more than an almost literal translation of JOSIPON ii. 1–2. DE ROSSI was certainly in error when he regarded this as a main proof for his theory, that originally there must have been a more copious book of Esther, out of which he took these Chaldaic passages to be the original documents preserved.

[The importance of these apocryphal additions to the book of Esther demands some further notice. We condense the following particulars from the article in MCCLINTOCK'S and STRONG'S *Cyclopædia, s. v.*:—

In the Septuagint and Old Latin versions these additions are dispersed through the canonical book, forming therewith a well-digested whole; and they therefore have in those versions no separate title. JEROME separated them in his edition, and removed (or rather added) them to the end of the book because they are not in the Hebrew, and they consequently appear in the Vulgate as the last seven chapters of the book. LUTHER entirely severed the apocryphal books from the canonical, placing the additions in question under a separate title; and the English Version has followed him in this, designating these pieces as "the rest of the chapters of the Book of Esther, which are found neither in the Hebrew nor in the Chaldee," and numbering them as "part of the tenth chapter after the Greek," and chaps. xi.—xvi.

The design of these additions evidently is to give a more decidedly religious tone to the record contained in the book of Esther, and to show more plainly how wonderfully the God of Israel interfered to save His people and confound their enemies. This the writer has effected by elaborating upon the events narrated in the canonical volume the following pieces:

1. Chap. i. 1 of the canonical book is preceded in the Septuagint by a piece which tells us that Mordecai, who was in the service of Artaxerxes, dreamed of the dangers that threatened his people and of their deliverance (vers. 1–12). He afterwards discovered a conspiracy against the king, which he disclosed to him, and was greatly rewarded for it (vers. 13–18). In the Vulg. and English this constitutes chap. xi. 2—xii. 6.

2. Between vers. 13 and 14 of chap. iii. of the canonical book the Septuagint gives a copy of the king's edict, addressed to all the satraps, to destroy without compassion that foreign and rebellious people, the Jews, for the good of the Persian nation, on the fourteenth day of the twelfth month of the coming year. In the Vulgate and English this is chap. xiii. 1–7.

3. At the end of chap. iv. 17 of the canonical book the Septuagint has two prayers of Mordecai and Esther, that God may avert the impending destruction of His people. In the Vulgate and English this is chap. xiii. 8—xiv.

4. In the midst of vers. 1 and 2 of chap. v. of the canonical book the Septuagint inserts a detailed account of Esther's visit to the king. This is chap. xv. of the Vulgate and English.

5. Between vers. 13 and 14 of chap. viii. of the canonical book the Septuagint gives a copy of the edict which the king sent to all his satraps, in accordance with the request of Mordecai and Esther, to abolish his former decree against the Jews. This is chapter xvi. of the Vulgate and English.

6. At the close of the canonical book, chap. x. 3, the Septuagint has a piece in which we are told that Mordecai had now recalled to his mind his extraordinary dream, and seen how literally it had been fulfilled in all its particulars (vers. 4–9). It also gives an account of the proclamation of the Purim festival in Egypt (vers. 10–13). This is given first in the apocrypha portion of the Vulgate, and English (as chap. x. 4–13).

7. The whole book in the Septuagint is closed with the following entry: "In the fourth year of the reign of Ptolemæus and Cleopatra, Dositheus, who said he was a priest and Levite, and Ptolemy his son, brought this epistle of Phurim, which they said was the same, and that Lysimachus, the son of Ptolemy, that was in Jerusalem, had interpreted it." In the Vulgate and English this forms chap. xi. 1.

The patriotic spirit with which the Jewish nation so fondly expatiated upon the remarkable events and characters of by-gone days, and which gave rise to those beautiful legends preserved in their copious literature, scarcely ever had a better opportunity afforded to it for employing its richly inventive powers to magnify the Great Jehovah, embalm the memory of the heroes, and brand the names of the enemies of Israel, than in the canonical book of Esther. Nothing could be more natural for a nation who "had a zeal of God" than *to supply the name of God*, and *to point out more distinctly* His interposition in their behalf in an inspired book, which, though recording their marvellous escape from destruction, had for some reasons omitted avowedly to acknowledge the Lord of Israel. The temptation was too great to be resisted, and, as in the case of all apocryphal writing, we are readily enabled by this meretricious embellishment to detect the false amid the genuine.

Besides the book implies and suggests far more than it records, and it cannot be doubted that there are many other things connected with the history it contains which were well known at the time, and were transmitted traditionally and otherwise to the nation. This is evident from the fact that JOSEPHUS (*Antiq.* XI. 6, 6 sq.) gives the edict for the destruction of the Jews in the Persian empire, the prayers of Mordecai and Esther, and the second edict authorizing the Jews to destroy their enemies, also mentioning the name of the eunuch's servant, a Jew, who betrayed the conspiracy to Mordecai, and citing other passages for the Persian chronicles, read to Ahasuerus, besides that relating to Mordecai, as well as amplifications of the king's speech to Haman, *etc.* The same appears in the fact that the second Targum, the Chaldee published by DE ROSSI, and JOSEPHUS BEN-GORIDON (ed. Breithaupt, p. 74 sq.) give the dream of Mordecai, as well as his prayer and that of Esther.

The first addition, in which Mordecai *foresees* in a dream both the dangers and the salvation of his people, is in accordance with the desire to give the whole a more religious tone. The latter part of this addition is intended to develope more distinctly the brief statement given in the canonical book of the loyal service of Mordecai, so as to explain so important an incident. In like manner the second addition originated from the fact that chap. iii. 13 of the canonical book speaks of the royal edict; hence this piece pretends to furnish said document in full. The same is the case with the third addition, which aims to supply the prayers said in chap. iv. 17 to have been offered by Mordecai and Esther. So also the fourth addition, giving a detailed account of Esther's interview with the king, originated in a desire to furnish more complete information upon a fact merely alluded to in the canonical passage. The fifth addition originated in the same manner as the second, namely, in an attempt to supply a copy of the royal edict; while the sixth addition ingeniously concludes with an interpretation of the dream in the first addition. The final entry was apparently intended to give authority to this Greek version of Esther by pretending that it was a certified translation from the Hebrew original. Ptolemy Philometor, who is here meant, began to reign B. C. 181. He is the same who is frequently mentioned in 1 Macc. (*e. g.*, x. 57; xi. 12; comp. JOSEPHUS, *Ant.* XIII. 4, 1 and 5; CLINTON, *Fasti Hellen.*, III. 393). Dositheus seems to be a Greeek version of Mattitiah. Ptolemy was also a common name for Jews at that time. Thus every one of these additions is naturally accounted for as a fabrication having an adequate and natural motive in the connection.

From what has been remarked above, it will be at once apparent that these apocryphal additions were neither manufactured by the translator of the canonical Esther into Greek, nor are they the production of the Alexandrian, nor of any other school or individual, embracing some of the numerous national stories connected with this marvellous deliverance of God's ancient people, the authorship of which is lost in the nation. Many of them date as far back as the nucleus of the event itself, around which they cluster, and all of them grew up at first in the vernacular language of the people (*i. e.*, the Hebrew or Aramaic), but afterwards assumed the complexion and language of the countries in which the Jews happened to settle down. Besides the above references which lead us to these conclusions, we refer also to the two Midrashim published by JELLINEK in his *Bethham-Midrash*, I. (Lpz. 1853), 1 sq.

It is of this Septuagint version that ATHANASIUS (*Test. Epist.*, p. 39, Oxford translation) spoke when he assigned the Book of Esther to the non-canonical books; and this also is, perhaps, the reason why, in some of the lists of the canonical books, Esther is not named, *e. g.*, in those of Melito of Sardis, and Gregory Nazianzen (see WHITTAKER, *Disput. on H. Script.*, Parker Society, pp. 57–58; COSIN on the *Canon of Scripture*, pp. 49, 50), unless in these it is included under some other book, as Ruth or Esdras (LEE, *Dissert. on 2 Esdras*, p. 25). The fathers, who generally regarded the Septuagint as containing the sacred Scriptures of the Old Testament, mostly believed in the canonicity of the additions likewise. Even ORIGEN, though admitting that they are not in the Hebrew, defended their canonicity (*Ep. ad Abiram*, ed. West, p. 225), and the Council of Trent pronounced the whole book of Esther, with all its parts, to be canonical. These additions, however, were never included in the Hebrew canon, and the fact that JOSEPHUS quotes them only shows that he believed them to be historically true, but not inspired. JEROME, who knew better than any other father what the ancient Jews included in their canon, most emphatically declares them to be spurious (*Præf. in Esth.*). SIXTUS SINENSIS, in spite of the Council of Trent, speaks of these additions in the same condemnatory manner.

See, in addition to the literature elsewhere cited in this connection, The Targum *Sheni* on Esther, in WALTON'S *Polyglott*, Vol. IV.; EICHHORN, *Einleitung in d. Apost. Schriften d. A. T.* (Leipzig, 1795), p. 483: HOTTINGER, *Thesaurus*, p. 494; SCHNURRER (ed.), *Variæ Lectiones Estheris* (Tüb., 1783); HERZFELD, *Geschichte d. Volkes Israel* (Nordhausen, 1857, Vol. I., p. 363 sq.); KEIL, *Lehrb. der Historisch-Kritischen Einleit.* (ed. 1859), p. 105 sq.]

§ 5. LITERATURE.

Jewish expositors, next to the Targums, Midrashim and Rabboth, of which ZUNZ speaks (*Gottesdienstliche Vorträge d. Yuden*, espec. p. 35, 61 and 170 sqq.), have published commentaries, some of which embrace the whole of the hagiographa (comp. the literature on Ezra and Nehemiah), while others are only on the five Megilloth (Canticles, Ruth, Lamentations, Ecclesiastes and Esther).

To the latter belong ביאור (Elucidation) על חמש מגילות by ABDIAS SPHORNI, an Italian physician, printed in Venice, 4to.; also פירוש or *exposition* of the five Megilloth by ELISA GALIKO, president of the Synagogue in Safed, publ. in Venice, in 1587, 4to.; also short explanations by JOSEPH TITATZACK or TAITZACK, a Spaniard, who likewise commented on Daniel (Venice, 1608, 4to.). So also ISRAEL ARAMAH, a Spaniard, who commented on the Pentateuch and the Megilloth ([Constantinople, 1518, 4to.], Venice, 1573); MOSES ALMOSHINUS (Venice, 1597, 4to.); R. ABRAHAM, of Heilbronn (under the title of אהבת ציון, *Amor Sionis*, Lublin, 1639), and others. As specially relating to Esther, we may mention the commentaries by R. ISAAK LEON, a Spaniard (Venice, 1565, 4to.; see BARTOLOCCI, in *Bibl. magna Rabb.*); by R. SALOMON BEN ZEMACH (תפ ארת ישראל); by R. ABRAHAM BEN ISAAK ZAHALON (Zabulon or Zebulon), which is a literal, allegorical and moral exposition (ישע אלהים, Venice, 1595, 4to.); by R. SAMUEL BEN JUDAH VALERIUS (יד המלך, Venice, 1585, 4to.; by R. SALOMON LEVI ALCABAZ, R. LEO and others (in CARPZOV, *Introd.*, I., p. 375).

Few Christian theologians have treated of the book of Esther. The Church-fathers have left us no exposition or treatment of it at all. Of Roman Catholic authors and their works we may mention: DIONYS. CARTHUSIANI, *Enarrationes in libr. Hester, etc.* (Coloniæ, 1534, fol.); a German exposition of Esther by JOHN FERNS (Mayence, 1567); FRANC FEUARDENTII *Commentaria* (Paris, 1585, Colon., 1595); SERARII *Comm. in Tobiam, Judith, Esther et Maccabæos* (Mayence, 1610); OLIVIERII BONARTII *Comm. literalis et moralis* (Colon., 1647); and DIDACI CELADÆIS *Comm. cum duplici tractatu de convivio Ahasueri mystico, i. e., De Eucharistia et de Esther figurata i. e. beata Virgine* (Lugduni, 1648, fol.). The commentary of FEUARDENTIUS, which is written in easy and almost too flowing Latin, far surpasses all those before mentioned. All the others savor of an intolerably insipid allegorical identification of Esther with the *beata cœlestis Regina* (the Virgin Mary); whereas this of Feuardentius is marked by sober, sound and very practical exegesis, and is based on much general reading. Although he now and then includes the Lutherans among the Hamanites to be exterminated, still Feuardentius has very perceptibly and early taken pattern after the evangelical exegesis, and copied some of the work of BRENZ almost literally.

On the part of the Evangelical Church BRENZ treats of the book of Esther in [*Commentarii* (Tübing., 1575); in Engl. by Stockwood, Lond., 1584, 4to.; also in] *Operr.* II.; also VICT. STRIGEL, *Libri Esdræ, Nehemiæ, Esther et Ruth, ad Ebraicam veritatem recogniti et argumentis atque scholiis illustrati* (Lips., 1571, 1572, 8vo.). There follow: COUR. PELLICAN, *Comment. Bibl.* (Figuri, 1583, fol.); LUD. LAVATER, *Homiliæ* (Figuri, 1586); RUD. WALTHER (Gualtherus) *Homiliarum sylva* (Figuri, 158, 8vo.); FRANZ BURMANN, a German Commentary published at Frankford, 1695; BALTH. KERNER, *Ehren-Krone der demuthigen Esther* (Ulm, 1666); GOTTFRIED MEISNER, *Niedrigen aber nachmals erhohen Esther, mit biblisch-historischen Schmuck angethan* (Hamburg, 1687); COM. ADAMUS, *Observatt. theol. phil.* (Gron., 1710, on chap. ii.).

Among those of more modern date may be mentioned a work which has not been referred to in the literature on Ezra and Nehemiah; CRUSIUS, *De usu libri Estheræ ad praxin vitæ Christianæ* (Ultraj.,1775).

The question: Who is to be understood by the Ahasuerus of our book? [which will be fully discussed in the Exegetical Notes on ch. i. 1] has been treated by FRANC. WOKENIUS in his *Commentatio in l. Estheræ* (1730), and by ASTER in his *Diss. phil. de Esteræ cum Ahasuero conjugio* (Wittenberg, 1730), both of whom held that Astyages is meant, although JOS. SCALIGER had given the correct interpretation, as also JOH. WAUCKEL, in his *Dissert. de Assuero Estheræ marito*, which he directed specially against JOS. SCALIGER.

As introductory works we may notice: SCHULZE, *De fide historica l. Estheræ*, in the *Bibl. Hagana*, V., VI.; KELLE, *Vindiciæ Estheræ* (Frib., 1820); MICH. BAUMGARTEN, *De fide libri Estheræ Comm. hist. crit.* (Hal., 1839); J. A. NICKES, *De Estheræ libro et ad eum quæ pertinent vaticiniis et Psalmis libri tres* (Romæ, 1856); also the articles on Esther by ROEDIGER in Ersch and Gruber's *Encycl.*, by BAUMGARTEN in HERZOG'S *Real-encycl.*, and by REUSS in SCHENKEL'S *Bibel-Lexikon.*

[**Additional Literature.**—RABAN MAURUS, *Commentaria* (in his *Opera*); BANOLAS, פירוש (Riva di Trento, 1560, 4to.); ASHKENAZI, יוכף לקח (Cremona, 1576, 4to., *etc.*); MELAMMED, מאמר מרדכי (Constantinople, 1585, 4to.); DRUSIUS, *Annotationes* (Leyden, 1586, 4to.); ALSHEICH, משאת משה (Venice, 1601, 4to.); COOPER, *Notes* (London, 1609, 4to.); D'AQUINE, *Raschii Scholia* (Paris, 1622, 4to.); MOLDER, *Dispositiones* (Dantzig, 1625, 4to.); SANCTIUS, *Commentarii* (Lyden, 1628, fol.); COUZIO, *Commento* (Chieri, 1628, 4to.); DURAN, ספר מגלת (Venice, 1632, 4to.); CROMMIUS, *Theses* (Lovan, 1632, 4to.); MERKEL, מירא דכרא (Lublin, 1637, 4to.); MONTANUS, *Commentarius* (Madrid, 1648, fol.); TRAPP, *Commentary* (London, 1656, fol.); JACKSON, *Explanation* (London, 1658, 4to.); BARNES, *Paraphrasis poetica* (London, 1679, 8vo.); RAMBACH, *Notæ* (in his *Adnot. V. T.* II. 1043 sqq.); HEUMANN, *Estheræ auctoritas* (Gotting., 1736, 4to.); MEIR, משתה יין (Furth., 1737, 8vo.); NESTORIDES, *Annotazioni* (Venice, 1746, 4to.); AUCHER, *De auctoritate Estheræ* (Hanniæ, 1772, 4to.); VOS, *Oratio* (Ultraj., 1775, 4to.); ZINCK, *Commentarius* (Augsb., 1780, 4to.); DE ROSSI, *Variæ Lectiones* (Rome, 1782, 8vo.); PERELES, גלת הכתרת (Prague, 1784, 4to.); WOLFSSOHN, אסתר (Berlin, 1788, 8vo.); SAMSON, *Discourses* (Edinburg, 1804, 12mo.); LOWE, אור הרש (Nouydwer, 1704, 4to.); SCHIRMER, *Observationes* (Vratiolav, 1820, 8vo.); CALMBERG, *Commentarius* (Hamburgh, 1837, 4to.); MCCRIE, *Lectures* (in his *Works*, 1838, 8vo.); MORGAN, *Esther typical* (London, 1855, 8vo.); CORDTHWAITE, *Lectures* (London, 1858, 12mo.); DAVIDSON, *Lectures* (Edinburgh, 1859, 8vo.); BERTHEAU, *Kommentar.* (in the *Kurzgefastes exeget. Handbuch des A. T.*, Leipzig, 1862, 8vo.); OPPERT, *Commentaire d'après les inscriptions Perses* (Paris, 1864, 8vo.); WORDSWORTH, *Notes* (in his *Commentary on the Bible*, Lond., 1866, 8vo.); KEIL, *Biblical Commentary* (translated from the German of Keil and Delitzsch, *Commentary on the O. T.*, Edinburgh, 1873, 8vo.); TERRY, *Commentary* (in WHEDON'S *Commentary on the Old Test.*, New York, 1873, 12mo.); RAWLINSON, *Commentary* (in the *Speaker's Commentary*, London and New York, 1873, 8vo.]

THE BOOK OF ESTHER.

PART FIRST.

ORIGIN AND INCREASE OF DANGER TO THE JEWS.

CHAPS. I.—V.

INTRODUCTION:

The Occasion of the History. The Feast of Ahasuerus and Vashti's Rejection.

CHAP. I. 1–22.

I. *Ahasuerus assembles the princes of his empire around him, and prepares a great feast, in which he endeavours to show his power and glory.* Vers. 1–8.

1 Now [And] *it* came to pass [was] in *the* days of Ahasuerus [Achashverosh], (this
is Ahasuerus which reigned [the *one* being king] from India [Hodu] even unto
2 [and till] Ethiopia [Cush], *over* a hundred and seven and twenty provinces,) *That*
in those days when [as] the king Ahasuerus sat on *the* throne of his kingdom, which
3 *was* in Shushan the palace,[1] In *the* third year of his reign, he made a feast[2] unto all
his princes and his servants; the power[3] of Persia [Paras] and Media [Madai], the
4 nobles[4] and [*the*] princes of the provinces, *being* before him. When he showed *the*
riches of his glorious [*the* glory of his] kingdom, and *the* honour of his excellent
5 [*the* excellence of his] majesty, many days, *even* a hundred and fourscore days. And
when these days *were* [*had*] expired, the king made a feast[2] unto all the people
that *were* present [found] in Shushan the palace,[1] both unto great and [to great and
6 even to] small, seven days, in *the* court of *the* garden of the king's palace; *Where*
were white [linen], green [cotton], and blue [violet] *hangings*, fastened with cords
of fine linen and purple to [on] silver rings and pillars of marble: *the* beds *were*
of [*there were* beds of] gold and silver, upon a pavement of red [white] and blue
7 [marble], and white [pearl], and black marble [colored stone]. And *they* gave
them [*there was* a giving of] drink in vessels of gold, (*the* vessels being [and the
vessels *were*] diverse one from another,) and royal wine in abundance, according to
8 *the* state [hand] of the king. And the drinking *was* according to the law; none
did compel: for so the king *had* appointed [ordained] to [upon] all the officers [every
great *one*] of his house, that they should do [to do] according to every man's plea-
sure.

II. *Queen Vashti refuses to appear before the king, and he is very much incensed thereat.* Verses 9–12.

9 Also Vashti the queen made a feast[2] for [of] *the* women *in* the royal house which
10 *belonged* to king Ahasuerus. On the seventh day, when [as] *the* heart of the king
was merry [good] with [the] wine, he commanded [said to] Mehuman, Biztha, Har-
bona, Bigtha, and Abagtha, Zethar, and Carcas, the seven chamberlains [eunuchs]

11 that served in *the* presence of Ahasuerus the king, To bring Vashti the queen be-
fore the king, with *the* crown royal [of royalty], to show the people [peoples] and
12 the princes her beauty: for she *was* fair to look on [good of appearance]. But
[And] the queen Vashti refused to come at *the* king's commandment [word] [which
was] by [*the* hand of] *his* [the] chamberlains [eunuchs]: therefore [and] was the
king very wroth, and his anger burned [heat devoured] in him.

III. *In accordance with the counsel of his wise men the queen is rejected by a public decree of the king.*

Verses 13–22.

13 Then [And] the king said to the wise *men*, which knew [knowers of] the times,
(for so *was the* king's manner [word] toward [before] all that knew [knowers of]
14 law and judgment: And the next unto him *was* Carshena, Shethar, Admatha, Tar-
shish, Meres, Marsena, *and* Memucan, *the* seven princes of Persia [Paras] and Me-
dia [Madai], which saw [seers of] *the* king's face, *and* which sat [the sitters] *the*
15 first in the kingdom); What shall we do [*is there* to do] unto [in *the case of*] the
queen Vashti according to law, because [upon *the fact* that] she hath not performed
[done] *the* commandment of the king Ahasuerus by [*the* hand of] the chamber-
16 lains [eunuchs]? And Memucan answered [said] before the king and the princes,
Vashti the queen hath not done wrong to [upon] the king only, but [for] *also* to
[upon] all the princes, and to [upon] all the people [peoples] that *are* in all the
17 provinces of the king Ahasuerus. For *this* deed [word] of the queen shall come
abroad [go forth] unto [upon] all [the] women, so that they shall [to cause *them* to]
despise their husbands in their eyes, when it shall be reported [in their saying], The
king Ahasuerus commanded [said] Vashti the queen to be brought [to bring] in
18 before him, but [and] she came not. *Likewise* shall *the* ladies [princesses] of Per-
sia [Paras] and Media [Madai] say this day unto all *the* king's princes, which
[who] have heard[5] *of the* deed [word] of the queen. Thus [And] *shall there arise*
19 too much [according to plenty] contempt and wrath. If *it* please [*be* good upon]
the king, let *there* go [forth] a royal commandment [word] from [before] him, and
let it be written among the laws of *the* Persians [Paras] and *the* Medes [Madai],
that [and let] it be not altered [not pass], That Vashti come no more [not] before
king Ahasuerus; and let the king give her royal estate [royalty] unto another [her
20 neighbor] that *is* better than she. And *when the* king's decree which he shall make
shall be published [heard] throughout [in] all his empire [kingdom], (for it *is*
great,) [and] all the wives [women] shall give to their husbands honour, both to
21 great and small. And the saying [word] pleased [was good in the eyes of] the
22 king and the princes; and the king did according to *the* word of Memucan: For
[And] he sent letters into [unto] all *the* king's provinces, into [unto] every province
according to *the* writing[6] thereof, and to [unto] every people after their language,
that every man should bear rule [for every man to be prince] in his *own* house, and
that it should be published [spoken] according to *the* language of every [his] people.

TEXTUAL AND GRAMMATICAL.

[1] [Ver. 2. בִּירָה, whence *βάρις*, denotes properly a *fortress*, hence the *capital*.—Tr.]

[2] [Ver. 3. מִשְׁתֶּה, *a drinking, i. e., a banquet*, in which the wine was the principal feature, as represented freely on the Assyrian monuments.—Tr.]

[3] [Ver. 3. חַיִל, military *force*.—Tr.]

[4] [Ver. 3. פַּרְתְּמִים, a Persian word Hebraized. As it is here in the "absolute form," it does not qualify "provinces" following, but stands as an official designation, probably of civil rank at court.—Tr.]

[5] [Ver. 18. The English Version has unwarrantably transposed this clause ("which have heard," *etc.*), which belongs to "ladies," *etc.*, above.—Tr.]

[6] [Ver. 22. כְּתָב here evidently signifies the *style of writing* peculiar to each province. Thus the cuneiform differs according to the several districts of the Persian empire.—Tr.]

EXEGETICAL AND CRITICAL.

Vers. 1–8. *The King's Banquet.*—The point of departure in this history is formed by a feast at which Ahasuerus was unexpectedly humbled and provoked to wrath, while purposing to show his great majesty.

Ver. 1. **Now it came to pass,** *etc.* The sentence begun here, in its chief fact really follows ver. 3. There it is stated that Ahasuerus made a feast in the third year of his reign. The ו at the beginning has not the conjunctive sense that it has in Ezra i. 1, but stands more indefinite. A Hebrew would understand this as a matter of which much had already been related, and of which the following is only a continuation. Thus he would proceed often with a ו without attaching any definite meaning to it. וַיְהִי has come to be a *conventional formula for a beginning*, comp. Jonah i. 4; Ez. i. 1; Isa. liii. 2, *et al.* **Ahasuerus** (Achashverosh) written in cuneiform letters (comp. Lassen, *Zeitschr. zur Kunde des M. L.* VI., p. 123 sqq.; Benfey, *Die pers. Keilinschrift*, p. 63 sqq) *Khsy-arsha*, whence *Cyaxares* (comp. Dan. ix. 1), or *Khsay-arsha*, whence *Xerxes* (comp. Ezra iv. 6), early interpreted by Herodotus (vi. 98, *etc.*), as meaning ἀρήϊος, according to Spiegel (*Eranische Altherthumskunde*, II. p. 377), *a mighty man*, here does not mean, as in Dan. ix. 1, *Cyaxares* I, the father of Astyages, as Ferrand holds (*Réflexions sur la religion Chrétienne*, I., p. 159), and Des Vignoles (*Chronol.* II., p. 274), and Nickes (*De Estheræ libro*, I., p. 43–59) would have it, since they especially insist that, according to chap. ii. 5 sq., Mordecai belonged to the first period of the exile, and that our book nowhere indicates that a new people had again arisen in Jerusalem. Nor is the monarch referred to the same as *Astyages*, as is asserted in the works referred to in § 5; and still less *Artaxerxes*, as Josephus assumes out of regard to the Septuagint version; but he is certainly *Xerxes*, as has been well proved by Scaliger (*De emend. temp.*, ed Genev., p. 591 sqq.); also by Justi (in Eichhorn's *Repert.* XV., p. 338), and still more emphatically by Baumgarten (*De fide l. Esth.*, pp. 122–151, and in his treatises respecting Cyrus the Great, in the *Stud. u. Krit.*, 1853, p. 624 sqq.). On the different views in reference to Ahasuerus, see especially Feuardent on our book, and Pfeiffer, *Dubia vex*, p. 481 sqq. Against the identification with either Cyaxares or Astyages, are the following facts: (1) Shushan was already the capital of the empire, which it became through Cyrus (comp. Strabo, XV.); (2) the Persians are now the chief people (comp. the frequent collection of פָּרַס וּמָדַי, *e. g.*, in ch. i. 3); (3) the number seven indicates that of princes at the court of the king (comp. chap. i. 14); (4) many other specifically Persian peculiarities. Further, the empire at the time in question extended from India to Æthiopia, and stretched also to the coasts and isles of the Mediterranean sea (comp. chap. i. 1 and x. 1), as was the case since the time of Darius Hystaspis. The Jews, moreover, are here represented as scattered over all parts of the empire (comp. iii. 7, 8) and particularly numerous in the city of Shushan (comp. chap. ix. 12, *etc.*). On the contrary Artaxerxes is called in the Bible (in Ezra and Neh.) *Artachsharshta* or *Artachshasta*. For Xerxes, on the other hand, we may claim the identity of names (comp. Ezra ix. 6). In his favor is also the whimsical and tyrannical character manifested by the Ahasuerus of Esther (chap. i. and elsewhere). Besides, there is the remarkable circumstance that Vashti was rejected in the third year of Ahasuerus, although Esther was not made queen till the seventh year of his reign, which in the case of Xerxes may be explained on the basis that between his third and seventh year he made war on Greece.* The clause beginning with הוּא (comp. Gen. ii. 11) and referring us back—**this is Ahasuerus which reigned from India even unto Ethiopia**, *etc.*—is no doubt intended to designate Ahasuerus more distinctly,† but at the same time to make known his greatness of dominion and power. Thus the danger that threatened the Jews, as well as the elevation of Esther and Mordecai, and of the Jews through these, is more powerfully brought out. הֹדּוּ stands for the original הִנְדּוּ, as *Hidku* in the cuneiform inscriptions of the Persians stands for *Hindhu* (in Zend and Syrian *Hendu*), and is therefore *India*, in the Sanscrit *Sindhu* which is really the river *Indus*, then the inhabitants along the Indus, and at last the land of the Indus (comp. Lassen, *Judische Altherthumskunde*, I., p. 2); so also in the Vedas *Sapta, Sindhavas*, or "the seven streams," really stand for India (comp. Rödiger in Gesen. *Thesaurus*, Append. p. 83). The *o* sound in הֹדּוּ, and the tone falling on the first syllable are quite remarkable, but perhaps only a provincialism. Herodotus testifies to the great extension of the Persian empire under

* [We condense the following summary of the argument on the identity of the Ahasuerus of the book of Esther, from McClintock & Strong's *Cyclop. s. v.* Ahasuerus. "From the extent assigned to the Persian empire (Esth. i. 1), 'from India even unto Ethiopia,' it is proved that Darius Hystaspis is the earliest possible king to whom this history can apply, and it is hardly worth while to consider the claims of any after Artaxerxes Longimanus. But Ahasuerus cannot be identical with Darius, whose wives were the daughters of Cyrus and Otanes, and who in name and character equally differs from that foolish tyrant. Josephus (*Ant.* XI. 6, 1) makes him to be Artaxerxes Longimanus; but as his twelfth year (Esth. iii. 7) would fall in B. C. 454, or 144 years after the deportation by Nebuchadnezzar, in B. C. 598 (Jer. lii. 28), Mordecai, who was among those captives (Esth. ii. 6), could not possibly have survived to this time. Besides, in Ezra vii. 1-7, 11-26, Artaxerxes, in the *seventh* year of his reign, issues a decree very favorable to the Jews, and it is unlikely, therefore, that in the *twelfth* (Esth. iii. 7) Haman could speak to him of them as if he knew nothing about them, and persuade him to sentence them to an indiscriminate massacre. Nor is the disposition of Artaxerxes Longimanus, as given by Plutarch and Diodorus (XI. 71), at all like that of this weak Ahasuerus. It therefore seems necessary to identify him with Xerxes, whose regal state and affairs tally with all that is here said of Ahasuerus (the names being, as we have seen, identical); and this conclusion is fortified by the resemblance of character, and by certain chronological indications (see Rawlinson's *Hist. Evidences*, p. 150 sq.). As Xerxes scourged the sea, and put to death the engineers of his bridge because their work was injured by a storm, so Ahasuerus repudiated his queen, Vashti, because she would not violate the decorum of her sex, and ordered the massacre of the whole Jewish people to gratify the malice of Haman. In the third year of the reign of Xerxes was held an assembly to arrange the Grecian war (*Herod.* VII. 7 sq.); in the third year of Ahasuerus was held a great feast and assembly in Shushan the palace (Esth. i. 3). In the seventh year of his reign Xerxes returned defeated from Greece, and consoled himself by the pleasures of the harem (*Herod.* IX. 108); in the seventh year of his reign 'fair young virgins were sought' for Ahasuerus, and he replaced Vashti by marrying Esther. The tribute he 'laid upon the land and upon the isles of the sea' (Esth. x. 1) may well have been the result of the expenditure and ruin of the Grecian expedition."—Tr.]

† [The principal purpose of this clause is to distinguish the Achashverosh in question from all other Persian monarchs bearing that general or regal title, by adding the extent of his dominion. It thus becomes, as was evidently intended, an important chronological datum.—Tr.]

Xerxes, and in chap. xii. 9 he says that Mardonius reported to Xerxes that the Saccæ and Assyrians, as well as the Indians and Æthiopians, had been conquered. See also vii. 97, 98, and viii. 65, 69, where the Æthiopians and Indians are enumerated as being under tribute. According to Arrian, Cyrus extended his conquests up to India, and the people of the Açvaka were by him made to pay tribute. Darius added still greater parts of northwestern India to the Persian empire (comp. Duncker, *Gesch. d. Altherthums*, 3d ed., II., page 468). The auxiliary sentence: **A hundred and seven and twenty provinces,** is merely to be regarded as an additional sentence in loose apposition, to indicate what provinces were included in the region just mentioned. If this sentence depended upon הַמֶּלֶךְ, it should have עַל [or בְּ] before it. According to Herod. III. 89 sqq., Darius Hyst. on account of the raising of taxes divided the empire into twenty ἀρχαί which were termed σατραπίηαι. A further division into lesser portions was not thereby excluded; with so many petty tribes and peoples this came as a matter of course. So there were contained in the fifth satrapy (comp. Herod. III. 91) a small Jewish people, a separate מְדִינָה, which really means a judicial or official *circuit* (comp. Ezra ii. 1). Our 127 provinces remind us of the 120 Satraps whom Darius the Mede placed over his empire (Dan. vi. 2).

Ver. 2. **In those days, when the king Ahasuerus sat,** *etc.*—Sitting is a posture common to judges and kings, but more particularly characteristic of the kings of Persia. The Persian kings are always painted as sitting on a throne under a lofty canopy. This is true of them even in the time of war, and in their journeys. Xerxes, indeed, was present in the battles sitting; thus it was at Thermopylæ according to Herodotus (VII. 102), and at Salamis according to Plutarch (*Themistocl.* 13). See also Baumgarten, *l. c.*, p. 85 sqq. **Which was in Shushan the palace.**—He had a royal establishment in several cities; but at the time here referred to it was in Shushan, which was his favorite winter and spring residence (comp. Neh. i. 1). Æschylus calls it the palace ornate with gold of the Cissians, and Strabo asserts that every Persian king built his own palace there. מַלְכוּת was in use in later language, and מַמְלָכָה in earlier times.

Ver. 3. **In the third year of his reign he made a feast,** *etc.*—All his princes and servants, for whom this feast was made, are specified as follows: **The power of Persia and Media, the nobles and princes of the provinces (being) before him.**—These words form an explanatory sentence, and assert distinctly that all the princes and servants were really gathered around Xerxes. We are to understand by the "power," the representatives of the same, who probably consisted of the body-guard of the king, which formed the flower of the entire army-power. According to Herod. VII. 40 sqq., this was in itself sufficiently large, and consisted of two thousand picked horsemen, two thousand lancers, and ten thousand common foot-soldiers. The פַּרְתְּמִים, who are mentioned also in chap. vi. 9, and Dan. i. 3, were the *principes*, chief men (in Sanscrit we find it *parthama* = "first;" in the Behistun Inscription *fratama*, in Pehlevi *pardom*), *i. e.*, the magnates. [" It is a superlative from a root *fra*, equivalent to the Greek πρό, "before." — Rawlinson]. The princes of the provinces are the Pashas or governors of those one hundred and twenty-seven provinces. That פַּרָס is more correct than פָּרָס has been mentioned in the note on Ezra i. 1.

Ver. 4. **When he shewed the riches of his glorious kingdom,** *etc.*—Keil connects these words with the inserted explanatory sentence, " the power — before him," and thus he gets the sense, not that the feast itself, at which Xerxes showed his riches, lasted one hundred and eighty days, but that he prepared a feast for the army lasting seven days, after they had viewed his riches for one hundred and eighty days (ver. 5). But the connection of our verse with the main assertion in ver. 3: "He made a feast" is much closer; as may be seen in the fact that nearly all exegetes have declared themselves for this rendering. Something again different seems to be meant in the seven days' feast of ver. 5, which Xerxes had caused to be made, not for the army, but for all the people in Shushan the palace. The feast during a hundred and eighty days may have been only for the purpose of consultation, and the real feast may have followed in the seven days succeeding. Keil's objection, that then the mention of the preceding feast of a hundred and eighty days was purposeless, does not hold, since the fact that Xerxes could entertain his princes and servants so long, is a proof also to the reader of his great riches. That such magnificent, long and great feasts were very popular at the Persian court, is elsewhere stated (comp. Duncker, as above, p. 609 sqq.). Herod. vii. 8 informs us that after the re-subjection of Egypt, Xerxes called the magnates of his empire to Shushan, in order to consult with them in reference to the campaign against Greece; and in vii. 2, he further states that the preparations for this undertaking lasted four years. Hence the assumption is not unfounded that in these long assemblages it was specially designed in the third year to counsel together regarding the war with Greece. This is the more evident since in the inserted clause of ver. 3 the power of the Medes and Persians is prominently stated. If Xerxes ascended the throne in the year B. C. 486 then there were still three or four years until this happened. There were three years until the battle of Salamis (480) beginning with his first year of empire. Clericus asserts that these princes of the provinces could not possibly have remained away so long a time as a hundred and eighty days from their provinces and governmental activity. Hence he would have them entertained one after the other; a view which is without foundation. They doubtless had subordinate officers, who ranked high enough to take their places for one half year.*

* [" We are not obliged to suppose that all or any of the governors were present during the whole period of festivity. Rather we may conclude that the time was extended in order to allow of the different persons

Ver. 5. **And when these days were expired, the king made a feast to all the people.**—This does not, as Keil would have it, take up the third verse again, but forms the transition from the counseling to the purely festive entertainment to which the king invited (in addition to those already assembled to the army and great rulers, comp. ver. 11) all the people at Shushan the palace. מִלּוֹאת is not an abstract form with an infinitive signification, which would properly have to be punctuated thus מְלוֹאֹת, as are שִׁכְבַת, יְבֹשֶׁת (comp. Ewald, § 239 *a*), but the ו stands in the wrong place in the originally defectively written מִלֹּאת (comp. Lev. xii. 6), in order that it might be known as having been added later (comp. Joh. xx. 22).—To all these people who were invited, belonged also the lower classes of servants, and probably the common inhabitants likewise, as is evinced by the phrase **both unto great and small**—from the highest to the lowest. But these were only the male population, as is shown in ver. 9. In reference to הַנִּמְצְאִים comp. the note on Ezra viii. 25. לְמִגָּדוֹל, with לְ, as in 2 Chron. xv. 13; without it 1 Sam. xxx. 19.—**In the court of the garden of the king's palace.**—בִּיתָן for בֵּית occurs often in our book, but is found connected with גִּנַּת as also in chap. vii. 7. The kingly palace or series of houses was situated, in Oriental manner, as is customary also to-day, in a large park (Xenoph. *Cyrop.* I. 3, 12, 14).

Ver. 6. The language describing the court of the garden where this entertainment took place, *i. e.*, the tent-like, enclosed, and covered space of the park, specially prepared for this festive occasion, and likewise the entertainment itself in vers. 7, 8, must be understood as explained by the exclamations of wonder, **white, green, and blue (hangings)**, *etc.*, these latter being employed as coverings. חוּר designates the white cloths as to color, not as to a certain quality of cloth; from חָוַר, *to be white.* כַּרְפַּס, occurring in the Sanscrit, Pers., Armen., and Arab., corresponds to the Greek κάρπασος; designating *cotton* cloth; and, because of the two preceding and corresponding words, a splendid parti-colored fabric. תְּכֵלֶת is the glistening blue-black hyacinth color, and here means any kind of cloth which had this particular hue. White and blue were, according to Curtius VI. 6, 4, the regal colors of Persia (comp. also Duncker, as above, pp. 891 and 951). These cloths were held fast (אָחוּז) with cords to rings, and by these to the pillars.* The last words: **The beds** (divans) **were of gold and silver** (lying) **upon a pavement of red and blue, and white and black marble,** *etc.*, describe the seats for the guests. *Gold and silver* here mean the cloths, which were woven with gold and silver threads. Hence they were *brocades* with which these divans were covered. But they lay upon רִצְפַּת, Sept. ἐπὶ λιθοστρώτου, a tessellated (mosaic) flooring, which was formed of various kinds of stones. בַּהַט, in Arab., a false stone, accords to the Sept., σμαραγδίτης, a stone of a green color, similar to the emerald (smaragth), is perhaps malachite or serpentine. שֵׁשׁ is white marble; דַּר, in Arab. *darun* and *darratun*, pearl, is, according to the Sept., πίννινος λίθος, a stone similar to pearl, perhaps mother of pearl. סֹחָרֶת (from שְׁחַר=סְחַר, *dark*), is very likely black marble, with scutiform spots.*

Ver. 7. **And they gave (them) drink in vessels of gold.**—This actually occurred, or was seen transpiring. הַשְׁקוֹת, Infin. Hiph., is a substantive here. **The vessels being diverse one from another,** *i. e.*, very different drinking-vessels were in service. According to Xenoph. *Cyrop.* VIII. 8, 18, these constituted an essential part of Persian luxury. **And royal wine,** *i. e.*, such as was drunk from the royal vaults, as especially costly, perhaps coming from Chalybon, which it was usual for Persian kings to drink (comp. Ez. xxvii. 18). **In abundance, according to the state of the king.**—כְּיַד, *according to the hand*=power of the king, means that the great quantity did honor to the power of the king, or that it corresponded to the ability and riches of the king (comp. chap. ii. 18; 1 Kings x. 13; also Neh. ii. 8).

Ver. 8. **And the drinking was**—*i. e.*, went on—**according to the law** (custom); **none did compel,** *etc.* כַּדָּת hardly means a law enacted for this special occasion; for this purpose the expression would be too general;—but as custom, especially Persian royal etiquette required. This means, not *moderately* (as Clericus,—moralizing was not here intended), but on the contrary that the guests in a courageous and vigorous carousing should show their appreciation of the liberal hospitality of the king, and at the same time evince their ability to do something in their drinking worthy of the royal table. The Greeks knew how to do justice to hospitality (see Baumgarten, p. 12 sq.). While דָּת was held to be a special law made for this occasion, it was thought that its substance was contained in אֵין אֹנֵס, אֹנֵס being taken in the sense of *urging.* The meaning is that the drinking was not to occur, as was usually the case, in compliance with the wishes or encouragements of the court officers. In contrast with the customary excessive drinking, because of too frequent urging, this should remain free to all to remain sober. While the Septuagint, in a free rendering, has joined אֵין אֹנֵס with כַּדָּת (οὐ κατὰ προκείμενον νόμον), the Vulgate has it thus: "*Nec erat, qui*

making their appearance at the court successively." Rawlinson.—Tr.]

* ["Nothing could be more appropriate than this method at Susa and Persepolis, the spring residences of the Persian monarchs. . . . . A massive roof, covering the whole expanse of columns, would be too cold and dismal; whereas curtains around the central group would serve to admit both light and warmth." Loftus.—Tr.]

* [Herodotus mentions (IX. 80-82) the immense quantities of gold and silver vessels of various kinds—which we know from the monuments were of the most elegant style and costly ornamentation—together with couches and tables of the precious metals, besides various colored *awnings* (παραπετάματα), which Xerxes carried with him on his expedition to Greece.—Tr.]

nolentes cogere ad bibendum." But the true interpretation of the phrase evidently is as already indicated; every one having entire liberty to drink of the wine, without urging. The whole tone of the passage expresses abundance and luxuriance: yet we need not make "urging" out of אָנַס, but rather "creating a real necessity, preparing difficulty, standing in the way in a preventive manner." In Dan. iv. 6, at least, it has this signification. It may possibly be an additional form for אֱנַשׁ (Hitzig on Ez. xxiv. 17). At any rate it frequently stands in the Targums for the Heb. גָּזַל, עָשַׁק, and רָצַץ. That no one should hinder another in drinking must have been self-evident and understood at a decently-conducted feast. But here it is stated: **For so the king had appointed to all the officers of his house**; here not our own, but Persian customs, give the key. Besides there is a negative hindrance in drinking, which obtains even among us, and which would seem to have been necessary in a company where high and low mingled together, namely that of not so frequently filling the cups. יִסַּד means, as it does in 1 Chron. ix. 22, *arranging* (ordering). With עַל it is, first of all, *giving orders* in reference to or for some one. רַב־בֵּיתוֹ = the chief of the house, *i. e., court-officer.*

Vers. 9–12. *The Queen's Banquet, and her Refusal to appear in the Royal Presence.*—The festival of the king went hand in hand with that of the queen, which doubtless was intended to bring into view at the same time the royal majesty and magnificence. Usually the queen ate with her husband (see Herod. IX. 110), and even in greater feasts she was not under all circumstances excluded, as is proved by the reference to Lucian by Brissonius, *De regio Pers. princ.* I., c. 103. At this time she was compelled to remain away, since she also gave entertainment to the ladies. To permit the participation of women in all the feasts of the men would certainly not have been very desirable, since it was a mixed company.

Ver. 9. The name *Vashti*, וַשְׁתִּי, has probably a connection with the Old-Persian *vahista* ("the best"), or with the related *behisht* ("*paradisiacus*"); comp. Pott, *Ueber alt-pers. Eigennamen*, in the *Zeitschrift, d. D. M. G.*, 1859, p. 388. In modern Persian Vashti signifies a *beautiful woman.* Vashti gave the feast to the ladies in the king's palace, *i. e.*, either in her own apartments, which also were in the royal residence, or in some other dwellings there which were placed at her disposal for this festive occasion.*

Ver. 10. **On the seventh day**, as the last of the feast, in which perhaps there was the greatest joviality. **When the heart of the king was merry with wine**, *i. e.*, well disposed, happy (כְּטוֹב, as in 2 Sam. xiii. 18; Judg. xvi. 25; טוֹב is the infin. constr. Kal, with an intransitive signification), would grant a still greater favor to his guests, and one too which he would not have been willing to grant in a more sober mood. He turned to the seven eunuchs that served before him, אֶת־פְּנֵי, together with שֵׁרֵת, as in 1 Sam. ii. 18. Their names signify nothing for the present purpose; and there are no certain data for their interpretation.* But our author names them because they were transmitted to him, and in order that the historical character of his narrative may be strengthened thereby. Certain it is, they were the medium between the king and the ladies. They were to transmit the commands of the former to the latter. Their number, *seven*, has close connection with that of the Amshaspands. This number was peculiarly sacred to the Persians, see ver. 14.

Ver. 11. They were to bring the queen in the regal crown, כֶּתֶר, κίδαρις or κίταρις, *i. e.*, in a high, pointed turban, and consequently bring her in her entire royal apparel, in order to show her beauty to the prince, as well as to the entire people, of whom at least there were representatives present. Xerxes was desirous of glory, not only because of his riches, but also because of his beautiful wife.†

Ver. 12. **But the queen Vashti refused to come.**—כִּדְבַר הַמֶּלֶךְ here has reference to the word of the king, as in chap. iii. 15; viii. 14; 1 Ki. xiii. 1, 8. **By (his) chamberlains**, *i. e.*, which was brought to her in a formal manner, and which therefore ought to have been obeyed all the more (comp. ver. 15). Persian etiquette gave to ladies, and especially to the queen, a certain reserve, and this under all circumstances. It was regarded as something unheard of if the queen appeared in public unveiled. But here, where there was no doubt of the fact that she should become the gazing-stock of a drunken company, that, so to speak, she should make a show of herself to the lascivious eyes of so many —according to the extremely literal view of the Targums, she was to appear naked—she had a right, indeed she was compelled to guard and keep in mind her dignity. There is no doubt that as the queen she was safe from such shameless proceedings as Herodotus (ver. 18) relates of Persian foreign ministers. But instead of being rejoiced at the modesty of his queen the king felt deeply humbled in the eyes of those to whom he would have shown himself in his highest glory. It is possible, and even probable, that a well-known self-assertion of Vashti had something to do in the matter. But this we need not necessarily assume in connection with his peculiar character in order to explain his wrath. Pride and self-exaltation perhaps so blinded him

* ["If the Ahasuerus of Esther is rightly identified with Xerxes, Vashti should be Amestris, whom the Greeks regard as the only legitimate wife of that monarch, and who was certainly married to him before he ascended the throne. In that case the name may be explained either by corruption of Amestris, or as a title; and it may be supposed that the disgrace recorded was only temporary; Amestris in the latter part of Xerxes' reign recovering her former dignity." RAWLINSON.—TR.]

* ["These names, being those of eunuchs, are not unlikely to be of foreign origin. They have generally but little resemblance to known Persian names." RAWLINSON.—TR.]

† ["It has been said that this is invariable, and indicates an ignorance of Persian customs on the part of the author. But even De Wette allows that such an act is not out of harmony with the character of Xerxes (*Einleitung*, § 198, a, note 6); and it is evidently related as something strange and unusual. Otherwise the queen would not have refused to come." RAWLINSON.—TR.]

that he did not dream of such a rebuff. Perhaps, too, she might have found some way, had she been wise, in which without compromising herself she might have rendered obedience. But however bad the fact, the unfavorable light does not fall on her, but upon the king. He appears so thoughtless that one is quite prepared to expect still other rash and inconsiderate acts from him.

Vers. 13–15. *The King's Inquiry.*—**When the king said to the wise men, which knew the times.**—To know the times means to judge the times as did the astrologers and magicians, according to the heavenly phenomena, and to give counsel corresponding thereto, (comp. Dan. ii. 27; v. 15; Isa. xliv. 25; xlvii. 13; Jer. l. 35). But it also means in a general sense *to be learned;* for according to the expressions following, these wise men were likewise those skilled in the law. **For so,** adds the author, **(was) the king's manner toward all that knew law and judgment.**—דְּבַר הַמֶּלֶךְ does not here mean *the word of the king,* for then we might expect, instead of לִפְנֵי, a preposition expressive of direction; but it is *a matter of the king, i. e.,* all that relates to the king, or what he undertakes.

Ver. 14. **And the next to him** or *standing nearest to him,*—thus the explanation becomes clear, **were Carshena, Shethar,** *etc.*—There is no doubt that all seven should be named as standing before the king, and not the first only.* The sing. הַקָּרֹב אֵלָיו has application to the second and third no less than to the first, and is, therefore, equal to a neuter plural. The sense, however, is clear. By these words, the wise were meant, the chief persons, who during and after consultation were to have a word before the king in this matter. The clause **which saw the king's face,** expresses their intimate relation to the king, and their great and high preference in an especially significant manner, since the approach to the king was very difficult. The seven princes that had conspired against the Pseudo-Smerdis had a perfect understanding that it should be permitted them to enter at any time into the presence of the king, who had been elected from their midst, and that, too, without previous announcement (see Herod. iii. 84). But that these princes themselves formed the court either before or after the event spoken of here, although mentioned "as the seven princes of the Medes and Persians," is not to be assumed. Those seven before mentioned did not, as did these, belong to the learned class, to the selected counsellors of the king, although they had intercourse with the king. These were the seven supreme counsellors (comp. Ezra vii. 14), who formed a complement to the seven Amshaspands.† The number seven, which is retained by the Persians in ver. 5, and again in chap. ii. 9, was originally instituted because of the seven planets, or the weekly cycle, or finally with regard to the seven Amshaspands. Perhaps its being composed of the numbers three and four gave it significance. הַיֹּשְׁבִים רִאשֹׁנָה, *first =presiding,* is, first of all, to preside, constituting the highest authority. The feminine רִאשֹׁנָה is a substitute for the adverb (comp. Gen. xxxiii. 2; Num. ii. 9).

Ver. 15. First, here, the discourse of the king follows. They are asked: **What shall we do unto the queen Vashti according to law?** כְּדָת is expressly prefixed here, and that without the article; hence, *legally.* **Because she hath not performed the commandment of the king Ahasuerus.**—Thus the king expresses himself, instead of simply saying: *my word;* since this was just the matter that came into consideration, that it was the king's word. For the rest comp. ver. 12 and notes.

Vers. 16–20. *The Courtier's Reply.*—Memucan, although last mentioned among the seven, is spokesman, doubtless after the wise men had had a consultation. For מומכן is here the same as ממוכן in ver. 14, as is shown by the Keri. The assumption is natural that the *Scriptio defectiva* was really employed, and that the ו was added later by the Masoretes. This is evident, further, in ver. 5, where the full form is distinguished as having been added by them at the wrong place. Feuardent thinks that, according to a more general custom, the last of the seven responded first "lest he might seem to say aught in view of the favor and protection of the chiefs and elders, but on the contrary out of mere liberty, and the full determination of his own will and judgment." But Memucan seems to have spoken first not only here, but also above; hence he seems to have been chairman (spokesman). He judges the offense of the queen very strictly in order to justify a severe verdict. But he also correctly premises that the offenses of persons high in office, on account of the influence which their examples will have, are punishable in a very high degree. **Vashti the queen hath not done wrong to the king only,** *etc.*—עָוָת with עַל occurs only here.*

Ver. 17. **For (this) deed of the queen shall come abroad to all women.**—יָצָא with עַל, usually with אֶל־. **They shall despise,** properly, *make them to despise,* **their husbands in their eyes.**—Those that despise are of course the wives, as is clear from the connection with בְּאָמְרָם. The masc. form of the suffix is substituted for the fem. form.

Ver. 18. **(Likewise) shall the ladies of Persia and Media say this day unto all the king's princes.** הַיּוֹם הַזֶּה is used in its

---

* ["These names have a general Persian cast, though they are difficult of identification. They have probably suffered to some extent for corruption (*i. e.,* transcription into Hebrew); and perhaps they were not even at first very close to the Persian originals. In *Marsena* we may perhaps recognize the famous *Mardonius,* and in *Admatha* Xerxes' uncle, *Artabanus.*" RAWLINSON.—TR.]

† ["According to Herodotus (III. 84), there were seven families of the first rank in Persia, from which alone the king would take his wives. Their chiefs were entitled to have free access to the king's person. The Behistun Inscription, which gives Darius six coadjutors in his conspiracy, confirms the Greek writer." RAWLINSON.—TR.]

* ["It is not surprising that the judgment delivered by Memucan was one of condemnation, for it was rarely indeed that any Persian subject ventured to offer opposition to the mildest caprice or to the most extravagant whim of the monarch. (See Herodotus III. 31, 35)." RAWLINSON.—TR.]

direct meaning. What the speaker means to say is, *as regards the rest of the lower women*, who were referred to in ver. 17. It may take a long time before the new law of the court shall have come to the knowledge of all, because some will hear of it later. But the princesses who live at the court and who have immediate news of Vashti's conduct, will relate what has been indicated in ver. 17. After תֹּאמַרְנָה the same sentence is to be understood as follows: כְּאָמְרָם in ver. 17; for the last words of the verse: **Thus (shall there arise) too much contempt and wrath,** cannot be construed into the definition of an object in view, as Bertheau would have it, as if the ו stood before כְּדַי only as an attachment to the long phrase, but these form a separate sentence. The predicate; *thus there shall arise*, must be supplied. כְּדַי, really *for a sufficiency*, is by *litotes, e. g.*, "more than enough."

Ver. 19. This contains the verdict.—**If it please the king, let there go a royal commandment from him.**—טוֹב עַל occurs often in our book as also in Neh. ii. 5. דְּבַר מַלְכוּת, *a word of the kingdom* or *a king's word* (comp. ver. 8), hence first of all a *royal order*. **And let it be written among the laws of the Persians and the Medes, that it be not altered,** *i. e.*, let it have express legal authority, so that it must remain unaltered (comp. Dan. vi. 9).* **That Vashti come no more before king Ahasuerus; and let the king give her royal estate unto another that is better than she.**—מַלְכוּת = מַמְלָכָה (comp. ver. 2), *royal state, royal government*, here means *royal highness, dignity*, רְעוּתָהּ = *her female companions*. טוֹב, as to its connections, is especially referable to *obedience*. It may be that Vashti was hated as being a proud, assuming person. But the severity of the sentence against her is explainable also in this, that there remained no alternative to the judges either to declare her innocent, which, as respects Ahasuerus, they could not do, or to make her for ever harmless. Even if she had again obtained an influence with the king, they would have had to expect her wrath.

Ver. 20. We here notice the consequence of the decree of the king.—**And when the king's decree, which he shall make, shall be published—all the wives shall give to their husbands honour,** *etc.* The predicate נִשְׁמַע is chosen, since it makes a presupposition for the יִתְּנוּ which is expressed. It is first of all neuter: *when it shall be published* (heard). פִּתְגָם, as in Ezra iv. 17. אֲשֶׁר יַעֲשֶׂה may mean: *which he shall execute*, inasmuch as this decree would be sanctioned by the example of the king himself; otherwise: *which he shall decree*. Memucan reminds him of the greatness of the empire, since the success of the punishment and its importance is connected with it. לְמִגָּדוֹל, as in ver. 5.

Vers. 21, 22. *The Decree Issued.* The king accepts the proffered counsel and rejects Vashti; indeed he does even more. In order that her punishment may become as well-known as her offense, he sends letters into all the provinces;* and in order that these may be intelligible, he writes according to the language of every province, and to every people in their own language.† **That every man should bear rule in his own house, and that it should be published according to the language of every people.**—לִהְיוֹת does not really indicate the substance of what was written—this consists of the rejection of Vashti and the reasons therefor—but only its aim. Yet this object, strange as it may have sounded, has nevertheless received sufficient prominence. Feuardent thinks that the edict may be explained on the ground that there was too much petticoat government in Persia. But there exists no proof of such an assertion. It is true, in chap. v. 10, that Haman drew his wife into the council of consultation, but his friends first. It may be asked, what is the sense and connection of the phrase, **and (it) should be published according to the language of every people.** Older commentators and also Keil find therein only a command, that a man in his own house should speak his own native language. Hence if he was possessed of one or more foreign wives, who spoke a different language, they should be compelled to learn his language and speak only in it. Thereby the man was to show his authority as master of his own house.‡ But if we apprehend this decree in such a general manner, it would not only have been a very peculiar, but also a separate edict, and it would apply in fact to the rejection of queen Vashti, neither in its object, nor yet in its communication. It might much better have read thus, "that the wives speak the language of their husbands' people." Hence Bertheau, according to Hitzig's advice, changed כִּלְשׁוֹן עַמּוֹ to כָּל־שֹׁוֶה עִמּוֹ: *(and every one) shall speak what to him is appropriate;* but

* ["The theoretical inviolability of the laws of the Persians is often touched on by the Greek writers. Practically the monarch, if he chose, could always dispense with the law. It was therefore quite within his power to restore Vashti to her queenly dignity, notwithstanding the present decree, if he so pleased." RAWLINSON—TR.]

* ["The Persian system of posts is described with some minuteness both by Herodot. (VIII. 98) and Xenophon (*Cyrop.* VIII. 6). The incidental notices in this Book (see chaps. III. 12-15; VIII. 9-14) are in entire harmony with the accounts of the classical writers. Herodotus describes the system as in full operation under Xerxes." RAWLINSON.—TR.]

† [The practice of the Persians, to address proclamations to the subject-nations in their own speech, and not merely in the language of the conqueror, is illustrated by the bilingual and trilingual inscriptions of the Achæmonian monarchs, from Cyrus to Artaxerxes Ochus, each inscription being of the nature of a proclamation." RAWLINSON—TR.]

‡ ["This decree has been called 'absurd' and 'quite unnecessary in Persia' (Davidson). If the criticism were allowed; it would be sufficient to observe that many absurd things were done by Xerxes (see Herod. VII. 35; IX. 108-111). But it may be questioned whether the decree was unnecessary. The undue influence of women in domestic, and even in public affairs, is a feature of the ancient Persian monarchy. Herodotus tells us that Alesia 'completely ruled' Darius (VII., 3). Xerxes himself was, in his later years, shamefully subject to Amestris (*ib.* IX., 111). The example of the court would naturally infect the people. The decree, therefore, would seem to have been not so much an idle and superfluous act as an ineffectual protest against a real and growing evil." RAWLINSON.—TR.]

this would introduce a thought foreign to the subject, and besides שׁוה according to chap. iii. 8, should have לְ before it. Perhaps the meaning is this: *that he speak, etc.*, in short, that he have the right to use his people's language in his own house, even though he have a foreign wife; moreover that it is obligatory upon his wife to so far learn the language of her husband that she may understand the orders he may give in it. This phrase receives further light from the consequence which would follow upon the usurpation of the wife, since she would then compel her husband to learn her own language.

DOCTRINAL AND ETHICAL.

On vers. 1–12. 1. Ever and anon the question arises, whether there is not upon earth somewhere, a condition of true satisfaction and unclouded happiness. One very much desires such a state of things, and one is tempted to believe it, especially when regard is had to the most beautiful dreams of the past, which had the appearance of bright promises. But this is not all. In spite of all assurances and experiences to the contrary, one is ever inclined to think that the world, and especially its lords, could give an affirmative answer to our question.

At the very beginning of our book there is unfolded to our eyes a picture full of riches and affluence, full of splendor and glory. Whatever is beautiful to look upon, whatever is enjoyable to the taste, whatever could rejoice the heart and elevate the soul, is here combined. A ruler, whose height of power leaves hardly anything to be desired, who has united under his sceptre the most powerful, the richest, and most celebrated nations, from India to Æthiopia, has called together the chief men of the various countries, and they are gathered around him in the beautifully situated and magnificently built city of the lilies, the most beautiful of all Persian residences (comp. Neh. i. 1), there to revel in luxury and enjoyment. He, it seems, is happy to be their ruler, and they are happy as his subjects. At the same time the women are also called to this festive enjoyment. The higher in station mingle on equal terms with those lower, and all celebrate and enjoy the occasion together. It seems as if every one must feel happy in his place. Yet the old adage asserts itself that the world, the rich, the high, the proud world possesses least of that which we here seek. It may be said, indeed, of this world alone, that it passes away with all its pleasures, and that its apparent wealth at last becomes sheer poverty. Ahasuerus, who is admired because of his greatness and lauded as happy by so many, is deeply humiliated; a woman dares to defy his command, and his joy is changed to anger and chagrin. Again, all the efforts that he makes to remove the object of his disappointment serve but to complete his misfortune. However widely and effectually his power may be felt, he is still only a man, and as such he has human needs. The empire cannot displace his house. All the wealth of earth cannot give him the joy that one person does, who submits herself entirely to him. Her he cannot gain by his measures, but rather she becomes for ever lost to him by those very measures. Vashti, however, this second person at the highest point of worldly glory, now sees the crown of her exalted station and her happiness torn to pieces. For her the day of highest joy becomes the day of her misfortune. The subjects, who had to bear the cost of these feastings, must have groaned and sighed the most in advance, instead of rejoicing. Feuardent: "David once called water blood, because it had been drawn at the manifest risk of life on the part of his chieftains, and he therefore held it wrong to drink of it. But . . . . from another's hide, as the proverb goes, since shoe-strings are cut by chiefs."

1. There is but One, who—Himself ever blessed—can make all kings and nations truly happy with the great wealth of His treasury. He also will bring to pass that if those whose beauty ought to be His honor and joy—mankind, whose love would have given Him more pleasure than a man would find in the love of his wife—if these will not come to Him, will not honor nor rejoice Him, indeed if all but one family desire each to go their own way; yet has this its ground in His highest, in His most liberal greatness, by which He has found means from the very beginning to unfold more and more the wealth of His glorious kingdom, in contrast with such stubbornness, and especially to reveal to us the riches of His grace.

2. Ahasuerus, or Xerxes, who had received this great and powerful kingdom from Darius his father, and who now governed it in its fullest extent, possessed the greatest glory among the people of his own time and those succeeding, as being the greatest and most powerful king. And in the feast, which in our chapter he instituted, he made it his special business to maintain this distinction to its fullest extent. But it is this very feast that while it reveals his greatness, also reminds us of his weakness. Perhaps even then many of his friends felt that he did not quite deserve all the distinction that he claimed for himself. By reason of his thoughtlessness and folly—and this may not have been the first time when these were manifested, though he now revealed them in a more public manner before the eyes of his princes—he demanded of the queen what was against all custom and good breeding. This lapse in moral strength of which he was guilty—in that he lived more for sensual gratification than for the duties of his government—especially reveals the fact that, though never so mighty a king and ruler, yet in fact in himself he was nothing more than a poor slave.

3. While Ahasuerus was intent to show how far the limits of his empire extended, by calling to his court the governors of the most distant provinces, he found in close proximity, yea, in his very house, insubordination to his will. Though he knew how to punish it, yet he could not conquer it, nor turn it into obedience to his wishes.

There is, therefore, a power higher than that of man, were he even the mightiest ruler of earth. Though the latter may prescribe laws and issue commands, the former has long ago set in order His ordinances, indeed stamped them on the very face of nature so deeply, so ineffaceably and unchangeably, that in contrast with human commands, they appear holy and irrefragable, and in case of a conflict bear away the palm of victory. To obey human laws may be a sacred duty; but to follow dutifully the eternally divine ordinances, is a holy and most glorious privilege, which no one must permit to be abrogated. To disobey human commands may be dangerous, may bring temporal disadvantage, but to despise God's laws is degrading, and will bring eternal ruin. If an earthly ruler with his laws come into conflict with divine ordinances, he will begin a war in which he will finally be destroyed. Feuardent: "Not even the heathens were unaware, under the instruction of Plutarch, that a man ought to govern his wife as the soul does the body, not as a master does a beast."

STARKE: "Great pleasure is often followed by equally great displeasure. Occasions of joyous feasting commonly end in sorrow (1 Macc. ix. 41). Wine disperses sorrow and rejoices the heart of man (Sir. xxxi. 32 sq.). In a drinking-company all kinds of useless counsels are generally brought forth (Wis. ii. 10). Men with men, women with women, thus it was among the heathen, and so should it also be among us Christians. How much that is unchaste would thereby be avoided, which is usually found in such gatherings (Sir. xix. 2). Although beauty is a gift of God, still one should not make a boast of it nor yet be proud (Prov. xxxi. 30). Pride occasions much sorrow, and often plunges others into destruction (Sir. iii. 30; Prov. xxix. 23; 1 Pet. v. 5)."

On vers. 13–22. 1. The wise men, on whom Ahasuerus depends to give a decision as to how Vashti should be treated, are both judges and masters of ceremonies. They are to execute law and justice, but they are also to see to it that court-etiquette be maintained. Instead of at once following out the suggestions of his wrath, and doing what he thinks best to be done, Ahasuerus subjects himself to an objective will-power, namely that of law and custom. This in itself is great and beautiful. This is the victory of culture over crudeness and passion. But in the manner in which this is done here, it amounts to nothing after all. We seem to feel in advance that nothing good will come of it. It sounds to us as if the advice of Memucan came from a court of judgment: where what was held to be light is changed into darkness, and what was deemed to be sweet is changed into bitterness. The queen's act, which was at the most but a trivial mistake, is now stamped as a dark crime, and this sentence is supported by them with learned reasons and wise references. There is guardianship of justice and of morals which is nothing more than hypocrisy, by means of which injustice and violence are made a cloak for the performance of abominable deeds. Hence we must seek to know, not what pleases man, but what pleases God. What is good and beautiful in itself is to be sought after. Feuardent: "All might have been explained in a milder sense, and a reasonable excuse might have been offered. She was forbidden to enter that promiscuous assembly by the very modesty which is a woman's chief ornament."

2. However wisely the counsellors of Ahasuerus counsel together, yet all their wisdom in truth is nothing but folly; to such a degree as to cause us to smile, but yet pity. They would forestall the assumptions of the women, and would protect the respect due to men. They suppose that they firmly ground the honor of man, if they suppress the rights of woman. They do not perceive that if they compel woman to be subject to them, even to the sacrifice of her modesty, they will divest her of all humanity, and thereby make her truly and offensively bold and arrogant. Ahasuerus appears equally foolish. By not rendering a decision himself, but deferring to his court for judgment, he would protect himself from the reproach of cruelty and blind passion. But the real responsibility nevertheless falls upon him. Nor does he by any means guard himself against the great loss of a wife, of whom he has been so proud, and whose merits he will so soon be compelled to recognise. Now the question remains, Were other heathen princes or judges really any wiser? We know that it has ever pleased God to bring to shame the wisdom of the world; and we would not hazard much, were we to say that the folly of Ahasuerus and his counsellors would be found repeated more or less in all human measures and arrangements which have not proceeded from a fear of God, but have reference solely to human desire, inclination, and advantage. The divine law only is truly wise, and those who are led thereby are surely protected from loss. Though that law pronounces sentence of banishment against those who are rebellious, still it is just; and even those so banished, if they but come to themselves and look within, must recognise its justice. It only rejects these, to make room for all those who do turn within and strive to give place to grace.

STARKE: "Vers. 13–15. 'For the wrath of man worketh not the righteousness of God' (Jas. i. 20). Vers. 16–18. Thus it is ever in the world: as long as one is able to stand, others run to aid, knowing that their help is not needed. When, however, signs of falling are seen, all help to push him down. Ver. 19. True counsellors must set aside all respect for private interests, they must keep their eyes fixed upon public dangers. They must exert themselves to avert general misfortune, though thereby they even endanger their own welfare. Oh that all great lords would have respect to the laws of the great God, as they desire to have *their* laws respected! God's law is truly of such a nature and obligatory character upon us that it neither can nor should be changed. Vers. 20, 21. This is the manner of all great lords; when their honor is insulted, they are very severe, and promptly bring their laws into execution. But when God's honor is insulted, then they are easily quieted, and can readily and quickly change their purposes."

FIRST SECTION.

The Rise and Conflict of Opposite Elements.

CHAPS. II., III.

A.—ESTHER IS RAISED TO THE PLACE OF VASHTI, AND MORDECAI MAKES HIMSELF DESERVING OF THE FAVOR OF AHASUERUS.

CHAP. II. 1–23.

I. *Esther's Elevation.* Vers. 1–18.

1 AFTER these things [words], when [as] *the* wrath of king Ahasuerus was ap-
peased [subsided], he remembered Vashti, and what she had done, and what was
2 decreed against her. Then [And] said *the* king's servants [young *men*] that
ministered unto him [his waiters], Let *there be* fair [good of appearance] young
3 virgins sought [let them seek] for the king: And let the king appoint officers in
all *the* provinces of his kingdom, that they may [and let them] gather *together* all
the fair young virgins [every young virgin good of appearance] unto Shushan the
palace, to *the* house of the women, unto *the* custody [hand] of Hege *the* king's
chamberlain [eunuch], keeper of the women; and *let* their *things* for purification
4 be given *them* [*let there be a* giving their furbishments]: And let the maiden
[young *woman*] which pleaseth [that seems good to] the king be queen instead of
Vashti. And the thing pleased [seemed good to] the king, and he did so.
5 *Now* in Shushan the palace *there* was a certain [man] Jew, whose [and his]
name *was* Mordecai, *the* son of Jair, *the* son of Shimei, *the* son of Kish, a Benjamite,
6 Who *had* been carried away [made captive] from Jerusalem with the captivity
which *had* been carried away [made captive] with Jechoniah king of Judah, whom
7 Nebuchadnezzar *the* king of Babylon *had* carried away [made captive]. And he
brought up [was supporting] Hadassah (that *is* Esther) his uncle's daughter; for
she had neither father nor mother, and the maid [young *woman*] *was* fair [beauti-
ful of figure] and beautiful [good of appearance];[1] whom [and her] Mordecai,
when her father and mother were dead, took for his *own* [to him for a] daughter.
8 So [And] it came to pass [was], when *the* king's commandment [word] and his
decree was heard, and when many maidens [young *women*] were gathered *together*
unto Shushan the palace, to the custody [hand] of Hegai, that [and, *i. e.* then]
Esther was brought [taken] *also* unto *the* king's house, to the custody [hand] of
9 Hegai, keeper of the women. And the maiden [young *woman*] pleased him
[seemed good in his eyes], and she obtained kindness of [received favor before]
him; and he speedily gave [hastened to give] her her *things* for purification [fur-
bishments], with [and] such *things* as belonged to her [her portions], and seven
maidens [young *women*], *which were* meet [seen, *i. e.* chosen] to *be* given [give] her,
out of *the* king's house: and he preferred [changed] her and her maids [young
10 *women*] unto *the* best [good] *place* of *the* house of the women. Esther *had* not
showed [told] her people nor [and] her kindred [lineage]: for Mordecai *had*
11 charged [enjoined upon] her that she should not show [tell] *it*. And Mordecai
walked [*was* walking to and fro] every day [continually][2] before *the* court of *the*
women's house, to know how Esther did [the peace, *i. e.* welfare of Esther], and
what should become of [be done with] her.
12 Now [And], when every [each] maid's turn was come [approached] to go *in* to
[the] king Ahasuerus, after that she had been [at the end of her being] twelve
months, according to *the* manner [law] of the women, (for so were *the* days of their
purifications [furbishments] accomplished, *to wit*, six months with oil of myrrh,

and six months with sweet odors [spices], and with *other things for the* purifying
13 [furbishments] of the women,) Then [And] thus [in this *time*] came *every* maiden
unto the king; whatsoever she desired [might say] was [would be] given her, to
14 go with her out of *the* house of the women unto *the* king's house. In the evening
she went, and on the morrow [in the morning] she[3] returned *into the* second house
of the women, to *the* custody [hand] of Shaashgaz *the* king's chamberlain [eunuch],
which kept [keeping] the concubines: she came [would come] *in* unto the king
no more, except the king delighted in her, and *that* she were called by name.
15 Now [And] when *the* turn of Esther, *the* daughter of Abihail *the* uncle of Morde-
cai, who had taken her for his [to him for a] daughter, was come [approached] to
go *in* unto the king, she required [sought] nothing but what Hegai *the* king's
chamberlain [eunuch], *the* keeper of [keeping] the women, appointed [might say]:
and Esther obtained [was receiving] favor in *the* sight [eyes] of all *them* that looked
16 upon [seeing] her. So [And] Esther was taken unto [the] king Ahasuerus *into*
his house royal in the tenth month, which *is the* month Tebeth, in *the* seventh year
17 of his reign. And the king loved Esther above all the women, and she obtained
[received] grace [favor] and favor [mercy] in his sight [before him] more than all
the virgins; so *that* [and] he set *the* royal crown upon her head, and made her
18 queen instead of Vashti. Then [And] the king made a great feast [banquet] unto
all his princes and his servants, *even* Esther's feast [banquet]; and he made a
release [rest] to the provinces, and gave gifts [a contribution] according to the
state [hand] of the king.

II. *Mordecai makes himself deserving of the favor of Ahasuerus.* Vers. 18–20.

19 And when *the* virgins were gathered *together* the second *time, then* Mordecai sat
20 [*was* sitting] in *the* king's gate. Esther *had* not *yet* showed [*was* not telling] her
kindred [lineage] nor [and] her people, as Mordecai *had* charged [enjoined upon]
her: for Esther did the commandment [saying] of Mordecai, like as [what she
21 was] when she was brought up [in her being supported] with him. In those days,
while [and, *i. e.* when] Mordecai sat [*was* sitting] in *the* king's gate, two of *the*
king's chamberlains, Bigthan and Teresh, of *those* which kept [keeping] the door
[threshold] were wroth [was enraged], and sought to lay hand on the king Aha-
22 suerus. And the thing [word] was known to Mordecai, who [and he] told *it* unto
Esther the queen, and Esther certified [said to] the king *thereof* in Mordecai's
23 name. And *when* inquisition was made of [they sought] the matter [word], [and]
it was found *out;* therefore [and] they were both hanged on a tree: and it was
written in *the* book of *the* Chronicles [words (*i. e.* deeds) of the days] before the
king.

TEXTUAL AND GRAMMATICAL.

[1] [Ver. 7. Of the two expressions here used, the former refers to general *symmetry* of person, יְפַת־תֹּאַר, and the latter specially to *comeliness* of countenance, טוֹבַת מַרְאֶה. Esther had not only a fine form, but also a fine face.—Tr.]

[2] [Ver. 11. The expression here used is doubly emphatic, בְּכָל־יוֹם וָיוֹם, to show Mordecai's intense solicitude for his ward.—Tr.]

[3] [Ver. 14. The pronoun, being expressed, is here emphatic = *each* individual singly.—Tr.]

EXEGETICAL AND CRITICAL.

Vers. 1–4. *Plan for procuring a new Queen.*—The history which informs us how Ahasuerus caused virgins to be brought together from all the parts of his kingdom; how in consequence he loved Esther in the place of Vashti, begins properly here, at the point when the anger of the king against Vashti had allayed, and when he thought of what she had done, and what was determined respecting her. In view of ver. 16 we would be led to assume, since Esther was brought to the king's palace in the seventh year, and the tenth month of the year, that now we stand in the fifth or even the sixth year of the reign of Ahasuerus. Hence there would be between ch. i. (comp. ver. 3) and chap. ii. a period of nearly three years. We may assume that it did not take longer than a half year to execute the order here given; and the preparation of the virgins described in ver. 12 did not continue more than a year. Meanwhile Ahasuerus was employed in Greece during the sixth year of his reign, but he returned in the seventh. In all probability we are still in the time of the Grecian war. We may also very naturally conclude that under the circumstances many years were not suffered to pass before it was thought to find a substitute for Vashti. This resolution was formed soon after the rejection of Vashti, but its execution may have been delayed because of the newly undertaken Grecian war. The literal meaning of ver. 1 seems to be that Ahasuerus rued in his sober moments what had passed, that hence the fear might have arisen lest he would now direct his anger from Vashti and let it fall upon his counsellors.

שֹׁךְ from שָׁכַךְ, *to let down*, to lie down, is here and in chap. vii. 10, spoken of the swellings of anger, in Gen. viii. 1, of movements of water, and is related to שָׁחַח, *to be low* or become low. גָּזַר is *to decide*, to *conclude firmly*, irrevocably, comp. גְּזֵרָה, Dan. iv. 14.

Ver. 2. The youths* that served before the king sought to avert the danger that threatened. Those here mentioned are his attendants (comp. Neh. iv. 10), who were employed about his person (comp. chap. vi. 3, 5). They advised that maidens, virgins, be brought to the king, and that these should be beautiful to look upon. יְבַקְשׁוּ, the 3d pers. plur., represents, as is usual in the Aram., the impersonal "one," as a passive expression. נְעָרוֹת, *marriageable* persons, is in itself too indefinite to be other than an appendage to בְּתוּלוֹת.†

Ver. 3. They also gave the plan of execution of this project: The king, through his appointed officers, or through specially authorized men, was to cause to be brought together from all the provinces of his kingdom the most beautiful virgins, and placed under the hand of Hege in the house of the women. This Hege was the chief eunuch of the king, the keeper of the women, under whose care and direction every young maiden taken into the harem was placed, and by him prepared for one whole year to go into the presence of the king (comp. ver. 12). הֵגֶא in vers. 8 and 15 called הֵגַי, was, as above stated, the chief overseer of the king's harem.‡ **And let their things for purification be given (them).**—וְנָתוֹן, the infin. absol., gives prominence to the act purely as such, since it presupposes the subject as being self-evident: "Let them be given" [rather, "Let there be *a giving*"]. תַּמְרוּק (comp. vers. 9 and 12), from מָרַק, *to rub*, to cleanse, to make clean, is an abstract image, *purification* in the sense of cleansing; while מְרוּקִים in ver. 12 means rather [passively] *become cleansed*, or pure. Evidently such a purification meant a cleansing and anointing with precious oils, ver. 4. Their purpose was that the one who should please the king might become queen in the room of Vashti. מָלַךְ here speaks of the queen, as it elsewhere does of the king. Ahasuerus approved of this proposition also (comp. chap. i. 21).

Vers. 5–7. Now our author can and must make a reference to Mordecai and Esther as the chief persons on the one side in the conflict that is to follow. Ver. 5. **A certain Jew**—remained about there—**in Shushan the palace—whose name (was) Mordecai.**—It is a characteristic of our author in his vivid mode of statement that, instead of continuing the connection, he makes use of וַיְהִי, so taking a fresh start (comp. chap. i. 9, 10). Thus a new element, which comes into play in this history, receives greater prominence.

The name *Mordecai*, which in the later recensions is not written מָרְדְּכַי, but מָרְדֳּכַי, has perhaps connection with the Persian *mordkai*, "little man" (mannikin). Its derivation from the name of the Chaldee God, *Merodach*, is, however, extremely improbable. Its import is equally as uncertain with that of most of the names mentioned in chap. i.* **The son of Jair, the son of Shimei, the son of Kish, a Benjamite.**—According to most commentators, also Clericus and Rambach, Jair, Shimei and Kish were the nearest antecedents of Mordecai.† Still it is much more natural to hold with Josephus, who traces the genealogy of Esther to a royal house, that King Saul is meant (*Arch.* XI. 6); while both Targums hold both Shimei and Kish as being much earlier in the line, namely, identical with the men mentioned in the Books of Samuel, Shimei, the son of Gera, who cursed David (2 Sam. xvi. 5 sqq.; 1 Ki. ii. 8, 36 sqq.), and Kish, the father of Saul (1 Sam. ix. 1; 1 Chron. viii. 33). This agrees with the statement that the former Shimei, the same as the one here mentioned, should have been a son of Kish. In 1 Sam. xvi. 5 he is designated as being of the lineage of Saul. Further we discover that Mordecai, by this derivation, was a Benjamite, and that already by this genealogical descent he is placed in opposition to Haman as his enemy. This is most clearly shown by our author in designating

* [נַעַר, however, like παῖς in Greek, and *boy* in English, often denotes merely a male *domestic*, with little regard to age.—Tr.]

† [It here, however, denotes something additional to the charms of the candidates for the queenly state. All young females are not virgins, nor are all virgins young. These were to be both, and more besides, to be fair.—Tr.]

‡ ["The 'gynæceum' or 'harem' was always an essential part of an Oriental palace (comp. 1 Kings vii. 8). In the Persian palaces it was very extensive, since the Persian monarchs maintained, besides their legitimate wives, as many as 300 or 400 concubines (Parmen. *ap.* Athen. *Deipon* XIII. p. 608 *a*). Hege, strictly speaking, seems to have been 'keeper of the virgins' only, since the concubines were under the care of Shaashgaz (ver. 14)." Rawlinson.—Tr.]

* ["Mordecai has been probably identified with a certain *Matacas*, who, according to Ctesias, was the most powerful of the eunuchs during the latter part of the reign of Xerxes. ...... That Mordecai was a eunuch is implied by his adoption of a young female cousin, and also by the ready access which he had to the harem of Ahasuerus." Rawlinson.—Tr.]

† [So also Rawlinson: "If the writer had intended to derive Mordecai from a royal stock, he would scarcely have omitted the name of Saul himself. Nor would he have designated Kish as a mere "Benjamite." The same writer adds that on the supposition "that the list is simply the true line of Mordecai's descent from a certain Kish otherwise unknown, who was his grandfather," and had been carried away by Nebuchadnezzar; then "the four generations, Kish, Shimei, Jair, Mordecai, exactly fill up the space of 130 years from Jeconiah's captivity to the latter half of Xerxes' reign. ...... The age of Mordecai at the accession of Xerxes may have been about 30 or 40; that of Esther, his first cousin, about 20." Still these coincidences seem to be outweighed by the considerations advanced by our author.—Tr.]

the latter as an Agagite (comp. ch. iii. 1). It is also well known that it was a custom of Biblical historians not to give the genealogy complete, but rather to form a connection more or less close with celebrated names of the older times (comp. *e. g.* Maaseiah in Neh. xi. 5, the son of Shiloni; or Pethahiah, Neh. xi. 24, the son of Judah; or Shallum, 1 Chron. ix. 19, the son of Korah). The relative sentence in ver. 6: **Who had been carried away from Jerusalem with the captivity, which had been carried away with Jeconiah king of Judah, whom Nebuchadnezzar the king of Babylon had carried away** cannot by any means be referred to the last named Kish, as is thought by older commentators, and also by Clericus and Baumgarten (I. c. p. 127), but only to Mordecai, to whom special reference is made as being a Benjamite. Not only the analogy of similar personal designations found in the Scriptures demands this, but especially the circumstance that this reference to Kish as a Benjamite would be purely arbitrary. Thus it gives the appearance as if Mordecai had himself belonged to the first period of the exile, and not his great grand-father, and as if the history of our book, instead of belonging to the period of Xerxes, really belonged to the period of a pre-existing king of Media (perhaps to that of Cyaxares, comp. chap. i. 1). For the assumption that Mordecai had lived from the beginning of the exile up to the time of Xerxes, and then, being perhaps 120–130 years old, had become prime minister, is quite improbable. So is also the statement that he was identical with the Mordecai mentioned in Ezra ii. 2; Neh. vii. 7, an exile returned to Jerusalem with Zerubbabel and Joshua, but afterwards coming back again to Chaldæa, or rather to Shushan (Rambach). The contrast with the youth of Esther renders it in that case well nigh impossible then that she should come into notice here. Still this natural consideration may be deceptive. Since all the other incidents point to the later time of Xerxes, we are justified, indeed compelled, to bear in mind that mode of speech which was then employed. This treats of things done by predecessors as having been witnessed by their progeny, who had a certain part in them; such an analogy is found in Gen. xlvi. 8 sqq. Perhaps also the expression here indicates in advance that Mordecai had been carried away not only along with Jeconiah, but also together with the captives led away at the time of Jeconiah.* One thing, however, is clear: that though a Benjamite, he belonged to the "captivity" of Judah, and not to that of Israel, to which Joachim Lange would assign him. But in this place reference is made to him, as is indicated in ver. 7, because of his relationship to Esther. **And he brought up Hadassah [that is, Esther] his uncle's daughter.**—אֹמֵן, a participle connected with an accus., means a *guardian* (2 Ki. xi. 5; Num. xi. 12), but it may also mean one *who cares for*, or who is a foster-parent (Isa. xlix. 23). הֲדַסָּה, *myrtle*, usually masc. הֲדַס, plur. הֲדַסִּים, may be compared with the Greek names for maidens, Μυρτία, Μυῤῥίνη. The phrase, "that is, Esther," has joined with it also the other name by which she has become known. Without doubt she received this at the Persian court. אֶסְתֵּר is old Persian *stara* with א prosth.: see the term for *star*, modern Persian *sitareh*, Greek ἀστήρ. As the daughter of his uncle, his father's brother, hence also his cousin, it was very likely that she was somewhat younger than her foster-father, but not one hundred or more years younger, as would be the case if he had lived at the beginning of the exile. Her father's name, according to ver. 15, was Abihail.

In vers. 8–11 it follows how Esther, and through her Mordecai, were involved in the history of Ahasuerus. Ver. 8. **So it came to pass** (literally "when was heard," comp. chap. i. 20 and Neh. vi. 1), **when the king's commandment and his decree was heard**—*i. e.*, the decree of the king as expressed in the publicly proclaimed law, so that all were obliged to give it obedience; among other maidens **Esther was brought also into the king's house.**—Perhaps quite a time was allowed to elapse before executing the decree, on account of the war with Greece, which had broken out meanwhile. It is quite certain, according to what follows, that Esther was not brought into the palace of the king Ahasuerus before the sixth year of his reign.

Ver. 9. Now since Esther appeared very beautiful in the eyes of Hegai, and found favor in his sight נָשָׂא חֶסֶד or נָשָׂא חֵן (vers. 15, 17; chap. v. 2) occurs only in our book, commonly מָצָא חֵן, to *obtain* or bear away *grace* or favor—**he speedily gave her her things for purification with such things as belonged to her** (comp. ver. 3). מָנוֹת are *portions*, not so much of oils for anointing as rather *good food* (comp. chap. ix. 19, 22). Perhaps those maidens that were selected by the king received during their time of purification an especially good diet (comp. Dan. i. 5). But they were prepared one after the other. Hegai expedited matters that Esther should be counted among the virgins of the harem as soon as possible. The accus.: *the things for her purification and such things as belonged to her*, does not depend upon יְבַהֵל, but upon לָתֵת לָהּ; the object is placed before the infin. according to Aramæan usage. But the infin. is here added after the following object; and "the seven maidens selected" is repeated, lest the previous objective statement might seem too long. The seven maidens selected, *i. e.* from the king's service, were by law given to her as servants and to keep her company. רְאֻיוֹת means primarily *selected* for a definite purpose (comp. חֲזָא, Dan. iii. 19); in the Talmud and Rabbins רָאוּי takes the meaning of *dignus, decens, conveniens.**—**And he preferred**

* ["The relative clause, 'Who had been carried away,' need not be so strictly understood as to assert that Mordecai himself was carried away; but the object being to give merely his origin and lineage, and not his history, it involves only the notion that he belonged to those Jews who were carried to Babylon by Nebuchadnezzar with Jeconiah, so that he, though born in captivity, was carried to Babylon in the persons of his forefathers." KEIL.—TR.]

* [It is implied that each concubine received seven maidens, but that by the favor of Hegai, Esther received *picked* maidens. RAWLINSON.—TR.]

her and her maids unto the best (place) **of the house of the women,** *i. e.* an especially good and beautiful part of it, the staterooms of the women's house. Thus she might in every respect live as belonged to the distinction awaiting her.

Ver. 10. Esther owed this fortune next to her fairness to the shrewdness of Mordecai. Because of his advice **Esther had not showed her people nor her kindred,** as being one of the captive and despised Jews, else she would soon have been set back. Mordecai showed his love and shrewdness also in this, that even now he kept up his relationship to her. **And Mordecai walked every day before the court of the women's house, to know how Esther did, and what should become of her.**—This was to find out whether she was really in preparation for the king. It appears that he could still approach her without hindrance, whereas in chap. iv. it is stated, that when he put on clothes of mourning, he was no more permitted either to stand in the gate of the king, or to pass up and down before the house of the women. Perhaps the laws of the harem were in those days not so strict that, though he could not speak to Esther directly, still he could find out about her by her associate maidens. We have neither a right nor claim on the explanation of Jewish commentators that he was a Persian official high in rank, and therefore he had admittance to her (comp. ver. 19).*

Vers. 12–18. Esther was preferred before all the other virgins. But in order to give prominence to the modesty and simplicity of Esther, our author tells us beforehand, in vers. 12–14, what would have been granted her in this decisive hour had she requested it. **Now when every maid's turn was come to go in to king Ahasuerus,** *etc.*—תּוֹר, really *order*, according to Ewald, § 146 *d*, probably connected with תּוֹרָה (comp. 1 Chron. xvii. 17), here in our verse corresponds to "turn," "row" (ver. 15); comp. תּוֹרִים, *rows*, chains, Cantic. i. 11. So instead of saying: "When the turn of each maid came," we would say: "When it was the turn of each maid." **After that she had been twelve months, according to the manner of the women.**—One would be led to expect: "At the end of twelve months, after that," *etc.* But the author desires to give expression to the thought: "At the end of the purifications and necessary preparations." The "manner of the women" does not mean the *custom of the women* (Gen. xviii. 11; xxxi. 35, Clericus), for it would not then be necessary to add "twelve months;" but it is the law prescribing those preparations which are more fully set forth in what follows. The term "women" instead of "maidens" must not seem strange to us at this place any more than תַּמְרוּקֵי at the end of the verse. **Six months with the oil of myrrh,** *etc.*, is more fully supplemented by: "They were purified" or prepared. The purifications of the women last mentioned are still other means which were employed by the women for this purpose. The clause following in ver. 13 should perhaps read: "At the coming of every maiden to the king all these things were given her," *etc.* For this is really the declaration upon which a fact is based, namely, that when Esther came, she required nothing more of Hegai than what he appointed, as is stated in ver. 15. The expression: "At her coming" is made with a previous clause of condition, and is attached by the conjunction "and" to the sentence gone before; and it is also connected in its participial form with the principal sentence, so that it is best introduced by the terms "and when" or "now when" (comp. Job i. 13, 16, 17 seq., and Ewald, § 341 *d*). Such participial sentences of condition as are found in ver. 14 correspond to the nominative absolute, somewhat like the genitive absolute of the Greeks. **Then thus came (every) maiden unto the king; whatsoever she desired was given her to go with her.**—בָּזֶה may be understood to mean *from that time*, as does also the Sept., *i. e.*, *illo, sc. tempore;* but it may also have reference to the condition, *hoc modo, sc. ornata* (comp. בְּכֵן, chap. iv. 16). The subject, "whatever" (all that), precedes for emphasis, and does not mean a companion (Rambach)—opposed to this is ver. 15—but all kinds of articles of decoration and of precious value with which she would decorate herself to appear before the king. The lot that befel most virgins in spite of all preparation and decoration is also on this account made note of by the author in ver. 14, in order to give due prominence to the good fortune that came to Esther in her simplicity and attractive demeanor by placing it in such contrast. **In the evening she went, and on the morrow she returned into the second house of the women, to the custody of Shaashgaz,** *etc.*—שֵׁנִי is for שֵׁנִית, as in Neh. iii. 30; another part of the harem which was occupied by the concubines. Shaashgaz, who had the special oversight over the concubines, may have been a subordinate officer. **She came in unto the king no more, except the king,** *etc.*—We find that נִקְרָאָה is in other good MSS. also written with the usual punctuation נִקְרְאָה.

Following ver. 15 we have Esther's conduct and success. **Now when the turn of Esther, the daughter of Ahihail, the uncle of Mordecai, who had taken her for his daughter, was come,** *etc.* Thus fully is this account given, since now the decisive moment had come, in which she should come into such an important relation to her people. **She required nothing but what Hegai the king's chamberlain, the keeper of the women, appointed.**—Not, perhaps, because of shrewdness, as if she depended on the fact that Hegai understood best the taste of the king; she did not design to please the king by means of ornamentation, and only put on what was deemed

* ["Mordecai occupied, apparently, an humble place in the royal household. He was probably one of the porters or door-keepers at the main entrance of the palace (see ver. 21, and comp. ch. iii. 2; v. 13, *etc.*). This position separated him from his adopted daughter, and some effort was needed to keep up communication with her." RAWLINSON.—TR.]

indispensable by Hegai.* **And Esther obtained favor in the sight of all them that looked upon her.**—She was attractive, *sc.* in this momentous hour. נָשָׂא חֵן, like נָשָׂא חֶסֶד, in ver. 9.—[Ver. 16. **The month Tebeth.**—"This word, which does not occur elsewhere in Scripture, is singularly like that of the corresponding Egyptian month, *Tobi* or *Tubai*. A name but slightly different is found in the Palmyrian inscriptions (Gesenius, *Thesaur*, p. 543). Tebeth corresponded nearly to our January."—Rawlinson.]

Ver. 17. **And the king loved Esther, and made her queen instead of Vashti:** no doubt at the time of the first interview.

Ver. 18. In addition he also made a joyous marriage-feast, *viz.:* **a great feast unto all his princes and his servants (even) Esther's feast.**—Perhaps such a feast, named in honor of the queen, was a custom on these occasions, and its import is this: Esther's marriage with the king was thereby celebrated in due form. To this it may be added that Ahasuerus gave to the provinces **a release, and gave gifts, according to the state of the king.**—The verbal form of the Hiphil of הֲנָחָה in Chaldee may mean a *release from taxes;* the Sept. has it more indefinitely as ἄφεσις. But the Vulg. has it *requies*, as if it meant only a day of rest, for which עָשָׂה may be more appropriate. מַשְׂאֵת, according to Amos v. 11; Jer. xl. 5, is a *gift* of corn or articles of food. כְּיַד הַמֶּלֶךְ, as in chap. i. 7.

Vers. 19–23. The author connects with the elevation of Esther a meritorious act of Mordecai, namely, the discovery of a conspiracy against the life of Ahasuerus. This fact, though not at once apparent as to its present bearing, became of very great importance in the history yet to be developed. And it could even now serve to confirm the hope, by means of Esther's elevation, that henceforth an especially good time was coming for Judaism in Persia. Mordecai, who had previously shown himself a very shrewd man, now also reveals himself as a righteous subject. It seems that he, even more than Esther, was to be celebrated. The introductory sentences in vers. 19 and 20 are very obscure. **And when the virgins were gathered together the second time, then Mordecai sat in the king's gate.**—It may be asked what is meant by this second gathering of virgins. Clericus thinks "they seem on the first occasion to have been collected into the various provinces, and afterwards at Susa, before they were introduced into the royal *gynocæum*. The writer returns to what had happened before the marriage of Esther." So likewise Grotius: "It is an ἐπάνοδος or retrogression; for reference is made to the incidents in chap. ii. 2."

* ["No doubt the virgins generally took the opportunity—one that would occur but once in their lives—to load themselves with precious ornaments of various kinds, neck-laces, bracelets, ear-rings, anklets and the like. Esther allowed Hegai to dress her as he would."—Rawlinson. Thus, as ever, it proved that true piety is the highest ornament, even in a heathen's sight; and modesty is the brightest jewel of female beauty (1 Pet. iii. 3, 4).]—Tr.]

But the word שֵׁנִית does not well correspond to this, nor the circumstance that, now, according to ver. 20 sqq., Esther is already queen; so that Mordecai now no more takes his post at the inclosure of the house of the women, but in the gate of the king, and thus through him she is enabled to give information to Ahasuerus. Drusius and Bertheau assume that the writer speaks here of the gathering or transfer of those maids who had been with the king into the other part of the house of the women which was under the care of Shaashgaz. Thus we may explain the fact that Mordecai no longer walked up and down before the house of the women, but stopped in the gate of the king, and was at his post when the virgins were conducted from the house of the king back to the house of the women, where he might expect that Esther would pass, since as the beloved queen she frequently came to the king. But then we would not read of a gathering, especially one of virgins, בְּתוּלוֹת. Besides שֵׁנִית does not well have a place in this explanation, and the idea that in the gate of the king one would be nearer to the women when returning from the king's palace is incorrect. The choice of the same expression קָבַץ, which was employed in verses 3 and 8 with reference to the first collection of women, as well as then שֵׁנִית, leads to the sense, as is recognised by Corn. à Lapide, as also by more modern expositors, Keil included, that after the elevation of Esther a still further collection of virgins was made, perhaps of such as came from distant provinces, and who arrived later. We must keep in mind that the selection of Esther did not prohibit Ahasuerus from loving other virgins also and crowning them queens, even though she had the preference before all the others. Solomon had seven hundred queens and three hundred concubines. The latter were only *secundariæ uxores* (concubines). Then it may further be asked, What purpose was served by the mention of the second gathering in this connection? Keil's assumption that thereby the period of the history following is designated, is insufficient, especially since it does not well serve as a designation of a period of time. The words immediately following make it probable that it was intended thereby to express how Mordecai could before this remain the more readily and oftener at his post in the gate of the king without attracting attention, or even without regard being paid to him. It may be assumed that at that time people did often come to the gate of the king except when the virgins had arrived, and in order to see them, while at other times they remained away. Usually, however, it was the seat for the officials, whether high or low in position (comp. chap. iii. 2, 3, and Dan. ii. 49; also Xenophon's *Cyrop.* VIII., 1, 6; Herodot. II., 120). We find nothing leading us to suppose that Mordecai was already an officer of the court, and as such had a place in the gate. If such had been the case it would have been mentioned, since, as an explanation to sitting in the king's gate, it was essential to the matter in hand. But, in chap. iii. 2, we again find him sitting in the king's gate, and that too, day after day. This may be accounted for. We may assume that, in consequence of the event stated of him in this place, he had in a certain sense obtained the right to stand among the servants of the king who had their position there. A confirmation of this view may be found in ver. 20, the object of which, without this connection, will remain obscure. **Esther had not (yet) shewed her kindred nor her people**, *etc.* If we look at what follows, where the door-keepers did not pay much regard to him, the sense seems to be: Mordecai did not remain there as the foster-father of Esther, for as such he would have been a distinguished personage, and one to be feared, but simply as an unimportant stranger. The reference is clearly to ver. 10. The author, in the repetition of this remark, and as is also clearly shown by the use of the participle, desires to indicate that Esther, as from the first so now also, maintained a strict secrecy, even after having become queen. Besides, the position of the word מוֹלַדְתָּהּ is notable. מוֹלֶדֶת, in distinction from עָם, signifies the family connection or relationship, *kindred.* This is here placed first, because the relation of Esther to Mordecai is under consideration. The strong emphasis laid on the fact that, Mordecai had so instructed her, that she only carried out his wishes, as when she was under his care, seems to oppose the opinion that she did it from other reasons, as that she was ashamed of her descent, and hence kept silence. כַּאֲשֶׁר here means "like as when;" comp. Job x. 19, where it signifies "as if." אָמְנָה, *education*, care, has the *raphe* over the ה, so that the ending may not be taken for a suffix.

Vers. 21–23. In these days when Mordecai sat in the gate of the king, **Bigthan and Teresh,* two of the king's chamberlains, of those which kept the door** (Sept. ἀρχισωματοφύλακες), or watchmen of the palace (comp. 2 Kings xii. 10), **were wroth**, became angry (קָצַף), **and sought to lay hand on the king.**† Contrary to ver. 20 the Sept. adds: *Because Mordecai had become distinguished.* But the matter became known to Mordecai in some way, according to Josephus through the Jewish slave of one of the conspirators; in truth, perhaps, because the lower officers, who had become party to the conspiracy, did not exercise sufficient discretion. Mordecai, through Esther, gave the king notice thereof.

Ver. 23. The matter was investigated, and it was so found, *i. e.*, established, and **they were both hanged on a tree**, *i. e.*, they were hung on a stake, or impaled; a customary mode of crucifixion (comp. chaps. v. 14; vi. 4; vii. 9, 10; Ezra vi. 11; and Herodot. III., 125).‡ These events were recorded in the book of the history of the reign, *i. e.*, in the chronicles of the empire (comp. chaps. vi. 1; x. 2; Ezra iv. 15), and that **before the king**, which may mean, either in his presence, so that he might be assured of their correct insertion, or that the chronicles of the empire were deposited before him, in his palace (comp. chap. vi. 1). It was a Persian custom to insert the names of those into the chronicles of the empire, who had deserved well of the king, as is confirmed by Herodot. VIII., 85. He also relates that Xerxes, on his campaign against Greece, had historians in his train, who were required to record the deeds of the Persians in a book.*

* ["*Bigthan* (the Bigtha of ch. i. 10) is probably the Old-Persian *Bagadana*, *i. e.*, God-given. *Teresh* is by some derived from *tars*, 'to fear;' but it is more like a foreign than a Persian name." RAWLINSON.—TR.]

† ["Conspiracies inside the palace were ordinary occurrences in Persia. Xerxes was ultimately murdered by Artabanus, the captain of the guard, and Aspamitras, a chamberlain and eunuch (Ctesias, *Pers.*, § 29; Diod. Sic. XI., 69, § 1). A similar fate befell Artaxerxes Ochus." RAWLINSON.—TR.]

‡ [Especially "of rebels and traitors in Persia (see Herod. III., 159; IV., 43; and the Behistun Inscription, *passim*)." RAWLINSON.—TR.]

* ["These royal chronicles were distinctly mentioned by Ctesias, who said that he drew his Persian history from them (Diod. Sic. II., 32)." RAWLINSON.—TR.]

DOCTRINAL AND ETHICAL.

It is of the every-day life of a purely worldly, of a heathen court, that the author of our chapter treats. This moves in the high places of this world, and yet it is a very low life. Ahasuerus begins to feel the loss which he has brought on himself by the rejection of his wife, and his courtiers advise him to procure for his lust another, most liberal indulgence. He lends an ear to their suggestion, and orders what might be expected to follow as a matter of course. Nothing seems more improbable in these events than a divine control and government; and we would hardly be led to expect the thoughts and guidance of God under such circumstances. Yet we are soon made aware that we are standing right in the midst of divine providence. Independent as the world may appear in its outward life, still the Lord knows how to make even the lowest impulses and movements — indeed even the sin present in them—serviceable to His purposes. While on the one side Ahasuerus desires nothing but to find the most beautiful of virgins, God on the other side places Esther in the right position, and through her brings help and protection to His people in the face of the dangers that threaten them on the part of the world. He permits His people to become involved in the low life of the world, nay, He has humbled them to such an extent that even *their* virgins must be brought to Shushan at the king's command. But in thus revealing the full depth of their degradation He also begins again to elevate them. Besides, it is remarkable, how the life of human love, even in its sunken state, can illustrate the work of divine Love. For just as Ahasuerus caused virgins to be brought together from all peoples and tribes, in order to select the most beautiful for himself, so God has in a certain sense tested all the peoples of mankind to see if He could find one that would be peculiarly His own. And then, in preference to all others, however many there might be, and however many excellencies they might have in certain directions, He would select the one least noticed as His bride and spouse.

On vers. 1–7. The author permits us here to take a hasty but deep insight into the domestic life of a powerful and wealthy heathen ruler, who lives in the world merely to live, and on the other hand he gives us a view into the every-day life of a seemingly poor Jew, who is also despised in the common lot of his people, but who nevertheless incontestably stands under the blessing of his fathers. Ahasuerus, amid all his wealth and splendor, feels an oppressive want. He remembers his wife whom he has rejected, and especially regrets the wrong which he has done her. Without doubt the feeling gains a place in him that the loss of a personal being whom he could call peculiarly his own, was a loss which could not be made good by any other possession, however precious. And the wrong which he thinks he had experienced from her, is, like all the wrongs of men of the world of which they accuse each other, rather of a doubtful kind. It may be a question whether it could not have been excused, or even taken in a good sense. In truth it was only because of his despotic and mistaken view of common rights, which even the wife has, that caused him to reject her. He had trampled under foot her feminine feelings. Nevertheless she was now for ever lost to him. He was not prudent, not cautious enough. He must even confess to himself that though he had consulted his counsellors, he still had acted in a passionate manner, and given too free a rein to his wrath. Though surrounded by affluence, he is yet discontented, more especially with himself; he is filled with vexation and conflict, though no one has dared to oppose him. Of course there are not wanting those who recommend to him means and ways for shaking off this oppressive feeling. One thing, however, is evident: he cannot attain to a true satisfaction in the manner which *they* recommend to him as regards the points in question. This can only be brought about by true love. But love, as is beautifully shown and carried out in Canticles, cannot be commanded nor yet purchased; it can only be won, and can only be brought into life and sustained by true love's labor. The view into the domestic life of Ahasuerus is, therefore, a view of the brilliant, but hopeless misery of heathendom, which only deceives the sensual fool with reference to its true nature, but which convinces those more circumspect of the poverty of those living without God in the world.

How different a picture is presented to us in the domestic life of Mordecai! Mordecai is a lowly descendant of a formerly distinguished, indeed royal family. He belongs to the scattered foreigners fallen under contempt, who were carried away captives from Jerusalem. He is in a strange land. He has, it appears, neither father nor mother, neither wife nor child. Even his relatives, his uncle and his aunt, are dead. But the latter left an orphan; he is to her a father, she to him a daughter, indeed a precious treasure. Doubtless he is aware how great a trust was left to him in her and with her, how God is justly called the Father of orphans, and that He especially blesses those who pity and minister to them. He knows his duty toward her, and its fulfilment brings to him satisfaction, makes him happy. God has blessed her with beauty, but what is more, He has bestowed on her an obedient, humble, and unassuming spirit, as is afterward fully shown by her conduct in the royal house of the women, and as had doubtless been often manifested before. She loves her people, and surely also its customs, laws, and religion. Thus she is to him indeed a Hadassah, a *myrtle* in the true sense of the word, an unpromising and yet promising bud. Indeed to him she has developed into a lovely flower of hope; and though it happen that she is taken into the royal house of the women, she will still be to him a lovely flower, whose presence he seeks, whose prosperity lies at his heart day by day, whose development will cause him to rejoice. Again she will more and more become to him a brilliant *star*, an Esther (*aster*), in whose light he views his own and his people's future. In this manner his life is not poor, though he appear insignificant and obscure, though it be filled with painful reminiscences and great perplexities which he must combat daily in his heathen surroundings. On the contrary he is rich in light and hope; and even if he had realized the latter in a less degree than he eventually did, still his existence would not have been in vain.

On vers. 8–11. That which gave Esther distinction above all the other virgins, who were at the same time selected with her, and whereby she obtained first the favor of the keeper of the harem, and then the love of Ahasuerus, was certainly not merely greater personal beauty. This would hardly have made such a favorable impression upon the eunuch. But it was rather a certain graciousness of being and carriage, which could only be present where the spiritual element does not occupy a lower plane than the physical, as was the fact with most Persian poorly-trained maidens, but rather where the spiritual element elevates and transfigures the mere bodily element. This grace had its ground partly in her fortune, but also for a great part in the spiritual nature of Judaism through the blessing of an adoration of the true, exalted, and spiritual God. It was therefore not without reason that the then existing Jews thought themselves recognised and honored in the preference of Esther, which, no doubt, they did to its full extent. They all more or less participated in her spiritual advantages, or at least all could or should have participated in them. This, however, affords little ground for beholding in the victory she won an indication of the triumph which Judaism, then so oppressed and despised, should obtain over proud heathendom at large. Nevertheless in the before insignificant but lovely Hadassah, who is now the powerful Esther, we see a symbol of the weaker but better element in Israel perfecting itself as the powerful community of the Spirit in the Christian church, which will yet conquer the world.

Luther: "Whatever heart is thus minded, will bear ornamentation without danger to itself; for it bears and yet does not bear, dances and yet dances not, lives well and yet not well. These are the heavenly souls, the sacred brides of Christ; but they are scarce. For it is difficult not to have a lust for great ornamentation and display." Stolberg: "Undazzled by splendor and royalty, the tender virgin rejected all these things. With noble simplicity she took the ornaments, neither selecting nor demanding anything, which the chief chamberlain brought to her. Even after she became queen above all the wives of the king, her heart still clung not only with gratitude, but with childlike obedience, to her pious uncle and foster-father, as in the time when he trained her as a little girl."

On vers. 12–18. In the small compass of what has here been said respecting heathen virgins on the one hand and Esther on the other, we find a beautiful picture of the world and of the kingdom of God—the opposite tendencies as also destinies, by which these conceptions are designated. Doubtless the heathen maids decorated themselves with all possible precious things, for the evening for which they had so long prepared themselves by their purifications and anointings, in order to make the best possible impression upon Ahasuerus, upon whose favor or disfavor their whole future happiness of life depended. But by all this tinsel they gained nothing more than to look beautiful in their own eyes, and that for a moment which flew away so soon, and in which they were allowed to harbor hope. The majority were only permitted to see the king, and thereafter for ever to bury their hopes. For them there remained the sad lot of the concubines; they must bid farewell to the joys which they might have had in another sphere of life, without obtaining any compensation for that loss in their strict seclusion. The elevated feeling that they had fulfilled their life-work must for ever be denied them. They had missed their life-purpose; life became to them more and more a uniform dark monotony. In like manner the children of this world act and deceive themselves. Although they are firmly intent on enjoying the pleasures of life, although they direct all their endeavors to this one object, and prepare and decorate themselves in their way at their very best, still they enjoy it but for a single fleeting moment. Esther, on the other hand, was distinguished by her lack of desire or claim to shine in external decoration. She only put on, what so to speak, was forced upon her. But she was thereafter beautiful not only in her own eyes, but in the eyes of all that beheld her.

Thus also her fortune was not a speedy disappointment; she really obtained, not what she had desired, but what she had never hoped nor expected. She really obtained a favorable intercourse with the king; she became his choice, his wife, she became queen. All these things plainly indicate that she possessed in an unusual degree God's favor and friendship, which still accompanied her. The children of God enjoy a still higher happiness. They who reckon it to be a great favor to serve God in all simplicity, yea to be even door-keepers in His sanctuary, are made His chosen and loved ones, if in other respects they have properly decorated themselves for Him. He adopts them as His children, and cares for them according to what is needful for them, even with temporal blessings; for the meek shall inherit the earth. He also elevates them to kings and priests, and adorns them with the crown of life, for He brings them to the inheritance which is incorruptible, undefiled, and that fadeth not away, reserved in heaven for them (comp. 1 Pet. iii. 3; i. 7).

On vers. 17, 18. It is quite possible that Ahasuerus did not clearly know why Esther was preferred before her heathen virgin competitors, and what he was pleased with in her, why he crowned her as his queen. Still we can readily discover in his demeanor an indication that heathenism is always desirous, even when it has tasted to the full all that it can procure for its own enjoyment, to obtain something different and higher. Certain it is that these higher needs, which could be satisfied with nothing low, and which exhibited a higher receptivity, should arrive at this point. It was meet also that the heathen should see the fact fulfilled, that they themselves, their heathen kings and princes must pay homage to the people of the Lord, as to a queen who above all is worthy to be placed upon the throne, and to impart to the world her laws and ordinances (comp. Isa. xlix. 23; lxii. 4 sqq.). When this shall be entirely fulfilled, then the marriage-feast which Ahasuerus made in honor of queen Esther, with the edict proclaiming a temporary freedom from taxation of the people, and the relief from their oppressive yoke granted at the same time, shall correspond to the entire life of mankind.

On vers. 19–23. 1. Esther was silent in regard to her Jewish descent and religion, and this was permissible so long as she was not asked to reveal it, so long also as the weal of her people did not require a different course. This she could the more readily do, inasmuch as the Old Testament religion, by reason of its limitation, did not impose the duty of a missionary confession. Even the Christian can keep his faith out of sight so long as its confession will not benefit, but would rather do injury, and so long as the duty of veracity is not violated. At all events the martyr's crown, if it is not hastily seized, but rather borne with dignity, is far more glorious than a royal crown. Yet true faith will manifest its world-conquering power, and be encouraging to its devotees only when it is openly confessed, though its confessors stand at the martyr's stake, or die by the claws of wild beasts.

2. Nothing justifies us in assuming that Mordecai reported those conspirators because of selfish reasons, or in order to gain distinction and merit, or because Ahasuerus as the husband of Esther was nearly related to himself. Besides being an indication, it may be an expression of shrewdness, of his sense of duty. Although the Jew as such did not have a very warm feeling of attachment to the Persian king, still, in so far as he lived according to the divine Word, he sought to perform his obligations also toward the heathen governmental authority (comp. Jer. xxix. 7). Thereby he also becomes a practical illustration of the fact that the piety which is nurtured by God's Word is also of benefit to the heathen state and to heathen rulers. The governments of modern times, which treat religion not only with toleration but also with indifference, should remember that godly fear, as it is useful for all things, is also the most substantial bulwark for the continuance of the state.

Brenz: "We have here a daughter bereft of the protection of man by the death of her parents, but God elevated her to great distinction, so that all men gave her honor. Why was she carried into exile, but that she should reign? why bereft of parents, unless that she might become the favorite of God and man?"

Feuardent: On vers. 8, 9. "From this it may be concluded, as later is actually affirmed by Paul, that God hath chosen the foolish things of the world to confound the wise; and the weak things of the world to confound the things which are mighty; and the base things of the world, and things which are despised, and things which are not, to bring to naught things that are: that no flesh should glory in His presence. For what is weaker than a little girl, or what more lowly and contemptible than an exiled orphan, born among a people of all other nations the most ignored and hated? What, on the other hand, in the estimation of the flesh and this world, is more wise and prudent, more glorious and powerful than Ahasuerus, Vashti, Haman and the other Persian and Median satraps? Yet by the means of a single person, Esther, they are confounded, superseded, ejected. By her office, I said, but by the help of God, although by the authority and arrangement of judges, of whom Esther was only the organ; lest the flesh should have aught whereof to glory, but that all the praise of the church preserved in the Persian realms should be referred to God. He was able, as in former days, so to have rallied under a brave Samson or Gideon His entire people scattered hither and thither, and to have fortified them with arms and strength, as to destroy by mutual slaughter all His foes when the great battle was joined; but in that case men would have arrogated something to themselves, and perhaps have said: Our own right hand, and not God, has done all this."—On ver. 15: "Let then both men and women learn by this case so to direct all their aims and desires as to please God alone by the ornament of a good conscience and by the forms of minds well adjusted; but to despise the adventitious bodily ornaments of this world as vain in His sight, and by this piety gain the surer rewards of heaven. For this alone is the true beauty, which is precious in God's view, and which causes us to be approved by the King of kings, and joined to Him in spiritual matrimony. . . . . Surprising that even the heathen saw and taught this. For Crates says: 'That is ornament which adorns. But that adorns which makes a woman more adjusted and more modest. For this end neither gold nor gems nor purple avails, but whatever has the import of gravity, modesty, and chastity.' "

STARKE: On ver. 1. "Whatever has been undertaken in anger against God's command can well be changed (1 Sam. xxv. 34, 35)."—On ver. 2. "To heap sin on sin is the master work of art of all ungodly persons (2 Sam. xv. 1; xvi. 22; Isa. xxx. 1; Jer. ix. 3)."—On vers. 3, 4. "The advice of courtiers is most generally directed towards the object to which they think their lords are chiefly inclined, and they speak to their wishes (2 Sam. xv. 4; xvi. 21). Carnal ears love to hear nothing better than what will please their lustful hearts (2 Sam. xvi. 22)."—On vers. 5–7. "When orphans fear God, He will also care for them (Ps. xxvii. 10). In a pious and virtuous maiden beauty of person is a great gift of God (Prov. xi. 2). We should not neglect the orphans of blood relatives. God is the Father of orphans (Ps. lxviii. 6), and He knows how to open the hearts of pious people who will faithfully care for them (Ps.x. 14)."—On vers. 8, 9. "What care and cost is required for the decoration of the soul, when it would prepare as an acceptable bride for Jesus (Ps. xlv. 14.)"—On vers. 16, 17. "God will raise the miserable one from the dust, so that He may seat him next to princes (Ps. cxiii. 7, 8)."

B.—HAMAN ATTAINS TO POWER AND DISTINCTION. HE DETERMINES UPON THE DESTRUCTION OF THE JEWS.

CHAP. III. 1–15.

1. *Haman's elevation. His resolve with reference to the Jews.* Vers. 1–7.

1 AFTER these things [words] did [the] king Ahasuerus promote [elevated] Ha-
man *the* son of Hammedatha the Agagite, and advanced [make great] him, and set
2 [put] his seat above all the princes that *were* with him. And all *the* king's ser-
vants, that *were* in *the* king's gate, bowed [were bending] and reverenced [bowing
themselves to][1] Haman: for the king had so commanded concerning [enjoined for]
him: but [and] Mordecai bowed not [would not bend] nor did *him* reverence [and
3 would not bow himself][1]. Then [And] *the* king's servants, which *were* in *the* king's
gate, said unto Mordecai, Why transgressest THOU[2] the king's commandment?
4 Now [And] it came to pass [was], when they spake daily unto him, and he heark-
ened not unto them, that [and] they told [*it* to] Haman, to see whether Mordecai's
5 matters [words] would stand: for he had told them that he *was* a Jew. And *when*
Haman saw that Mordecai bowed not, nor did him reverence, then [and] was Ha-
6 man full *of* wrath.[3] And he thought scorn [despised in his eyes] to lay hands
[hand] on Mordecai alone; for they *had* showed [told] him *the* people of Mordecai;
wherefore [and] Haman sought to destroy all the Jews that *were* throughout [in]

7 *the* whole kingdom of Ahasuerus, *even the* people of Mordecai. In the first month,
(that *is the* month Nisan,) in *the* twelfth year of king Ahasuerus, they cast[4] Pur,
that *is*, the lot, before Haman, from day to day, and from month to month, *to the*
twelfth *month*, that *is the* month Adar.

2. *With the permission of Ahasuerus Haman issues the decree to exterminate the Jews.* Vers. 8–15.

8 And Haman said unto king Ahasuerus, *There* is[5] a *certain* [one] people scattered
abroad and dispersed among the people [peoples] in all *the* provinces of thy king-
dom; and their laws *are* diverse from all [every] people, neither keep they[6] the
king's laws, therefore [and] it *is* not for the king's profit [fit for the king] to suffer
9 them [let them rest]. If *it* please the king, let it be written that they may be de-
stroyed [to cause them to perish]; and I will pay ten thousand talents of silver to
the hands of those that have *the* charge [the doers] of the business [work], to bring
10 *it* into the king's treasuries. And the king took his ring [signet] from [off] his
hand, and gave it unto Haman *the* son of Hammedatha [the Medatha] the Aga-
11 gite, the Jews' enemy. And the king said unto Haman, The silver *is* given to thee,
the people also [and the people], to do with them [it] as *it seemeth* good to thee [in
12 thy eyes]. Then [And] were the king's scribes called on *the* thirteenth day of the
first month [in the first month in *the* thirteenth day in it], and *there* was written ac-
cording to all that Haman *had* commanded, unto the king's lieutenants [satraps],
and to the governors [pashas] that *were* over every [each] province, and to *the*
rulers [princes] of every [each] people *of* every [each] province,[7] according to the
writing thereof, and *to* every [each] people after their [its] language; in *the* name
of [the] king Ahasuerus was it written, and sealed with the king's ring [signet].
13 And *the* letters [books] were sent by posts [*the* hand of the runners] *into* all the
king's provinces, to destroy, to kill [smite], and to cause to perish all Jews, both
young and old [from lad even to old *man*], *little* children[8] and women, in one day,
even upon *the* thirteenth *day* of *the* twelfth month, which *is the* month Adar, and *to*
14 *take the* spoil of them for *a* prey. *The* copy of the writing, for *a* commandment
[law] to be given in every province,[9] *was* published unto all people [the peoples],
15 that they should be [to be] ready against [for] that day. The posts [runners] went
out, being hastened by the king's commandment [word]; and the decree [law] was
given in Shushan the palace [citadel]. And the king and Haman sat *down* to
drink; but the city Shushan was perplexed.

TEXTUAL AND GRAMMATICAL.

[1] [Ver. 2. The different degrees of deference are well expressed by these two terms, of which the first, כָּרַע, denotes a simple *inclination* of the body as to an equal in courtesy, and the latter, שָׁחָה, a complete *prostration* in Oriental style of homage to a superior.—Tr.]

[2] [Ver. 3. The pronoun is emphatic, being expressed.—Tr.]

[3] [Ver. 5. חֵמָה, a more intense feeling than the ordinary אַף.—Tr.]

[4] [Ver. 7. הִפִּיל is impersonal, *one caused to fall*.—Tr.]

[5] [Ver. 8. יֶשְׁנוֹ the נ is epenthetic for euphony between the verbal noun יֵשׁ and its suffix וֹ.—Tr.]

[6] [Ver. 8. The original is emphatic, "And *there is* none of them doing."—Tr.]

[7] [Ver. 12. The true construction is "*In* province by [*lit.* and] province *was it written*," *etc.*—Tr.]

[8] [Ver. 13. טַף, a collective term for *girls and boys*.—Tr.]

[9] [Ver. 14. The original is emphatic, "In every province, and province, *i. e.*, severally.—Tr.]

EXEGETICAL AND CRITICAL.

Vers. 1–7. **The author in very brief terms** places the elevation of Haman, the Agagite, by the side of the exaltation of Esther, as shown in the previous chapter. Hence it is the more surprising that he adds what we would least expect upon the elevation of Esther, namely, that Haman, provoked by the apparent irreverence shown to him by Mordecai, resolves to destroy the Jews.

Ver. 1. **After these things did king Ahasuerus**—in ver. 7 we are in the twelfth year of the reign of Ahasuerus, five years after chap. ii. 16, but here somewhat sooner—**promote Haman the son of Hammedatha.**—גִּדֵּל, usually used in bringing up children, here means to *make him a great man*—**and set his seat above all the princes that (were) with him,** *i. e.* above all those princes who were in his immediate presence, above his chief officers. He made him, so to speak, his Grand

Vizier. Haman from *humajun*=*magnus, augustus*, or according to Sanscrit *somán*, meaning a *worshipper of Somar*, was a **son of Hammedatha**, whose name is formed from *haomo, soma*, and signifies *one given by the moon* (Benfey, *Monatsnamen*, p. 199). Nowhere else do we find it Hammedatha, but rather *Madathas* (in Xenophon) or *Madathes* (in Curt. v. 3, 6). This form according to Pott (*Zeitschr. der D. M. G.*, 1859, p. 424) has the same signification; and probably the ה is placed at the beginning on the ground that it may readily have fallen away, and thus is regarded as the article and so pointed. It is quite possible that the author knew the meaning of these names, and found them significant in what follows. Haman would accordingly be noted as a representative of heathendom.* The epithet הָאֲגָגִי leads us to this conclusion. One thing is certain, that this designation with Jewish interpreters, as Josephus and the Targums, had in it a reminder of the Amalekitish king Agag in Saul's time (1 Sam. xv. 8, 33). But we have evidence more nearly at hand, since Esther and Mordecai in chap. ii. 6 are traced back to a family that had to do with the Agag just mentioned. Haman may not have been an actual descendant of the Amalekitish king, nor yet have been known as such. But possibly our author desired to designate him as a *spiritual* offshoot of that race.† Agag was a king, and hence also a representative of that people which had kept aloof from Israel from motives of bitterest enmity, and at decisive times had placed itself in the way in a very hateful manner (comp. Ex. xvii. 8 sqq. and my Comment. on Deut. xxv. 17), and against whom the Lord also declared an eternal war (Ex. xviii. 15; Num. xxiv. 20). As an Amalekite, he formed, as is fully shown in the Targums, a link for Haman with the equally rejected and hateful rival people, the Edomites. Again, the author would seem to indicate that the flame of conflict, which soon broke out between Haman and Mordecai, inasmuch as it was originally war between heathendom and Judaism, had burned from ancient ages; and when Mordecai so vigorously withstood his opponent, causing his fall and destruction, he thereby only paid off a debt which had remained due from the time of Saul upon the family of Kish, since Saul had neglected to manifest the proper zeal by destroying the banished king (Agag). In the second Targum (on chap. iv. 13) Mordecai gives expression of this view to Esther, namely, that if Saul had obeyed and destroyed Agag, Haman would not have arisen and opposed the Jews. The author doubtless placed Haman in relation to Agag in particular, and not to the Amalekites in general, since he was a leader and prince, and not a common man of the people. The Arabs and even later Jews applied such genealogical distinctions to Greeks and Romans (comp. *e. g.* Abulfeda, *Historia Anteislamica*). In the Old Testament the word כּוּשׁ in Ps. vii. 1 offers only a doubtful analogy; but on the other hand in Judg. xviii. 30 the change of *Mosheh* into *Menashsheh* is a parallel case wherein the faithless Levite Jonathan comes into a spiritual connection with the godless king Manasseh.

Ver. 2. All the servants of the king, who had their posts in the gate of the king, *i. e.*, all royal court-officers, were obliged to bow the knee before Haman and to prostrate themselves; **for the king had so commanded concerning him** (לְ, as with אָמַר and similar verbs, comp. *e. g.* Gen. xx. 13). It was a custom among the Persians to bow before the king, fall prostrate, and kiss the ground (Herodot. iii. 86; vii. 136; viii. 118; Xenophon, *Cyrop.* v. 3, 18; viii. 3, 14), so also before the high officials and other distinguished men (Herodot. iii. 134). Mordecai, however, refused to do reverence to Haman. He did this not from stubbornness or personal enmity. It is clear from ver. 4 that it was because of his character as a Jew alone; otherwise that fact would not have been mentioned in this connection. Again the Jews could not have thought such ceremony under all circumstances unfitting or non-permissible, as did the Athenians, perhaps, who regarded its observance (before Darius) by Timagoras, as a crime worthy of death; or as did the Spartans (Herod. viii. 136), and later still the Macedonians, who would not fall down before Alexander the Great according to Persian custom. This mode of obeisance was established and sanctified for the Jews by the manifold examples of the fathers (comp. *e. g.* Gen. xxiii. 12; xlii. 6; xlviii. 12; 2 Sam. xiv. 4; xviii. 28; 1 Kings i. 16). Even the Alexandrine translators and the authors of the Targums, as also the majority of modern interpreters, agree that bowing the knee and prostration upon the face has here a religious significance. Persians regarded their king as a Divinity, and paid him divine honors, as is abundantly attested by classical authors. In Æschylus, *Pers.*, 644 sqq., it is said: "Darius was called their Divine Counsellor, he was full of divine wisdom, so well did he, Persia's Shushan-born god, lead the army." Curtius says (viii. 5, 11): "The Persians not only out of devotion, but also from motives of policy, reverenced their kings as gods, for majesty is the safeguard of the empire." Comp. also Plutarch *Themist.* 27. In Haman as the chief officer it was doubtless intended to manifest a reflection of the divine dignity of the king, which should have reverence paid to it. Mordecai, it is held, thought that bowing the knee before Haman would be idolatry, and contrary to the commandment: "Thou shalt not make unto thee any graven image or any likeness." But this law in itself would hardly have restrained him

* ["The name *Haman* is probably the same which is found in the classical writers under the form of *Omanes*, and which in ancient Persian would have been *Umana* or *Umanish*, an exact equivalent of the Greek *Eumenes*. *Hammedatha* is perhaps the same as *Madata* or *Mahadata* ('Madates' of Q. Curtius), an old Persian name signifying "given by (or to) the moon." Rawlinson.—Tr.]

† ["It is certainly difficult to assign any other meaning to the word; but on the other hand it seems unlikely that Agag's children, if he had any, would have been spared at the time of the great destruction of Amalek, without some distinct notice being taken of it. Haman, moreover, by his own name, and the names of his sons (ch. ix. 7-9), and of his father, would seem to have been a genuine Persian." Rawlinson.—We may therefore conclude that the epithet "Agagite" is here used symbolically of a *heathen enemy* of the Jews. —Tr.]

therefrom. Against this speaks, not only ver. 4, which does not make a reference to the word of his God, nor yet to his monotheism, but only to his general character as a Jew; this, however, might be explained from the very slight indication in the style of our author. But the greatest difficulty in the way of this view is the circumstance that from such a conviction in regard to the act of bowing the knee, he must also refuse its performance even before Ahasuerus. In that case a later more intimate relation could not have subsisted between them. Moreover the facts seem against this view, since such Jews as Ezra, and especially Nehemiah, pious and loyal to the Law, found no difficulty at all observing the usual customs in their relations with the Persian kings of their time. It must certainly have been in his mind that to him Haman was an Agagite and Amalekite, *i. e.* a man placed under the curse and bann of God. He regarded bowing the knee before him as idolatry, if at all such, for the reason that a distinction only belonging to the representative of God would here be shown to one cast out and banished by God. Brenz says correctly: "The apocryphal statement (in the Sept. version) that Mordecai is said to affirm, that he would adore none but God, although a pious remark, is nevertheless not appropriate to this place. . . . Mordecai had in view certain passages (Exod. xvii. 15 and 1 Sam. xv.), from which he understood that the whole race of Amalek and all the posterity of Agag the king of the Amalekites, to which Haman belonged, were accursed and condemned by God. Therefore Mordecai, stirred by the Holy Spirit, confesses with magnanimous candor that he is a Jew, and is unwilling to bless by his veneration one whom God had cursed." In this view of the case Feuardent and Rambach substantially concur. If, on the contrary, we hold that Haman was not really an Agagite, and that the Jews regarded him as such only because of his disposition, then, of course, we must suppose that it was Mordecai's arbitrary will which regarded Haman as one rejected by God. Haman's inimical disposition against the Jews would not in itself have given a valid ground to the enmity of Mordecai. On the contrary it would still have been his duty to honor him because of his office. But this objection rests upon a stand-point such as we cannot assign either to Mordecai nor yet to the author of our book. It would have been different had it only had reference to a common personal enmity of Haman against Mordecai. But as the enemy of the Jews, who hates and persecutes them *in toto* because of their laws and religion, every one thought it proper to count him among those transgressors for whose extermination nearly all the Psalmists had prayed, over whom they had already seen the curse of God suspended, before whom one was not to manifest reverence, but rather abhorrence. It is well to bear in mind that Haman is not an enemy of the Jews, such as were so many heathen kings and rulers before him, but that in him the hate specially against the Jewish law was perfected, whereas other heathen magnates had usually manifested great indifference towards it. Mordecai had certainly abundant opportunity to become informed as to the kind of enmity thus exhibited. The author has not given this point great prominence because in his usual manner he thought he had done enough if he designated him as the Agagite. If this assumption be correct, then the import of our book is somewhat more general than is usually held; it does not in that case signify that the people of God can as such refuse to pay homage to men in certain definite ways and modes, but rather that to certain persons, as those who are rejected of God, *all* honorable distinctions may be denied. But it at all events amounts to this, that God's people may not lessen the reverence due to Him by doing reverence to others; for homage shown to those rejected of God would be against the honor of God, would be idolatry. In so far as Haman is an enemy of the Jews, who will not allow the observance of their law and religion, the final question would after all be whether the people of God, together with its law and religion, can be suppressed by heathendom, or whether it will have the victory. Comp. also Seiler on this chapter.

Vers. 3 and 4. The other officers daily questioned Mordecai because of his refusal, and finally reported him to Haman **to see whether Mordecai's matters would stand** (would withstand, succeed): **for he had told them that he was a Jew.**—By "his words," we can only understand an assertion that, as a Jew, he was prevented from participating in the ceremony of doing homage to Haman.

Vers. 5 and 6. Haman, when he had convinced himself of the conduct of Mordecai, regarded it lightly, and did not deem it sufficient to punish him alone; for the people to whom Mordecai belonged, had been told him, hence Haman knew that he belonged to the despised people of the Jews. But he rather strove to destroy all the Jews in the whole realm of Ahasuerus as being of the same mind with Mordecai.*

Ver. 7. Haman reasoned that for such a difficult and great undertaking he must select an especially appropriate day, and for this purpose he caused lots to be cast day after day throughout the whole year, and stopped at every day to see whether it was the one most proper for the undertaking. It was **in the first month, that is, the month Nisan, in the twelfth year of king Ahasuerus**, when this was done. Since he found a suitable day only in the twelfth month, namely, the thirteenth day of the month, according to ver. 13, it is clear that he manifested much persistency and endurance. Possibly, what in itself is not of great moment, namely, the time in which he examined every single day, is here given, in order to give due prominence to the greatness of his zeal. Possibly another reason may have obtained in this designation of time.

* ["In the West such an idea as this would never have occurred to a revengeful man; but in the East it is different. The massacres of a people, a race, a class, have at all times been among the incidents of history, and would naturally present themselves to the mind of a statesman. The Magophonia, or a great massacre of the Magi at the accession of Darius Hystaspis, was an event not fifty years old in the twelfth year of Xerxes, and was commemorated annually. A massacre of the Scythians had occurred about a century previously." RAWLINSON.—TR.]

If the day of extermination was determined on already in the month of Nisan, and proclaimed on the thirteenth of that month (comp. ver. 12) then it is clear that the Jews were for a whole year harassed in their mind regarding their fate in view of the edict which was now no longer a secret to them. Especially, if those living in and around Shushan had already heard on the 14th or 15th Nisan what was determined relative to them, then the most sacred joy which came to them in the Paschal festival was turned into utter sorrow. That it was the Paschal month in which their destruction was determined on, is by our author not so clearly expressed, since he seems to omit what might be understood as self-evident, but deserves consideration here. It seemed as if the old Paschal celebration, which indicated the ancient redemption out of the slavery from the world, was now to be abolished; as if Israel was now again to be handed over into the despotism and cruelty of foreign rulers. Instead of partaking of a feast it was enjoined on Mordecai, Esther and her friends to fast, as is shown in the old Targums (comp. chap. iv. 1, 16). But the more the ancient deliverance from Egypt seemed to be divested of its import, the more the new deliverance from Persia must have risen in significance; the more doubtful the joy of the Paschal-feast became, the more was the rejoicing of the feast of Purim enhanced. The feast of Purim as the second celebration of deliverance was hence co-ordinate with the Paschal festival as being the first deliverance, but in such a manner that the former became a vital support to the latter.

We do not regard Haman as the subject (Bertheau) to be supplied with הִפִּיל פּוּר, as is generally assumed according to ver. 6, but an indefinite "he," some one, *i. e.*, "they." The author seems to presume that casting of lots in such cases as the one in hand was not infrequent, and that some one had the office of casting the lots, so that the subject of הִפִּיל may be implied as impersonal. If Haman himself had been the subject, then the words לִפְנֵי הָמָן following הוּא הַגּוֹרָל would be remarkable, instead of which one would expect to find it לְפָנָיו. Bertheau connects this sentence with the explanatory phrase הוּא הַגּוֹרָל, as if the use of the foreign word פּוּר by the Jews did not mean every lot, but only that cast before Haman. But then the author would have expressed it more easily and shorter: This is the lot of Haman and not the lot before Haman. That פּוּר in the Old-Persian signified *lot* may not be doubted. Even in Modern-Persian it is *behr* and *behre*, "appointment," fate, *portio*, *pars;* so that a ground meaning, such as "lot," is not improbable (comp. Zenker, *Turkisch-arab.-pers. Handwörterbuch*, p. 229). It lies still more natural to compare it with, *para* or *pare* = "piece," *morceau*, *pièce*, originally perhaps also *portio* (*ib.* p. 162).* The casting of lots in ancient times was very common (comp. Van Dale, *Orac. ethn.* c. 14; Potter's *Archæol.* I. 730) and is especially mentioned of the Persians (comp. Herod. III. 128). The opinion, so closely connected with Astrology, that one day was favorable and another unfavorable for a certain undertaking, is met with also among other ancient peoples, and very extensively among the Persians. Indeed it obtains in those regions even to-day (comp. Rosenmüller, *Morgenland*, III., p. 302).*

The words: **from day to day, and from month to month,** are not to be understood as if the casting of lots had been continued from one day to another, *etc.*, and thus repeated over and over, but, as is clear from ver. 13, the meaning is that, in the first month every day of the year one after the other was brought into question.† It is noticeable that, in addition to the words: "from month to month," the number of the chosen month is added, *the twelfth.* One would expect such a sentence as this to follow: "And the month was chosen, and then the number." At least after the phrase, "from month to month," it would have been added "up to the twelfth month." Hence Bertheau concludes that the Sept. has given the words here: "And the lot fell upon the fourteenth day of the month, which is Adar," because they found them in the text, and that the eye of the copyist slipped all between the first לְחֹדֶשׁ to the second, after which latter follow the designation of the day and its number. But since the Sept. also adds: "In order to destroy the people of Mordecai in *one* day," it is plain that it supplemented our verse with the thirteenth verse; and since it was not the fourteenth day, but the thirteenth (according to ver. 13; chap. ix. 18, 19) that was designated, it is clear that the Sept. assumed to make changes arbitrarily. Probably the author in his customary short style spoke just as we read it. The use of the cardinal number instead of the ordinal made such a contraction possible; and the statement as to which *day* had been decided by the lot, might readily be wanting here.

Vers. 8–11. In order to gain the king also over to his own murderous plan, and to obtain of him a legal edict, Haman said to the king: **There is a certain people scattered abroad and dispersed among the people in all the provinces of thy kingdom.**‡—יֶשְׁנוֹ has the *Nun* inserted before the suffix as in 1 Sam. xiv. 39; xxiii. 23; Deut. xxix. 14 (Ewald's *Lehrb.*, p. 262 *e*). אֶחָד is a numeral. He means: "Only one of the many peoples has dared to disobey the

* ["*Pur* is supposed to be an Old-Persian word etymologically connected with the Latin *pars*, and signifying "part" or "lot." In modern Persian *parch* has that meaning. The recovered fragments of the old language have not, however, yielded any similar root." RAWLINSON.—TR.]

* ["The practice of casting lots to obtain a lucky day continues still in the East, and is probably extremely ancient. Assyrian calendars note lucky and unlucky days as early as the eighth century B. C. Lots were in use both among the Oriental and the classical nations from a remote antiquity." RAWLINSON.—TR.]

† ["A lot seems to have been cast, or a throw of some kind made, for each day of the month and each month of the year. The day and month which obtained the best throws were then selected." RAWLINSON.—TR.]

‡ ["Although a part of the Jewish nation had returned to Jerusalem with Zerubbabel, the greater portion was still despised among the provinces, in Babylonia, Mesopotamia, and elsewhere (see Ezra vii. 6; viii. 17; Neh. i. 1, 2, *etc.*)." RAWLINSON.—TR.]

laws of the king." This *one*, however, is so generally scattered and dispersed among the others that the evil example is of no small moment. It seems as if Haman here gave expression to a presentiment, whose fulfilment is declared by Seneca when he (*De superstit.* 3, p. 427) says: "Such power have the customs of this detestable people already gained that they are introduced into all lands; they the conquered have given laws to their conquerors." **Their laws (are) diverse from all (other) people,** especially from the laws of this realm (comp. in ver. 1, "above all the princes").* **Therefore it (is) not for the king's profit to suffer them.**—שֹׁוֶה, as in ch. iii. 8; v. 13, while in chap. vii. 4 it has a somewhat different sense. לְהַנִּיחָם, *to leave them in peace.*

Ver. 9. **If it please the king let it be written** = let it be commanded by a public announcement, which is as irrevocable as a formal edict of the empire (comp. chap. i. 19), **that they may be destroyed. And I will pay ten thousand talents of silver to the hands of those that have the charge of the business.**—Such a great sum (according to the Mosaic Shekel twenty-five million, and according to the common shekel, twelve and a half million *thalers; vide* Zöckler on 1 Chron. xxii. 14) does he hope to bring in by the confiscation of the property of the Jews.† "Those that have charge of the business," in 2 Kings xii. 11, designated builders (masons, *etc.*); but here and in chap. ix. 3 are meant the officers of the treasury ["the collectors of the revenue." Rawlinson].

Ver. 10. The proposal of Haman seems to have pleased the king so much that he gave him his seal ring, and thus empowered him not only to cause the before-mentioned public proclamation to be made, but also to issue other suitable decrees, and by imprinting the royal signet to give them the authority of irrevocable commands (comp. chap. viii. 8, 9). In private relations the present of a ring was the token of the most intimate friendship. Princes, however, thereby designated the one who held it as their empowered representative, (comp. chap. viii. 2; Gen. xli. 42; 1 Macc. vi. 15; Curt., X. 5, 4; Aristoph., *Eq.* 947; Schulz, *Leitungen, etc.*, iv. 218 sq.; Tournefort, *R.*, II. 383).‡ Sometimes successors to the crown were also thus appointed (comp. Josephus, *Ant.* XX. 2, 3). The significant designation of Haman as "the son of Hammedatha the Agagite, the Jews' enemy," points out how eventful this bestowal of authority upon Haman became to the Jews.

Ver. 11. The prospect of the great treasure thus to be acquired must have had considerable weight with Ahasuerus, who needed much money. Still it must not assume the appearance as if covetousness had anything to do with it. Hence he left the money to be gained to Haman, for thus he would also be the more sure of him in possible and coming events. **The silver (is)** (let it be) **given to thee, the people also, to do with them as it seemeth good to thee.**—The participle נָתוּן is a short mode of expression appropriate to the king. The sense is: "It is," or: "Let it be given." So also לַעֲשׂוֹת, "let it be," or: "It must be done."*

Vers. 12–15. Haman at once caused the necessary proclamations to be prepared, and had them sent into all the provinces of the kingdom. Ver. 12. [**Then were the king's scribes called.**—"The 'scribes' of Xerxes are mentioned more than once by Herodotus (vii. 100; viii. 90). They appear to have been in constant attendance on the monarch, ready to indite his edicts, or to note down any occurrences which he desired to have recorded."—Rawlinson]. In the very same month in which he had the lot cast, and on the thirteenth day of the same (בּוֹ, *in it*, the said month). Perhaps it appeared that the thirteenth day of the first month was favorably indicated together with the thirteenth of the twelfth month.† **And there was written according to all that Haman had commanded unto the king's lieutenants, and to the governors that (were) over every province, and to the rulers of every people of every province.**—אֲחַשְׁדַּרְפְּנִים and פַּחוֹת are here, as in Ezra viii. 36, placed together, the satraps of the larger provinces and the rulers among the separate peoples of the provinces. The שָׂרִים are the native so-called born *princes* of the different peoples. Before the following מְדִינָה, and likewise before עַם further on, it should really be repeated: *to the satraps, etc.* The sense is: "For the governors of each province according to their mode of writing (style), and to those of every people according to its language." In the addition: "In the name of king Ahasuerus was it written, and sealed with the king's ring," the perfect tense only is fitting, and not the participle. And though נִכְתָּב may have a *Kamets*, to give it greater distinctiveness, still this is not true of נֶחְתָּם, though so given in several editions.

* ["Compare the charges made against the Jews by Rehum and Shimshai (Ezra. iv. 13–16)." RAWLINSON. TR.]

† ["According to Herodotus (III. 95), the regular revenue of the Persian king consisted of 14,560 silver talents, so that if the same talent is intended, Haman's offer would have exceeded two-thirds of a year's revenue (or two and a half millions sterling). With respect to the ability of Persian subjects to make presents to this amount, it is enough to quote the offer of Pythius (Herod. vii. 28) to present this same monarch with four millions of gold darics, or about four and a half millions of our money, and the further statement of the same writer (Herod. i. 192), that a certain satrap of Babylon had a revenue of nearly *two bushels* of silver daily." RAWLINSON.—TR.]

‡ ["The signets of Persian monarchs were sometimes rings, sometimes cylinders, the latter probably suspended by a string round the wrist. The expression here used might apply to either kind of signet." RAWLINSON.—TR.]

* ["Some understand this to mean that Xerxes refused the silver which Haman had offered to him; but the passage is better explained as a grant to him of all the property of such Jews as should be executed. In the East confiscation follows necessarily upon public execution, the goods of criminals escheating to the crown, which does with them as it chooses (comp. ver. 13 *ad fin.*, and chap. viii. 1, and 11 *ad fin.*). RAWLINSON.—TR.]

† ["Haman had apparently (comp. ver. 7 with ver. 13) obtained by his use of the lot the 13th day of Adar as the lucky day for destroying the Jews. This may have caused him to fix on the 13th of another month for the commencement of his enterprise." RAWLINSON.—TR.]

Ver. 13. **And the letters were sent by posts,** *etc.*—נִשְׁלוֹחַ, infin. abs. Niph., instead of the finite verb in vivid description (comp. chap. vi. 9; ix. 6, 12). Letters, without the article, for the thought is: "Letters whose contents are that . . . . . should be destroyed." By the *runners*, by whom they were sent, are meant the posts, the *angari* or pressmen, who were posted on the main roads of the empire at definite distances from each other, from four to seven parasangs, and who rapidly expedited the royal (mail) letters or commands (comp. Herodot. V. 14; VIII. 98; Brisson, *De reg. Pers. princ.* I. c. 238 sq.). **To destroy, to kill, and to cause to perish, all Jews,** *etc.*—The crowding of verbs impresses the murderous import. **And to take the spoil of them**—*i. e.*, to thus obtain their property as spoils. Haman, of course, did not desire to come short in that which fell to him; but by giving the people the privilege of plundering, he desired to awaken their zeal the more. Thus they would either give him a share of the spoils, or else he hoped to obtain the sum before mentioned by the help of his servants or his coadjutors.*

Ver. 14. **The copy (contents) of the writing,** *etc.*—The statements respecting the contents in ver. 13 are too indefinite. It was not yet ordered that the officers only should fall upon the Jews, but that the people themselves should do this. This is expressly made to appear here. With reference to פַּתְשֶׁגֶן, see Ezra iv. 11. The substance does not there follow verbatim, but is indicated by the infinitive. **For a commandment to be given in every province.**—But the decree itself reads: **Let it be published unto all people that they should be ready against that day.**—What was to be published is also indicated, but briefly. Thus in the style of expression the details are noted as is common in edicts, with abbreviation of points referred to. Since דָּת is feminine, as is seen, for example, in vers. 8, 15, we cannot render: "That they should publicly proclaim the edict—make it manifest to all." Still less are we to understand it, as does Keil: "A copy of the writing of the substance that a law be given, and be declared to all peoples." Instead of גָּלוּי this verb would then have to be in the perfect tense, and נִגְלָה does not mean, as Keil interprets, *open* or unsealed in its transmission; neither does it mean *opened*, *revealed*, made known. גָּלוּי is rather in the optative, the same as is נָתוּן in ver. 11 (so also Bertheau).

Ver. 15. **The posts went out, being hastened,** *etc.*—דָּחוּף, *went speedily*, in haste; in 2 Chron. xxvi. 20 is the Niph. נִדְחַף. The additional clause: **and the decree was given in Shushan the palace** means to assert from whence they went out. But the remark: **And the king and Haman sat down to drink; but the city of Shushan was perplexed** reveals the terrible contrast between the gluttony of these men and the distress into which they plunged the land. It also indicates by what means Haman sought to draw the king away from the business of government. נָבוֹכָה primarily does not mean that it was *distressed* by terror or sorrow, but that it was *perplexed*, did not know what to think of such a terrible command (comp. Joel i. 18); in an external sense נָבוֹךְ means to have erred (Ex. xiv. 3).*

DOCTRINAL AND ETHICAL.

On vers. 1–7. 1. Mordecai's meritorious act, though recorded, had not yet been rewarded. One would naturally think that at this period he would obtain the deserved honor. But instead it is expected of him on his part to do honor to a man such as Haman, who was the sworn enemy of his people and a bitter opponent of the Jewish law; who finally, as an Agagite, was under the curse of God. Esther, who no doubt was true to Judaism, although she had not yet openly professed it, was seated on the throne as the chosen queen. And now one would be led to expect—certainly the Jews hoped—that she would bring the people relief from oppression, and restore for them liberty which would secure them from injuries such as they had hitherto experienced, or at least had been threatened with. Instead of this, Haman, empowered with full authority, resolves to wholly exterminate the people; indeed he is in haste, although this exterminating process was to begin only after eleven months, to make the people acquainted with their fate long before the event comes to pass. Now it happens that Haman thereby utterly ruins their holiest joy, and the season of Paschal rejoicing is converted into a time of distress and grief. It seems by such notice as if the people could no more place any reliance in their God as their Saviour; as if their Lord, who had at one time chosen them as His peculiar people, and who, if He would, could even now deliver them from the distress of exile, was no more to be the source of their joy. But, however unexpectedly these turns in their affairs may seem to some, and however the question might be raised, which is so often mooted, why it must thus transpire, seemingly against all hope; still that which came to pass was not so very surprising, but quite natural. One would very naturally expect of a prince

* ["By the issue of the decree at this time ('the first month') the Jews throughout the empire had from nine to eleven months' warning of the peril which threatened them. So long a notice is thought to be 'incredible' (Davidson), and the question is asked, 'Why did they not then quit the kingdom?' In reply we may say—(1) that many of them may have quitted the kingdom; and (2) that those who remained may have believed, with Mordecai (chap. iv. 14), that enlargement and deliverance would arise from some quarter or other. As to its being improbable that Haman should give such long notice, we may remark that Haman only wished to be quit of Mordecai, and that the flight of the Jews would have served his purpose quite as well as their massacre." RAWLINSON.—TR.]

* ["The remark that 'Shushan was perplexed' has been attributed to 'Jewish conceit,' but without reason. Susa was now the capital of Persia, and the main residence of the Persians of high rank. These, being attached to the religion of Zoroaster, would naturally sympathize with the Jews, and be disturbed at their threatened destruction. Nay, even apart from this bond of union, the decree was sufficiently strange and ominous to 'perplex' thoughtful citizens." RAWLINSON.—TR.]

who, like Ahasuerus, did not live to perform his duties, but to indulge in sensual gratification,—who sought, not the welfare of his subjects, but their wealth, would leave the power and government in the hands of men who knew how to flatter his weaknesses and to gratify his desires.

But above all, we cannot but notice the sharp contrast between the heathen state, as such, and the people of God. It looks very much like a merely casual human command, when Ahasuerus decreed that every one should bow the knee to such a man as Haman, and as if this single instance called forth a conflict. But in reality there is expressed the unconditional subordination which the state, especially the heathen one, must insist upon in reference to its laws and regulations. So long as the latter have proceeded not from the Spirit of God, but from the unregenerate heathen heart, so long will they contain demands to which the people of God cannot subject themselves. So long as the State is not entirely irreligious, it will be even inclined to operate within the religious domain, and thus the conflict takes its rise immediately between it and the people of God. We may also expect that the state will avail itself of such instruments to carry out its orders as of themselves are little disposed to be friendly to God's people; instruments who, because of that people's peculiarities, look upon them as a disturbing element, and are little disposed to exercise forbearance and toleration towards them. The people of God, on the other hand, have their obligation to obey all authorities under whose dominion they may be placed, even to the extent that they must endure condemnation to death, and suffer execution (Rom. xiii. 1 sqq.). But they are equally obligated to give honor to God and not to man. They can only give honor to man in so far as God has so ordered it. They must refuse honor to those who are opposed to God, at the risk of provoking the most powerful and dangerous men of authority in the government. There is in short a great contrast between those who know nothing higher than the law of the state and state religion and those who look above and beyond these to the true and living God, and who supremely reverence His law. This contrast in later times gave rise to the wars of the Maccabees, and still later, though differently in form, to the war against the Romans; and it was this, too, which more especially brought on the persecutions of the Christians. In short, it is the contrast which in the history of mankind has asserted its power even at the cost of conflict for life or death. It is so irreconcilable and so powerful that it could not and can not be removed by any compromise whatever, but only unconditional subjection on the one part—namely, of the kingdom of the world—and by victory on the other—namely, of the kingdom of God. This contrast has always revived anew where the powers of the world have thrown off from themselves the bands of the Lord and His anointed.

Berlenburg Bible: "That believers obey not the laws of the king has always been the chief complaint among the anti-Christian rabble, of which Haman furnishes a copy. The children of God, in their eyes, must ever be insurrectionists, disturbers of the peace, persons subject to no law or order, and by whom the public weal is endangered." Thus we have expressed the view in which Christ and His apostles were regarded (Luke xxiii. 2, 5). But this is the greatest of all falsehoods."

2. It is not only offended ambition that incites Haman against Mordecai; it is also hate against Judaism. It offends him that it has privileges and laws so different from those of the other peoples in the empire (comp. ver. 8). Hence he is not content to lay hands on Mordecai alone, but he resolves also to exterminate all Jews. As his offended ambition strengthens his hate against Judaism, his hate receives fresh occasion from the offence to his ambitious designs on the part of Mordecai. The contrast between him and Mordecai has therefore a more general and deeper reason. Even Mordecai's religion is endangered thereby. Haman demands the bowing of the knee, because according to the Persian notion, Deity is thereby honored in him. This is to him a religious rite. This is especially clear from the fact that he does not himself arbitrarily determine the day in which he will carry out his designs respecting the Jews, but he is rather dependent on the voice of Deity, as it is revealed to him by means of the casting of the lot. Nevertheless he gives religion a subordinate position in his thoughts, tendencies, desires and purposes,—so that the former really becomes merely a means to the latter. It is just the opposite with Mordecai. Had it lain in his power to determine, he would doubtless cheerfully have obeyed the king's order to bow the knee before Haman. He no doubt comprehended the greatness of the danger that threatened him in case of refusal. He would perhaps the more easily have given in, since no doubt a voice often whispered in his ear that it might be very questionable whether or not he should view Haman as an Agagite, as one rejected of God. But the facts were too plain, and God's Word required Mordecai to abominate instead of honoring Haman. This he must perform not only when it was most agreeable to his disposition, but also in the most opposite case. Viewed in this light Haman and Mordecai clearly indicate to us that the emphatic difference between heathen and Jew is true piety. The former serves when the worship of deity is only worship of self; in the lower plane it is only worship of nature and of the flesh; in the higher grades it has its basis in worship of human ideals. True piety, however, is a surrender to another will, to the will of the Holy God. Hence the former perfectly corresponds to the selfish manner of men, as they live at present, because of sin; the other opposes this in sharp contrast. But while the first is a flatterer, who, if any man will give heed, will deceive, the latter is a trusty friend who will lead upon a right way and toward salvation.

Brenz: "Satan, as Christ says, is a liar and a murderer. Hence he is ever busy in persecuting the church with his lying and murderous designs. You have heard before his lie: 'The people are using new laws and ceremonies, and they despise the edicts of the king.' Now hear his murderous words: 'If it pleases thee, decree that this people be destroyed.'" Feuardent: "The sorrowful condition of the Jews becomes very apparent and plain as here revealed; likewise the just judgment of God is here fulfilled. He says: 'They would not obey God in their own land, where they enjoyed such great freedom, but now they groan under the severe service that presses upon them, and they are brought into the risk of life itself. They refused to assemble in the sanctuaries of Jerusalem under their own kings, they ran after the golden calves, the sacred groves, and idols and superstitions of the heathen. Now they are placed and scattered under the most tyrannical form of government. They neither can nor dare congregate to offer a service of praise to God.'' STARKE: "A man resigned to the will of God will disregard the laws of men, whenever these stand opposed to the will and laws of God, however much he may suffer thereby (Acts v. 19; Dan. vi. 10 sq.). Although we should hold in honor those whom the higher authorities command to be honored, still such homage must not conflict with that due to God. When men disobey the laws of man and violate them, it is very soon taken notice of (Dan. vi. 11–13); but if they violate the law of God, then no one seems to observe the fact. We should not make man our idol, nor make flesh our arm (Jer. xvii. 5). Immoderate ambition generally breaks out into cruelty. The anger of great men is fierce (Prov. xvi. 14); hence one should have a care not to arouse the same against one's self."

On ver. 24. The people of God, in the conflict with their enemies, may rely on the protection of God, if they are morally in the right. Thus also the enemies of such people will be their own destroyers by virtue of their machinations. Such is the tenor of this whole book. But a more difficult question arises here, whether Mordecai, in refusing to bow the knee to Haman, and thereby bringing on the conflict, was really in the right. This question is the more grave, inasmuch as Haman could not properly be termed either an Agagite or an Amalekite; and all turned upon a form of homage proper and permissible in itself. The question would be more simple if Haman, as opposed to Mordecai, had been only a *private individual*. That in that case the latter's conduct would have been right and proper, cannot be doubted. As the Lord sanctioned enmity against all that are like-minded to Amalek in the command: "Remember what Amalek did unto thee" (Deut. xxv. 17), David justifies himself before God in hating those that hate God, and is grieved at those who raise themselves against Him; indeed he hates them with perfect hatred (Ps. cxxxix. 21, 22). When he would recount the chief characteristics of a truly pious person in the church, he makes this trait prominent (Ps. xv. 4). This, according to Luther, means that the just man is no respecter of persons; nor does he care how holy, learned, or powerful one be. If virtue be reflected from any one, the just man will honor him, though he were even a beggar. But if virtue be *not* found in him, then he will be esteemed as bad, and as nothing; the righteous man will tell him of it, and censure him. He will tell him, "Thou dost despise the Word of God, thou dost slander thy neighbor; therefore I desire no connection with thee." The Christian must in like manner perform this duty. He must do it for the sake of mercy, if no other means will avail; or for the sake of truth, which pronounces evil to be evil, and censures it. He must hold up to reproof him who by a persistent immoral life brings disgrace upon the name of Jesus Christ, or even by his conduct manifests enmity against the same. This the Christian should do often, not only as respects the particular person, but also as respects his acts or disposition. In regard to this, Harless says very justly: "It were a gross error to think that the Christian should content himself with reproving simply the offence and its tendency, but that thereafter he could nevertheless maintain personal and external relations with such a person. On the contrary, the blessings of the Spirit of Christ given to His church, will materially depend upon the principle that in the *selection of personal companionship* the consciousness and *true unity* which should unite the church must be maintained by external separation. The Christian, in so far *as it depends on his own selection and is consistent with his calling*, should avoid the society of those whose disposition he has found to be reprobate. We cannot term it other than a lack of Christian consistency when such Christians call it Christian love to seek out society from all the world in an indiscriminate manner, and cultivate it, and that according to *one's own choice* (comp. 1 Cor. xv. 33, *etc.*) " (*Christliche Ethik*, § 47, p. 456, 7th ed.). But all this has reference primarily only to the relation of the common intercourse of neighbors. Haman was to Mordecai an *official magisterial* person. Besides, it was expressly commanded by the king that he should be thus honored by bowing the knee before him. Hence the command: "Honor thy father and mother," and also the other that, " one should not revile the gods, nor curse the ruler of thy people" (Ex. xxii. 27), demanded respect. Neither was the precept to be forgotten: "My son, fear thou the Lord and the king" (Prov. xxiv. 21). In the New Testament the two chief apostles exhort us to submission under authority: Paul in Rom. xiii. 1 sqq.; Peter in 1 Pet. ii. 13 sqq. Peter closes the paragraph cited with the words: "Fear God. Honor the king." If by the word *honor* we are to understand merely the rendering of obedience, as seems to be implied in verse 13, then it would not be doubtful as to its proper limits. The word of the apostle: " We ought to obey God rather than man" (Acts v. 29) is very conclusive and direct, and needs no further confirmation. The church-fathers of the first centuries, in treating of this point, strongly assert that we should honor the authorities *in*, and not as *opposed to* God. Comp. J. Gerhard, in *De magistratu politico*, § 474. Then when the stability of order within an organized community is attacked and overthrown in defiance of right,—and such was the situation in Persia when Haman in an inimical manner attacked the Jews, who up to this time had had the undisputed right to live according to their law and faith; when he became to them an Agagite and an Amalekite,—then *resistance*, and individual participation therein, is justified and commanded. This, of course, holds within the limits of the existing order of a people and of the individual calling. Stahl (*Die Partheien in Staat u. Kirche*, p. 288), as also Harless (*Christl. Ethik*, § 54), is very clear on this point that, "the doctrine of the blamableness of any active resistance, and the unconditioned obligation of passive obedience is opposed to the Christian's sacred maintenance of right. So also is the assumption false that obedience must be rendered to authority because it is authority, even though it deny and disregard all right and law in the enforcement of its own claims to authority—an authority which it has not received for its own sake, but because of the right whose guardian and executor it is its calling to be" (Harless, as above, p. 541). Hoffmann (*Schriftbeweiss*, II., 2, p. 409) speaks from the same conviction: "It is certainly not morally permissible that one people rise against the righteous order in the existing government of another people, or of a foreign ruler. But it is a moral duty that it should not submit to be despoiled by a foreign power of that element, which, in God's order, is essential to its existence and to its substantial peculiarity." Experience has ever proved that resistance grounded upon a good conscience, and supported by so high and noble an enthusiasm, is indeed countenanced by God in so decided a manner, that no force, however great, can accomplish anything against it. It is worthy of notice that the command to honor the king and secular authority demands more than obedience, it embraces also regard and homage. Hence arises the question, whether or not we ought to meet certain persons with esteem and homage, to whom we must refuse obedience, indeed against whom—in contrast with Mordecai—we are compelled to offer resistance. There are doubtless many cases where these conditions obtain. Such a case would especially occur where the authorities think that right is on their side. When they proceed from a different view or conviction with reference to the case, they are by no means to be disregarded. The admonition in 1 Peter ii. 18 is in place here: "Servants, be subject to your masters with all fear; not only to the good and gentle, but also to the froward." Now if the authorities, as says Harless, really assume to disregard and deny right and law, in its claim of jurisdiction, which it can only have as the guardian and executor of justice, then practically it ceases to be authority. If it sanction oppression and pillage; if it touch the existing right, religion, and conscience, then it becomes a chief enemy of those who will not submit to the spoiling of these possessions—for so did Haman, nor otherwise could he justly be called an Agagite.

Hence homage can only be denied to the magisterial office where the bearer of the name is regarded as unworthy of the position he occupies. An external homage, in connection with which one must manifest hostility, would then become hypocrisy, and the more so since instead of giving the honor due from a sincere heart, we can only despise and execrate. To refuse it is only to act honestly, though it often requires courage. This is the more necessary since the opposition is grounded upon and confined to what is permitted according to right and calling. As was the case with Mordecai, we should take an early opportunity to manifest our determination to refuse homage to authority, since its false ways cannot be too severely condemned.

On vers. 8–15. 1. So long as Israel possessed a political independence the chief support of its religion had been the State. The State had jurisdiction over its own laws and those of religion. Now, however, the State takes an opposite stand to its religion. The complaint of Haman was, that this people had different laws from those of the other peoples of the kingdom, and hence did not obey those of the king (which was correct as regarded the laws that were opposed to its own). For this reason also, Ahasuerus permitted the decree for the extermination of Israel. The State, even at this period, could not avoid demanding decided submission; and where it encountered insuperable obstinacy it adopted extreme measures, even banishment and extermination. But it would have been better had it been tolerant to the last degree. All the means of might were at its command, by which to carry out its will. All the offices and organizations which the State had established for the weal of its subjects, as is indicated in vers. 12 and 15, could have been employed in their subjection. One might feel inclined to ask whether, in view of all these things, there remained any hope for Mordecai; whether his opposition did not, at the very beginning, promise to be futile. Doubtless his hope was in Him for whose honor he was jealous; namely, in the living God. That Being now desires to make manifest for all ages by a striking example, that He can sustain His people, not only without the aid of any civil power, but also in opposition to a foreign State. Indeed He can preserve it even amid the heathen, in spite of all distracting elements. Hence the church need not fear, be the relation of the State what it may. The Lord knows how to make even the most unfavorable circumstances serviceable and useful to the church.

2. If now we inquire upon what natural basis Mordecai could establish his hope, then we observe that truth was on his side. That which is rejected of God, instead of being honored, is to be abhorred. Hence for him who believed in the true God, no doubt existed but that this truth would eventually obtain a more general recognition. But in order to this, a still longer development was needed. Heathendom must first become conscious of itself, *i. e.*, of its own weakness and impotence, which were a part of its existence in spite of all external power; then only can it learn to know the true God. For the present, it was the weakness and failing, which attached to the leaders of heathenism, that offered resting-places for the helping hand of God. Whether these were already well known to Mordecai is doubtful; but to our eyes they are already manifest in this chapter. Haman would not venture to come before Ahasuerus and exhibit his wounded vanity and spirit of revenge; and Ahasuerus does not desire to reveal the fact that he is anxious to possess the money of the Jews. However, with the former vanity, and with the latter an inordinate desire for money, plays the chief part. They would have it appear as if their acts were done under the impulse of right and duty. They would kill off the people

of God with proper decency. They dissemble; but they thereby gain only a self-condemnation of their own evil motives. An official who is guilty of dissembling, is in danger of being unmasked; and a prince who is so weak as to be led by a motive of which he must needs be ashamed, especially in such a grave and extraordinary occurrence, easily exposes also other weaknesses. Hence it would not be difficult for others likewise to gain the ascendency over him, who could easily dissuade him from a purpose, even after the same had become an irrevocable edict. The remark at the close of the chapter is also very significant and characteristic. A prince and an officer who at the time when the inhabitants of their chief city are in the greatest consternation, when above all an entire people is thrown into mortal fear of their life, can sit down to eat and drink, manifest either an inhumanity, which would easily arouse a general revolt, or an evil conscience which already foretells the failure of their plans. If we ask respecting the natural foundations upon which the expectation of an eventual victory of Christianity is based, in the face of all the assaults and dangers to which it is exposed, then the power of truth, as it breaks its way and compels universal recognition, would emphatically answer the question, and be the main point of reliance. The experience of centuries teaches one fact definitely and variously, that there is salvation in no other, and that no other name is given to men whereby they may be saved, than the name of Jesus Christ. But the weaknesses of those who deem themselves strong will ever be a matter of observation. Christians should be better informed than they often are, of the impotency and nothingness of those in opposition to them. They have a clear right to the question: What can men do to us? Even their opponents must acknowledge, if they are not too much blinded, that in those nations among which the pure faith reigns supreme, there is a different type of fidelity, conscientiousness, devotion, and readiness to make sacrifices than among those who have been dried up by the sun of false enlightenment. The course of events will soon compel them to see their mistake.

Brenz: "This is plainly what Christ afterwards said to His little church; that is, His disciples: 'Verily, verily I say unto you, ye shall weep and lament, but the world shall rejoice: and ye shall be sorrowful, but your sorrow shall be turned into joy.' For as in the passion of Christ the chief priests triumphed, and the soldiers mocked, but Christ hung on the cross and was afflicted with exceeding misery, so the joy of the wicked will be at its highest over the sorrow of the godly. . . . But that is most true which we read: 'The triumphing of the wicked (is) short, and the joy of the hypocrite (but) for a moment. Though his excellency mount up to the heavens and his head reach unto the clouds; (yet) he shall perish for ever like his own dung: they which have seen him shall say, Where (is) he?'" Feuardent: "Observe now how active everything is in this matter, and how all conspires for the extermination of the people of God. The terrible sentence is defined and described in as many languages and modes as there are peoples in the empire. . . . . But while the godly are in great distress, as they anticipate the fatal day of the cruel execution, the king and Haman indulge in drunkenness and lust and joy. So perisheth the righteous, and no man layeth it to heart (Isa. lvii. 1). So the servants of God are oppressed by the agents of the Devil. So cruelty triumphs. . . . . But it is well. There is a God in the heavens." Starke: "When wicked men cannot otherwise persecute the pious, then his religion and laws must furnish them with a cause and a covering for their evil intentions (Acts xvi. 21, 22). In important matters it is not good to render a hasty judgment, it is better to reflect (Isa. xxviii. 7). God permits the wicked to have success beyond their own expectation at times, but afterward destruction will come all the more unexpectedly. (Ps. xxxvii. 35, 36; Job x. 45.")

SECOND SECTION.

The Conflict of Opposites.

Chapters IV. V.

A.—MORDECAI, GREATLY SORROWING WITH HIS PEOPLE, URGES ESTHER TO PLEAD FOR MERCY WITH THE KING.

Chapter IV. 1–17.

I. *Communication between Mordecai and Esther.* Vers. 1–5.

1 When [And] Mordecai perceived [knew] all that was done, [and, *i. e.* then]
Mordecai rent his clothes, and put on sackcloth with [and] ashes, and went out *into*
2 *the* midst of the city, and cried[1] *with a* loud [great] and *a* bitter cry; And came
even before the king's gate: for none *might* [*there was* none to] enter [go] into the

3 king's gate clothed *with* [in clothing of] sackcloth. And in every province,[2] whi-
thersoever [*the* place that] the king's commandment [word] and his decree [law]
came [*was* approaching], *there was* great mourning among [for] the Jews, and
fasting, and weeping, and wailing [smiting *the breast*]: *and* many lay in sack-cloth
4 and ashes [sack-cloth and ashes was strown for the many]. So [And] Esther's
maids and her chamberlains [eunuchs] came and told *it* her. Then [And] was
the queen exceedingly grieved; and she sent raiment to clothe Mordecai, and to
5 take away his sackcloth from [upon] him: but [and] he received *it* not. Then
[And] called Esther for [to] Hatach, *one* of the king's chamberlains [eunuchs],
whom he *had* appointed *to attend* upon [stationed before] her, and gave him a com-
mandment [enjoined him] to [upon, *i. e.* concerning] Mordecai, to know what it
was, and why it *was*.

II. *Mordecai commissions Esther to present his petition; but she raises a point of difficulty.* Vers. 6-11.

6 So [And] Hatach went forth to Mordecai unto *the* street of the city, which *was*
7 before the king's gate: and Mordecai told him *of* all that *had* happened unto him,
and *of the* sum [designation] of the money [silver] that Haman *had* promised
[said] to pay to [upon] the king's treasuries for [in consideration of] the Jews, to
8 destroy [cause them to perish]: Also [And] he gave him *the* copy of *the* writing
of the decree [law] that was given at Shushan to destroy them, to show *it* unto
Esther, and to declare [tell] *it* unto her, and to charge [enjoin upon] her that she
should go [to go] *in* unto the king, to make supplication unto him, and to make
9 request before him for [upon] her people. And Hatach came and told Esther *the*
10 words of Mordecai; Again [And] Esther spake [said] unto Hatach, and gave him
11 commandment [enjoined him] unto Mordecai; All the king's servants, and the
people of the king's provinces, *do* know [*are* knowing], that whosoever, *whether*
man [every man] or [and] woman, shall [who shall] come unto the king *into* the
inner court, who is not [shall not be] called, *there is* one law of his to put *him* to
death, except *such* to whom the king shall hold out the golden sceptre, that [and]
he may live; but I[3] have not been called to come *in* unto the king these [this]
thirty days.

III. *Mordecai presents his request still more urgently, and Esther promises to execute it.* Vers. 12–17.

12, 13 And they told to Mordecai Esther's words. Then [And] Mordecai commanded
[said] to answer Esther, Think not with thyself [in thy spirit] that thou shalt
14 escape *in* [to deliver] the king's house more than all the Jews. For [But] if thou
altogether holdest thy peace at this time, *then* shall *there* enlargement and deliver-
ance arise to the Jews from another place; but [and] thou and thy father's house
shall be destroyed [utterly perish]; and who knoweth whether thou art come [hast
15 approached] to the kingdom for *such a* time as this? Then [And] Esther bade *them*
16 [said to] return Mordecai *this answer;* Go, gather *together* all the Jews *that are* present
[found] in Shusan, and fast ye for [upon] me, and neither eat [eat not] nor drink
[and drink not] three days, night or [and] day: I also and my maidens will fast
likewise; and so will I go *in* unto the king, which *is* not according to the law;
17 and if [whereas] I perish [have perished], I perish [have perished]. So [And]
Mordecai went his way [passed] and did according to all that Esther *had* com-
manded [enjoined upon] him.

TEXTUAL AND GRAMMATICAL.

1 [Ver. 1. זעק, a later or Aramæan form for צעק, seems to be intensive of קרא, including the simple *call* for help, שוע, and the *shriek* from pain or danger, אנק, and denotes an earnest and vociferous demonstration. —Tr.]

2 [Ver. 3. See Note 7 in preceding section.—Tr.]

3 [Ver. 11. The pronoun, being expressed in the original, is emphatic.—Tr.]

EXEGETICAL AND CRITICAL.

The author manifestly desires to show in this chapter how very difficult it was for Mordecai to make even the one effort to save his people from destruction. But he was faithful and persistent; taking step after step until the object was attained. He here entered a conflict which was forced upon him, and which he was unable to avert. But thereby he ran the greatest danger both for himself and for Esther, whom he required to assist him. Three separate endeavors are recorded by our author as made on the part of Mordecai in order to involve Esther in this conflict. The first was preparatory, being designed simply to establish a connection with her; of the second the only result was the objections raised by Esther; and in the third she expressed her willingness and her resignation to a possible fate.

Vers. 1–5. Here is described *the first step*. The first thing Mordecai did was to take a leading part in the general sorrow of the Jews. Thereby he attracted the attention of Esther, and induced her not only to send him other garments than those of mourning, but also to send a confidential messenger through whom he could communicate with her. Ver. 1. **When Mordecai perceived all that was done.**—As is told us in ver. 7, Mordecai was even informed as to the sum of money which Haman expected to obtain by destroying the Jews. Possibly some of Haman's intimate friends heard of it and spoke of it in the king's gate where Mordecai could hear it. **Mordecai rent his clothes, and put on sackcloth with ashes**, *i. e.*, a garment of hair cloth, and with the same also put on ashes, by strewing ashes over his person and clothing (comp. Dan. ix. 3; Job ii. 12).* **And went out into the midst of the city.**—He did not conceal the fact that he was in deep distress, **and cried with a loud and bitter cry**; literally, occurs in Gen. xxvii. 34 with reference to Esau.

Ver. 2. **And came even before the king's gate**, *i. e.*, up to the free place that was before the entrance to the royal palace (comp. ver. 6),—further he could not come, no more could he come into the gate of the palace as before—**for none (might) enter into the king's gate clothed with sackcloth.**—So אֵין לָבוֹא, comp. Ewald, § 321 *c*.

Ver. 3. Many other Jews also mourned. The sorrow was general. Despite the elevation of Esther her people now had everywhere only distress and grief, instead of honor and joy. It seems as if the author would here describe how the Jews were treated contrary to what one would naturally expect after the elevation of Esther. He would here, doubtless, also give prominence to the remarkable mode which Mordecai adopted to secure the attention of Esther. Further in ver. 3 he would show us how pressing was the need of every possible endeavor for their preservation. **And in every province, whithersoever the king's commandment and his decree came**, *etc.*—מְקוֹם is the Accusative of place found in *stat. constr.* before אֲשֶׁר, as in ch. viii. 17; Eccl. xi. 3; comp. Lev. iv. 24 בִּמְקוֹם אֲשֶׁר. **And many lay in sackcloth and ashes.**—While all gave vent to their distress and tears, many manifested their sorrow by putting on sackcloth and sitting in ashes (comp. Isa. lviii. 5).

Ver. 4. The first object that Mordecai gained by his public grief was that he drew the attention of Esther's women-servants and eunuchs, *i. e.*, such as were assigned her for her exclusive service (comp. chap. ii. 9), and they gave notice to the queen. Though they had not as yet discovered the nationality of Esther, still they became aware of Esther's relation to Mordecai, who on his part was very diligent in his inquiries concerning her. Hence they delayed not to inform the queen of all that they know of him. Following the Kethib we should read וַתְּבוֹאֶינָה. As this prolonged form of the word does not usually occur after a *Vav. cons.*, the Keri has the form וַתָּבוֹאנָה. The object of יַגִּידוּ is found in what follows: the present appearance of Mordecai in mourning garments was not the cause (comp. ver. 5); but this was enough to give her considerable anxiety. וַתִּתְחַלְחַל, a passive intensive from חוּל, *they were seized as with pains of delivery*. She sent clothes to her guardian, that he might put them on, doubtless, that thereby he might again stand in the gate of the king, and so relate to her the cause of his grief. But he refused them, not only because he would wear no other than garments of mourning, but because he desired a private opportunity to communicate with her.

Ver. 5. Mordecai accomplished his object, and Hatach the eunuch was sent to him to obtain particulars. הֶעֱמִיד לְפָנֶיהָ, the king had appointed Hatach to serve Esther; hence he belonged to her eunuchs (ver. 4). וַתְּצַוֵּהוּ עַל, *she commissioned him with respect to* or עַל, substantially similar to אֶל, "she sent him to," (comp. ver. 10).

Vers. 6–11. Here we have *the second step*. In the face of the greatness of the danger that threatened the Jews it was hardly to be expected but that Mordecai should make a request of Esther whose fulfilment would be very serious in its consequences.—Vers. 6 and 7. When Hatach had proceeded to the open place before the palace, he found Mordecai, who in the hope that Esther would do something more, had remained there longer or more frequently resorted thither. Then Mordecai informed him of all that had occurred and that now threatened the Jews, and mentioned also the sum of money that Haman promised to place in the king's treasury, in return for the extermination of the Jews. This he did, no doubt, to show what low and despicable motives were at play in the matter; and thus he very naturally hoped to excite the greater indignation and wrath in Esther. She must not be left to think that Haman had found the Jews guilty of real transgressions when he obtained the consent of the king. That the king had remitted the money to Haman, is not referred to here because not pertinent. פָּרָשָׁה derived from פָּרַשׁ *to cut off*, separate, then to define correctly (comp. Lev. xxiv. 12), the exact statement of a thing, *i. e.*, here, of the amount, sum of money to be given. **For the Jews, to destroy them**, means when the Jews would be surrendered to him with permission to destroy them. The Kethib form of יְהוּדִיִּים is less frequently used for יְהוּדִים, which is found in chap. viii. 1, 7, 13; ix. 15, 18.

* ["To rend one's clothes in grief was as much a Persian as a Jewish practice (see Herod. viii. 99; Æschylus, *Pers.* 540–1, 1039, *etc.*)." Rawlinson.—Tr.]

Ver. 8. **Also he gave him the copy of the writing of the decree that was given at Shushan** (comp. chap. iii. 15), **to destroy them,** *i. e.*, which ordered them to be destroyed. פַּתְשֶׁגֶן could here have the meaning of "copy;" but the rendering "*contents*" of the writing of the decree is preferable, (comp. Ezra iv. 11). Possibly Mordecai had briefly noted down the substance of the decree. **To shew (it) unto Esther, and to declare (it) unto her, and to charge her that she should go in unto the king to make supplication unto him.**—וּלְהַגִּיד, contrary to the accents, is by Bertheau and Keil connected with what follows, as if it were the same in sense with לְצַוּוֹת עָלֶיהָ. But it rather belongs to what precedes according to its import. Hatach was to show the writing to Esther and give her the substance of the information it conveyed. It is quite possible that Esther could read it herself; Mordecai sent the copy for the purpose of enabling Hatach to give the proper meaning of its contents. The infinitives with לְ are here best translated by "in order that." **To declare** (explain) **it unto her, and to charge her to go in unto the king, to make supplication unto him . . . for her people.**—בַּקֵּשׁ with עַל here, as in chap. vii. 7, means: *to entreat*, supplicate for something diligently (comp. Ezra viii. 23). She should petition relief for her people.

Vers. 9–11. Mordecai elicited only the answer: **All the king's servants, and the people of the king's provinces, do know, that whosoever, whether man or woman shall come unto the king,** *etc.*—כָּל־אִישׁ וְאִשָּׁה is prefixed as a *Nom. absol.* The predicate with אַחַת דָּתוֹ follows as an *anacoluthon*: "one is his law," *i. e., one law extends to all.* דָּתוֹ is the law having reference in his case. Its substance reads briefly: לְהָמִית, *to kill, i. e.*, him. One was not even allowed to enter the inner court-yard, much less the king's palace. That the king resided in the inner court before the royal house (Bertheau and Keil), would not follow from chap. v. 1. Every one was to be killed, except him toward whom the king extended the golden sceptre. לְבַד מִן, *except*, as for example, Ex. xii. 23; Josh. xvii. 5. הוֹשִׁיט, from יָשַׁט, found only in this book (in chap. v. 2 and viii. 4), in the Aramaic tongue signifies "to reach out towards, to extend," and is connected with שׁט, שׁוּט. In the time of Deioces the Mede, approach to the king was already very difficult (Herod. I. 9); and among the Persians, with very few exceptions (Herod. III. 118), no one was permitted to approach the king without a notice (comp. chap. i. 14; and Herod. III. 140; also C. Nep. *Conon*, c. 3). According to our verse the sense of the law is not that no one should approach unannounced, but that no one should approach unless called. But the sense of both is the same. If one must give due notice of approach, one must first be also accepted; but to be accepted is to be called. As regards that law any one was free to give notice of his approach (comp. Herodot. III. 140), and hence arises the question, why Esther kept this privilege out of sight. Josephus says (*Antiq.* XI. 6, 3) that the husband of Esther (according to him Artaxerxes) forbade his people, by a special law, to approach him while he sat upon the throne. But he would manifestly give greater weight to our explanation. If we desire to find the correct answer we must not overlook the remark of Esther, that she had not been called to the king for now thirty days.* Possibly she apprehended that the king had become somewhat indifferent to her, and that, if she were to announce herself without being called by him, she would be refused admittance to his presence. This would have made the venture still more dangerous. According to chap. iii. 7, nearly five years had passed since their marriage. Hence she had possibly been somewhat forgotten. It could hardly appear otherwise in her eyes than that it was best to approach the king unannounced and place reliance on the fact that her appearance should kindle his love anew.†

Vers. 12–17. *The third step.* In order to move Esther to a compliance with his request, despite her hesitation, Mordecai had it reported to her (ver. 13): **Think not with thyself that thou shalt escape in the king's house, more than all the Jews.**—To be saved does not here mean, *if I only am saved, the others do not concern me*, as if Mordecai would warn her of a selfish and indifferent feeling toward her people. But the sense is: "Do not think that thou shalt escape, or that thou art better off." This is clear from ver. 14: **For if thou altogether holdest thy peace,** not making intercession with the king, **at this time, (then) shall there enlargement and deliverance arise to the Jews from another place; but thou and thy father's house shall be destroyed,** *i. e.*, be not better off, but worse. That the entire Jewish people cannot be thus destroyed is a matter self-evident to Mordecai. This is an incontestable truth, under all circumstances, which in his mind is made sure by the divine promises. And although neither God nor God's assurances are here mentioned, still, as is justly remarked by Brenz: "We have this noble and clearly heroic faith of Mordecai, which sees the future deliverance, even amidst the most immediate and imminent danger." Those Jews only can and must be destroyed, in his opinion, who, when it concerns the preservation of the people, do not perform their duty. It is very improbable that he should think that Haman has not power sufficient to cause the destruction of the Jewish nation as a whole, but merely of that detested Mordecai

* ["According to Herodotus (iii. 69), the wives of a Persian king, whether primary or secondary, shared his bed in rotation. As their number sometimes exceeded three hundred, the turn of a particular wife might not come for nearly a year." RAWLINSON.—TR.]

† [As to the *golden sceptre* Rawlinson observes. "A modern critic asks: 'Is it likely that a Persian king would always have a golden sceptre by him to stretch out towards intruders on his privacy?' It seems enough to reply that in all the numerous representations of Persian kings at Persepolis, there is not one in which the monarch does not hold a long tapering staff (which is probably the 'sceptre' of Esther) in his right hand." —TR.]

and his family, hence also Esther, must die (Bertheau,—otherwise he would not have said: "thou and thy father's house," but "thy father's house and thou, ye shall perish." He here makes reference rather to a divine punishment that shall come upon Esther first, but on her account also upon her father's house. רֶוַח = רְוָחָה (Ex. viii. 11) means relief from pressure because of want of air. עֲמַד in later language may have been given the meaning of קוּם, so that it should mean *to arise*, to go forth, to be (1 Chron. xx. 4). But it may also signify: *deliverance will be established* (Bertheau), or *stand ready*. The "*other place*" is not *God* as immediate for help, but *another agent of God*, in contrast with Esther. Mordecai means: God will find other instruments whom He will employ, if thou wilt not serve Him. The last sentence of ver. 14 is, by most interpreters, declared to mean: "And who knows but that thou hast been elevated to be queen for just such an emergency as this, where there is danger, which thou shouldst assist in averting, so that thou canst easily help. But if thou wilt not help, thou wilt not escape an especially severe sentence." But to take אִם in the sense of הֲלֹא, is to say the least, venturesome, and cannot be justified by the fact that מִי יֹדֵעַ is sometimes, (but without אִם) used in the sense of *perhaps* (2 Sam. xii. 22; Joel ii. 14; Jonah iii. 9). Again it does not correspond to the sense of "if," "whether;" and we may say with Bertheau: "Who knows, when thou hast approached the royal throne (beseechingly), what then shall happen, whether the king will not receive you graciously;" or again, as Keil says: "Who knows but that thou hast attained to royalty for just such a time as this (as was no doubt true), what shall then be done by thee?" Mordecai would perhaps say, by way of adding to the before-expressed threat, "Thou shalt be destroyed, if thou art silent: and who knows whether thou shalt really be courageous enough to speak for us, and thereby manifest to us that, for just such a time as this thou wast elevated to royal dignity?" A doubt such as this would evidently be the most powerful incentive to her to do what was requested of her.

Ver. 15. In fact this resolve was reached by her. She made request that Mordecai, together with the Jews in Shushan, should fast three days and nights in her behalf. Doubtless she thus expected to secure the help and protection of God for that eventful hour and step, and therefore she declared, with great resignation, that she would venture to fulfil their request. This fast could only mean that great misery impended over their heads, that with a contrite spirit God's hand was seen in this event, and that prayer was made to God for help (comp. 1 Kings xxi. 27–29; Joel i. 14; Jonah iii. 5). That Esther still does not make mention of God, no more than did Mordecai before this, when he asserted his faith in the indestructibility of the Jewish nation, may easily be explained, as has been observed in the Introduction, § 3, by remarking that it pertains to the style of the author. To the expression: **fast ye for me,** Esther adds: **and neither eat nor drink three days, night nor day,** in order to mark the severity of the fast. A strict fast of three days would indeed have been a severe task, and Esther would thereby have done injury to her appearance (J. D. Michaelis). But these *three days* seem, as in Jonah ii. 1, not to be clearly understood; hence the sense would be, from this day until the third day. For the fast must have begun on the same day that Esther's answer came to Mordecai. The "third day" mentioned in chap. v. 1 must mean the third day from that in which the decision of Esther was made. This decision was the main fact from which time was reckoned. Of course we cannot expect that Mordecai should that very day have induced all the Jews in Shushan to fast. Still it matters not so much that not *all*, if only *many*, fasted.—**And so will I go in unto the king, which is not,** *etc.*—בְּכֵן, *i. e. under such circumstances*, or under such conditions. אֲשֶׁר לֹא כַדָּת may simply mean: "which is not legally allowed," *although not, etc.* אֲשֶׁר may be taken in a neuter sense, although אֲשֶׁר לֹא reminds us of the Aramaic דִּי לָא, and hence it can easily be taken in the sense of "without" (comp. Ewald, § 322 *c*). The last words: **And if I perish, I perish,** are an expression of willing submission to the fate that may threaten her in the performance of her duty (comp. Gen. xliii. 14). Esther had great cause to prepare for her own destruction. She not only proposed to go to the king without being called, but also to request something of him, which, according to Persian custom, it was impossible to grant. She would by her petition recall the edict and thereby seem to disregard the royal majesty. She would and indeed must reveal herself as a daughter of this detested Jewish people thus given over to destruction. Last of all, she must thereby place herself in open opposition to that all-powerful favorite, Haman.

Ver. 17. Mordecai went forth to fulfil the wish of Esther. The verb עָבַר has induced the Targums and older interpreters, as J. D. Michaelis, to advance the opinion that he had violated, "passed over," namely, the law, which ordered the Paschal feast to be celebrated in a joyous manner (from chap. iii. 12 it might follow that we are still in the time of the Passover); but the word has the meaning of: *going away*, going further. It has its explanation as contrasting with what Mordecai had done before, since, so long as Esther's answer was not satisfactory, he remained standing there.

DOCTRINAL AND ETHICAL.

Ver. 1 sqq. 1. Mordecai rends his clothing, and puts on sack-cloth and ashes. He enters the city thus, and raises a great and bitter lamentation. So also the Church of God, in its development as regards the history of humanity, should again and ever anew put on the habiliments of mourning. "The world shall rejoice: and ye shall be sorrowful." The then existing nation of Jews could not manifest its loyalty to the law without coming into conflict with heathendom. Nor can the Church bring to development its inherent spiritual powers without challenging all the Hamans and their opposition in the world. Even this present period is an instance in proof. Following upon the great progress of the things of the kingdom of God since the time of wars for freedom, we must naturally expect reactions, such as have been manifest in the sphere of science and other relations. Indeed, we must constantly look for increasing opposition on the part of the world. But when the Church shall have most fully developed the gifts of grace granted to it, then conflict and sorrow will have reached its highest point at the end of days. The real cause of sorrow on the part of the true members of God's Church will not be, as was the case with Mordecai, their own distress, but that of the world. It will consist in the fact that the world is still devoid of the blessed society of the true God; that the kingdom of God is still rejected and even persecuted. What joy it would give, if, instead of enmity, recognition and submission, and, instead of disdain, a participation in the gifts and grace of our Lord were to become the universal experience!

2. The more difficult the position of the Church as in contrast with the world, the more favorable is her position for bringing to view her glory. Her glory is that of her Head. If even in the Old Testament times, and in the "dispersion" itself, there existed a Mordecai, who for love of the people manifested his firmness and strength in the hour of tribulation; and if there was found an Esther, who, when called upon, willingly came forward to bring about the salvation of her countrymen; how much more in New Testament times and in the modern Church will there arise individuals, who, in following the Lord, especially in evil days, will manifest a watch-care for others and a self-sacrificing spirit for them; who will show forth patience and meekness, as well as energy, fidelity and tenacity, a spirit of giving and an ability to make sacrifices; and withal will carry in their hearts joy and peace as the seal of their kinship with God. All these graces may be so many illuminating rays of the glorious life of their Lord and Saviour Jesus Christ, who more and more attains in them a full stature. May all seize the special opportunity, recognize the particular duty, and know when to perform it, which the times of distress of the Church place in their hand, of showing forth the power that dwells in them by their life and work!

3. Mordecai took an especially great part in the universal grief that overcame the Jews when the edict of their annihilation was issued and promulgated. It was not his personal danger that alarmed him, but, as may be expected of such a faithful follower of Judaism, it was the calamity threatening the whole Jewish people. While, however, thought and feeling were centred upon the event, he was free from despair. With him it was a settled conviction that the people of God, as a whole, could not be destroyed, and that deliverance must come from some source. Instead of giving way to despondency, he turned his distress into a power that urged him to still greater endeavors. There was no more a fear of appearing as a Jew, nor did he hesitate because his loud lamentation would attract general attention, and thereby expose him to the derision and disdain of many. However reluctant he might have been to expose his beloved Esther, whose welfare had ever been a matter of great concern to him, to extreme danger, still he persisted with the greatest determination that she should run the whole risk, and only rested when she gave her assent. It is barely possible that he attributed some blame to himself because of his firmness against Haman, or thought that on that account he more than any other was under obligation to remove the threatened danger. The sole moving impulse was doubtless his love for his people. But this should not be less in any true member of the Church. It should rather, in proportion as there are more members in the body of Christ, be the stronger than it was in him. Would that no one among us were behind him as regards energy, self-denial and a willingness to make sacrifices! There are doubtless many who are able to endure all this in their own person. But—if no lighter consideration—the thought that their relatives, yea, even wife and children, may suffer on account of their confession, bows them down. Would, if necessary, that we too may stand equal to Mordecai in willingness to surrender our dearest kin!

Ver. 6 sqq. Mordecai manifests a remarkable tenacity as opposed to Esther. He keeps his position at the gate of the king until she sends him not only her maids with garments, but also Hatach to transmit his message. He departs not thence until she has resolved to stand before Ahasuerus as a Jew pleading for the Jews. Under other circumstances he might have been thought to be tiresome by his persistency and demands; but his relation to her now justified it. When he had been accustomed to inquire concerning her health and well-being, to give her counsel, to care for her, he had shown no less persistency; and his demand that now she should reveal her Jewish descent, and as such should venture all, was equally in keeping with his character. So long as no danger threatened he counseled her to keep silence respecting her Jewish parentage; but now he had himself taken the lead in an open confession of the fact. Although it had before been difficult for him to approach Esther as the queen, or request any favor at her hand, now he hesitated no longer to implore her help, not so much for himself, as for the whole people. There was no motive for him to be selfish, or to conduct himself in a heartless or severe manner towards her. Hence there was no question but that his undertaking would succeed, that Esther would be willing to comply with his request. It is eminently desirable that those who, like him, must move and induce others to make sacrifices of self and possessions in the service of the kingdom of God, should stand on a level with him in this respect.

Brenz: "At first the lazy (*i. e.* Jews) do not snore. For the Holy Spirit exhorts us in all adversities to confide in the Lord; He does not exhort us to be indolent, indifferent and sleepy.

For our confidence in the Lord is a powerful and efficacious means of stimulating in His service all strength and limbs. . . . . Further, the Jews, though in the greatest peril, do not utter virulent words against the king, nor do they fly to arms. . . . Mordecai and the other Jews rend their garments, put on sack-cloth, strew ashes upon their heads, wail, weep and fast. These manifestations signify not that the Jews in Persia were turbulent, but that they take refuge in God; since help could not be discovered upon earth, they seek it from heaven. . . . 'The sacrifices of God are a broken spirit; a broken and a contrite heart, O God, thou wilt not despise.' . . . . By this example we too are taught that when afflictions are sent upon us, we should reflect that God then sets before us the fat oxen and calves which we may offer to Him. In this way we offer to God in our prayers the afflictions which we sustain, and call upon the name of the Lord that He may help us. . . . Behold, however, the reverse of this order of things. The palaces of princes are divinely instituted to be the places of refuge for the miserable. On the contrary in the palaces of Persia nothing is regarded as more odious and abominable than men with the signs of affliction. . . . Heaven is ever open to the cries of mourners, and God is never unapproachable to those calling on His name by faith."

Starke: "Temporal fortunes and successes are never so great as not to be subject to sorrow, terror and fear (Sir. xl. 3). God permits His Church to be plunged into sorrow at times; He leads her even into hell; but He also takes her out again (1 Sam. ii. 16). Though the Lord elevate us to high honors, we should never be ashamed of our poor relatives (Gen. xlvii. 2), but rather relieve their needs (1 Sam. xxii. 3). We should never reject proper and suitable means to escape a danger, but promptly use them (2 Cor. xi. 32, 33)."

Ver. 13 sqq. Mordecai manifests a precious sense of trust, saying: "For if thou altogether holdest thy peace at this time, then shall there enlargement and deliverance arise to the Jews from another place." But he who would save his soul will lose it. The risk which Mordecai called upon Esther to assume, that she should come to the king uninvited, and manifest herself as a daughter of the people thus devoted to destruction, was indeed great and important. Moreover, the hope that Xerxes would recall his edict, thus, according to Persian ideas, endangering the respect due his royal majesty, and likewise abandoning his favorite minister, was very uncertain of fulfilment. But Esther had been elevated to a high position. Mordecai, who in a doubting manner sends her word: "Who knoweth whether thou art come to the kingdom for such a time as this?" doubtless did it from a conviction that she must now prove herself worthy of such distinction, if she would retain it. He also conveys the idea that the higher her position the greater her responsibility, and consequently, in case of failure because of carelessness or fearfulness, the more intense her guilt. In these convictions of Mordecai are contained the most earnest exhortations even for us. This is especially true since we are all called to be joint heirs of Jesus Christ to the throne of the heavenly kingdom. In the deportment of Esther a no less reminder to duty is contained. It appears quite natural that Esther should order a fast not only to be observed by Mordecai and the rest of the Jews, but she also imposed on herself this fast of three days' duration. Had she had a little more of the common discretion of her sex, she would have feared the effects of the fast upon her appearance. Hence she would have adopted quite a different plan or preparation previous to her entrance into the king's presence. Here also she reveals the same attractive feature of mind and manner as when she was first presented to the king. Instead of placing reliance upon what she should externally put on or adorn herself with, we find her trust placed upon something higher. She well knows that she will only succeed if the great and exalted Lord be for her, who, notwithstanding His glorious majesty, yet dwells among the most lowly of men. It is in just such times as these, when we are raised to the greatest endeavors and self-sacrifices, that we must not expect to accomplish these things by our own power, but only through Him who in our weakness is our strength. Otherwise, despite our best intentions and most successful beginnings, we shall soon grow discouraged and fail. Our own weakness is but too often made manifest to our eyes. It is only when we consider and remember that the hand of the Lord is in it all that we will be saved from a lack of courage.

Brenz: "As it is the most pleasing worship to God to support the Church with all our strength, so He execrates no one more than him who withholds from the Church when in danger that help which he is able to render. . . . . If the cry of a single poor man is so availing that although unheard by man, it finds an avenging ear in God, what must be the influence of the cry of the whole Church in her affliction imploring assistance from Him who it hopes is able to help? . . . This teaches us that God confers power upon princes, riches upon the rich, wisdom upon the wise, and other gifts upon others, not that they may abuse them for their own pleasure, but that they may assist the Church of God, and protect it in whatever way they can. For the Church on earth is so great in the eyes of God, that He requires of all men whatever may serve her. 'The people,' He says, 'and the king that will not serve thee shall perish, and the nations shall dwell in a solitary place.'"

Starke: "Our flesh is always timid when it has to encounter a hazard (Exod. iv. 13). My Christ in His divine majesty stands at the entrance into the faith, and sounds the free invitation to each and all, 'ever frequent, ever dear, ever happy' (Sirach xxv. 20, 21). One should succor his neighbor in peril and need (Prov. xxiv. 11; Ps. lxxxii. 3), and especially the brethren in the faith (Gal. vi. 10), even at the peril of one's own life (1 John iii. 16). We are born for good not to ourselves, but to others, and thus God oftentimes shows us that through us He aids our own, our country and the community (Gen. xlv. 5). Faith is the victory that overcomes the world (1 John v. 8). We may use ordinary prayer for important blessings (James v. 14; Gen. xxiv. 7; xliii. 14). Life can never be spent better than when it is the aim to lose it (Matt. xvi. 25; Acts xx. 24; xxi. 13)."

B.—ESTHER IS GRACIOUSLY RECEIVED BY THE KING; BUT HAMAN, HIGHLY DISTINGUISHED BY THE QUEEN, RESOLVES, BECAUSE OF THE REFUSAL OF MORDECAI TO BOW THE KNEE BEFORE HIM, TO HAVE HIM HUNG.

CHAPTER V. 1–14.

I. *Esther finds favor with the King, and invites both him and Haman two separate times to a banquet prepared by herself.* Vers. 1–8.

1 Now [And] it came to pass [was] on the third day that [and] Esther put on
her royal *apparel*, and stood in the inner court of the king's house, over against the
king's house: and the king sat [*was* sitting] upon his royal throne in the royal
2 house, over against *the* gate [opening] of the house. And it was *so*, when [as] the
king saw Esther the queen standing in the court, *that* she obtained [received] favor
in his sight [eyes]: and the king held out to Esther the golden sceptre that *was* in
3 his hand. So [And] Esther drew near, and touched *the* top of the sceptre. Then
[And] said the king unto her, What wilt thou [*is* to thee], queen Esther? and
what *is* thy request? [*ask*, and] it shall be *even* given thee to *the* half of the king-
4 dom. And Esther answered [said], If it *seem* good unto [upon] the king, let the
king and Haman come this [to-] day unto the banquet that I have prepared
5 [made] for him. Then [And] the king said, Cause Haman to make haste, that
he may do [to do] as Esther hath said [*the* word of Esther]. So [And] the king
6 and Haman came to the banquet that Esther had prepared [made]. And the
king said unto Esther at *the* banquet of wine, What *is* thy petition? and it shall
be granted thee: and what *is* thy request? even [*ask*, and] to *the* half of the king-
7 dom it shall be performed [done]. Then [And] answered Esther, and said, My
8 petition and my request *is;* If I have found favor in *the* sight [eyes] of the king,
and if it please [*seem* good upon] the king to grant [give] my petition, and to per-
form [do] my request, let the king and Haman come to the banquet that I shall
prepare [will make] for them, and I will do to-morrow as the king hath said [ac-
cording to *the* mind of the king].

II. *Haman, encouraged by the remarkable distinction extended to him, at once resolves upon the immediate destruction of Mordecai.* Vers. 9–14.

9 Then [And] went Haman forth [on] that day joyful and with *a* glad [good]
heart: but [and] when [as] Haman saw Mordecai in the king's gate that [and] he
stood [rose] not *up*, nor moved [*or* trembled] for [on account of] him, [and, *i. e.*
10 then] he [Haman] was full of indignation against Mordecai. Nevertheless [And],
Haman refrained [restrained] himself: and *when* he came home [to his house],
[and] he sent and called for [brought] his friends [lovers], and Zeresh his wife.
11 And Haman told [recounted to] them of the glory of his riches, and the multitude
of his children, and all *the things* wherein the king *had* promoted him [made him
12 great], and how [that] he *had* advanced [raised] him above the princes and [*the*]
servants of the king. [And] Haman said *moreover*, Yea, Esther the queen did let
no man come *in* with the king unto the banquet that she *had* prepared [made] but
13 myself; and to-morrow *am* I[1] invited [called] unto her also[2] with the king. Yet
all this availeth me nothing, so long as [in all *the* time that] I see [*am* seeing]
14 Mordecai the Jew sitting at [in] the king's gate. Then [And] said Zeresh his wife
and all his friends [lovers] unto him, Let *a* gallows be made [Let them make *a*

tree] *of* fifty cubits high [*in* height], and to-morrow [in the morning] speak [say] thou unto the king that [and] Mordecai may be hanged [they will hang Mordecai] thereon: then [and] go thou in merrily [joyful] with the king unto the banquet. And the thing [word] pleased [*was* good before] Haman; and he caused the gallows to be made [made the tree].

TEXTUAL AND GRAMMATICAL.

1 [Ver. 12. The pronoun, being expressed, is emphatic.—Tr.]

2 [Ver. 12. The position of גַּם before לְמָחָר gives the latter emphasis; this was a fresh token of favor. —Tr.]

EXEGETICAL AND CRITICAL.

Vers. 1–8. Mordecai's opposition against Haman receives fresh support by the movements of Esther. But they have as a first result that Haman on his part also determines the utmost extreme against Mordecai. Hence the conflict against Mordecai is here also the chief feature, as was that of Mordecai against Haman in the previous chapter. Esther risks an unannounced entrance to the king—so it seems—only that she might together with him invite Haman to the banquet in order to distinguish the latter before all other officers. Thereby the arrogance of Haman is extraordinarily strengthened.

Ver. 1. **On the third day**, viz., after her interview with Mordecai (comp. chap. iv. 14 sqq.), **Esther put on (her) royal (apparel).**—If we will not with Bertheau on chap. vi. 8 and viii. 15 sanction the rejection of לְבוּשׁ before מַלְכוּת, then we must accept the fact that מַלְכוּת in itself signifies *royal* dignity (comp. chap. i. 19), but also means *royal apparel;* or that it was usual in poetic language to say לָבַשׁ הוֹד וְהָדָר (comp. civ. 1; Job xl. 10), as also לָבַשׁ מַלְכוּת. An accusative of limitation, "according to the king's manner," is highly improbable here. Esther *posted herself*—so here תַּעֲמֹד, according to 1 Kings xx. 38; 1 Sam. xvii. 51; not: *stood*, remained standing,—in the inner court in such a position that the king, who sat upon his throne in the king's house, could see her. He sat נֹכַח פֶּתַח הַבָּיִת, not: *before*, but *opposite*, over against *the door of the house.* Since נֹכַח may easily be rendered "before" in the sense of "opposite," it is well so to translate it. Perhaps the king had selected this position in order the more easily to see what transpired in the court of the house. Perhaps also the throne was situated not far from the farthest wall, and nearer to the door.*

Ver. 2. As his eyes fell on Esther she found grace in his sight, see chap. ii. 9. As he extended the golden sceptre to her she touched its point, possibly, as is indicated by the Vulg., kissing it.

Ver. 3. [**What wilt thou?** "Rather, 'What ails thee?'"—Rawlinson.] He promised her: **it shall be given thee to the half of the kingdom,** viz., she might make bold request, and it should be granted her what she desired; similarly as in the case of Herod in Mark vi. 23.* Feuardent: "Observe, I pray you, the promise, so thoughtless, rash, and imprudent (a common fault among kings), which, without consideration, is here repeated for the third time (comp. chap. vi. and vii. 2). So excessive and prodigal are princes as regards women, good-for-nothing, gluttons, sycophants, traitors, and such like." But here it is in point to notice the greatness of that object which is capable of calling forth true love, and for it nothing is too great.

Ver. 4. The first and simplest thing that Esther dared to request was to invite Haman and the king to dine with her. אִם טוֹב עַל, as in chap. i. 19. She would doubtless first convince herself whether the impression which she made on the king was deep enough to encourage her to express such a great request as she intended to present.† She desired Haman to be present, in order, as Calov remarks, that "she might charge him by name in the presence of the king with the decree surreptitiously obtained against her people, and to his very face cut off every possibility of cavil;" perhaps also in order to make his confusion the more complete.

Ver. 5. The king ordered Haman to be quickly called, and with him accepted the invitation of Esther. מַהֲרוּ, *hastened, i. e.*, to cause to make haste, comp. 1 Kings xxii. 9; 2 Chron. xviii. 8. לַעֲשׂוֹת, as an infin., may have Haman as its subject: "that he may do as Esther hath said." This also would explain the phrase, in order that one do, *i. e.*, the words of Esther.

Ver. 6. **At the banquet of wine** (comp. chap. vii. 2),—thus is indicated the more advanced stage of the banquet, where drinking was the chief thing, and where, in consequence, the most cheerful feeling prevailed (Bertheau), the king repeated his question and reasserted his promise.‡ וַתֵּעָשׂ (chap. vii. 2; ix. 12), "and it

* ["This is the usual situation of the throne in the 'throne-room' of an Oriental palace. The monarch, from his raised position, can see into the court through the doorway opposite him, which is kept open."—Rawlinson.—Tr.]

* ["According to Herodotus (IX. 109), Xerxes, on another occasion, when pleased with one of his wives, offered to grant her any request whatever, without limitation."—Rawlinson.—Tr.]

† ["Esther seems to have been afraid to make her real request of Xerxes too abruptly, and to have wished to impress him favorably before doing so. She concluded that the king would understand that she had a real petition in the background, and would recur to it, as in fact he did (ver. 6, and chap. vii. 2)."—Rawlinson. —Tr.]

‡ ["After the meats were removed, it was customary in Persia to continue the banquet for a considerable time with fruits and wine (Herod. I., 133). During this

shall be granted thee," is the shortened form of the imperf., the so-called jussive future, instead of וְתֵעָשֶׂה.

Vers. 7, 8. Still Esther hesitates with her principal request. It is true she begins: **My petition and my request (is)**; as if she would now express herself, but she breaks off as if courage failed her, or as if she reflected upon it; and she leaves it there, simply again inviting the king and Haman to another banquet, at which she obligates herself to make her petition known. She doubtless was not yet sure of the success of her undertaking.*

Vers. 9–14. Haman, completely puffed up because of the distinction shown him on the part of the queen, felt all the more bitterly the apparent stubbornness of Mordecai, which still continued, and resolved, aided by the counsel of his friends and wife, on the following day to request his execution from the king.

Ver. 9. On the same day he again met Mordecai in the gate of the king. It must needs be that on this very day Mordecai must provoke his anger to the highest degree, and thereby unconsciously assist in precipitating the inimical orders of Haman. The whole plan of the book is thus brought out in its correspondence to the conception and development of the present treatment. Mordecai could now again stand in the gate of the king. The garments of mourning which had prevented him from this, were doubtless laid aside when he assuredly knew that Esther would take the step promised to him, *i. e.*, go to the king. Fasting no doubt also ceased at the same time. In consequence he was doubtless more than ever drawn to that position where he might first hope to hear of the success of Esther. To the expression: **But when Haman saw Mordecai in the king's gate**, there is added the statement, **that he stood not up, nor moved for him**.—Such sentences of condition may be inserted without a copula (comp. Ewald, § 346). The וְ before לֹא־קָם, therefore, instead of being a copula, is a correlative to the following וְ before לֹא־זָע; so that we have an apposition, "neither"—"nor." Still it is more common and natural to accept a connection by means of וְ, "and" (comp. Gen. xviii. 11; xxiv. 21; Joshua vi. 1). קָם and זָע are not participles—for then their subject would be made prominent—but they are third pers. *præt.* But זָע with מִן does not mean: *neither did he even move from before him* (Vulg. and most interpreters), but according to Dan. v. 19; vi. 27: *he trembled not*, was not terrified before him, as he should have done had he violated the law of the king (chap. iii. 2).

Ver. 10. Haman controlled himself, but only to consult soon after with his friends and wife, *i. e.*, those who he knew would sympathize with him, and who would restrain him from too great rashness in determining upon radical measures against Mordecai.*

Ver. 11. The author, with great art of statement, gives Haman an opportunity to recount all that would make him great and happy, but yet so as to make him admit that there is one thing missing for the completion of his happiness, and this is indispensable, namely, the destruction of Mordecai. The higher the fortune and honor in which he rejoiced, the greater would be the fall, so soon to be realized; and the more impressive must be his history upon those who read it. Next to the **glories of his riches** he makes mention of the **multitude of his children** (sons). According to chap. ix. 7–10 there were ten of them. Bertheau thinks these do not belong here, and he would change the reading. But Haman was obliged to mention them in honor of his wife. What indeed would his riches have been to him had he possessed it for himself only, or if he had not hoped to cause his sons to inherit after him, in whom, so to speak, he continued to live on? Not only among Persians, but also among Israelites, the happiness of parents depended largely upon the multitude of children; especially of sons. Likewise also the esteem in which they were held, particularly with the king, who sent presents annually to parents having the greatest number of children (comp. Herod. I. 136). Then also he recounted all **wherein the king had promoted him**, *etc.* אֲשֶׁר is here the second accus., depending on גִּדַּל, and one of definition or of instrument.

Ver. 12. As the highest point of his distinction, and the very latest, he mentions the circumstance that, above all others, he alone was invited to the banquet of the queen to be given the day following. This is the most direct proof that the author regarded these invitations as the very highest point of distinction. And he lays great stress thereon in order the more powerfully to show the overwhelming disaster that befel Haman, and also to prepare the reader for the climax of the story. אַף, *also*, moreover, indicates in advance that what follows is a new ascending period. אֲנִי קָרוּא־לָהּ means *she has invited me* (see Ewald, § 295 *c*).

Ver. 13. **Yet all this**—thus he himself must make prominent his folly and insatiableness, and at the same time pronounce his own sentence—**availeth me nothing**, is not satisfactory to me, **so long as I see Mordecai the Jew sitting at the king's gate**.—בְּכָל־עֵת אֲשֶׁר may mean: *at all times*, every time, when I; so that the sense is that the feeling of dissatisfaction comes to the surface each time. But it may also mean: *during the whole time* when I, *i. e.*, so long as I (comp. Job xxvii. 3, according to Schlottmann and the older interpreters). The fact that such a Jew may defy him unpunished seems to be a counter-proof against his dignity and power.

Ver. 14. **Then said Zeresh his wife and all his friends**.—Zeresh being first, and also

part of the feast the king renewed his offer."—Rawlinson.—Tr.]

* [" Esther still cannot bring herself to make the request on which so much depends, and craves another day's respite. She will soften the king's heart by a second banquet, and then she will submit her petition to him. There is something extremely natural in this hesitation."—Rawlinson.—Tr.]

* [" The name *Zeresh* is probably connected with the zered *zara*, 'gold.' Compare the Greek *Chrysis*." Rawlinson.—Tr.]

the singular form of the verb, indicates that she led the counsel. Even kings as well as their chief officers doubtless often allowed themselves to be directed by their wives. **Let a gallows be made,** *i. e.*, erected, **of fifty cubits high.**—The third person plural here, as also in what follows, again points to an indefinite "one," "let one," "let them." The height of the gallows should intensify the disgrace of hanging, but should also serve to make manifest the dreadful punishment, and to terrify as many as possible from being discourteous to Haman. Feuardent well says: "But why make it so high (*i. e.* the tree, gallows)? In order that his disgrace might be plainly observable to the eyes of all, and the more striking. Wherefore should he be in such haste about it? Lest there should be danger in delay or procrastination. For what reason have it erected before his own house? So that he and all his family going in and out, seeing Mordecai hanging, might mock and feast their cruel eyes and minds with so miserable and foul a spectacle." **Speak thou unto the king that Mordecai be hanged thereon,** *i. e.*, speak, that they hang. תָּלָה as in chap. ii. 23. These advisers take it for granted that the king will give his consent.* Hence the gallows should be already prepared in order that the execution may come off that very morning. Then, of course, his joy can be unclouded for his noon meal.†

DOCTRINAL AND ETHICAL.

Vers. 1–8. 1. The destiny of God's people depended not only on the humors of this Persian king in general, but also upon the impression which a woman might make upon that monarch. This must appear as very peculiar and highly significant. Women have often exerted a decisive influence upon the destinies of nations. But here it seems as if this was not quite consonant with the dignity of the people of God, as they were still worthy of being called. It seems as if such a state of things could only be true of a degenerate cause. At present we have the view of Esther standing before the king, not as a wife before her husband, but as a petitioner before a sovereign, imploring protection, and anxiously waiting whether he would graciously reach out his sceptre to her. This truly represents the condition of dependence and lowliness of the Church of the Diaspora. In contrast with it Ahasuerus represents the dignity of the worldly power bearing rule over the people of God. For all this, however, every one feels that true dignity does not dwell with the former; he would else not have been taken captive by the charms of a woman, nor have made such unlimited promises, as he expressed. But true worth dwells with Esther, who, impelled by love for her people, risks even her life. Judgment concerning him would be vastly different if his liberality were to remind us that divine love above is prepared to give the better (godly) people all that is needed for its salvation and welfare. At any rate Esther here very well represents the better people. There are found in her beautiful countenance traces of the deep grief which fills her heart. She has become weakened by the fasting which she has imposed upon herself. She is pale in consequence of fear, which she cannot suppress. Hence her appearance is all the more noble and winsome to us. And if in Ahasuerus we regard the power which must be overcome, and in her the possibility of Israel's power, then it can no more be doubtful, how great will be the victory of Israel.

BRENZ: "This is truly heroic magnanimity, by which Esther declares as great a faith towards God, as love towards His church. Her trust in Him is such that she incurs the peril of her life in obedience to His call. For though all the circumstances of the case threaten her destruction, still she hangs by faith upon the divine promises. For whom God calls and leads into danger, to him He has also promised preservation and deliverance in those dangers. To Abraham He said: 'Get thee out of thy country and thy father's house.' This was a call to face danger. But He also added the promise: 'I will make of thee a great nation.' It is love alone that exposes itself in behalf of the church of God, and would rather risk its own life than leave the Church of God in danger. We may at the same time observe the modesty of Esther. Though elevated to regal majesty she does not disregard nor despise her relatives, even when most unfortunate and outcast; but condescends even to run the hazard of her life for them. How very far are some men, who have obtained a dignity beyond others, from exhibiting this modesty!"

2. We may recognize the picture of a soul praying to God in the image of Esther standing with humble and imploring attitude before Ahasuerus. Sacred poetry, especially, has made use of single features or expressions of this history in this regard. So Dressler in his beautiful hymn: "My Jesus to whom seraphim," *etc.*, causes the pious supplicant to say: "Reach thy sceptre to my soul, which like an Esther bows to thee, and shows herself thy bride to thee. Speak: 'Yea, thou art she whom I have chosen.'" The representative signification of the persons in this history have, as it were, brought with them their own recognition. The Christian may certainly employ them in this sense. So STARKE when he says: "If a heathen king can willingly grant such grace, how much more willing is the most faithful Lord to receive all poor destitute sinners coming to Him in faith, and in the good time to come to place them upon His throne." Ahasuerus paid no regard to the fact that Esther had violated his commandment, but received her very graciously, although his irrevocable edict stood in the way of granting her petition. The father heart of God, although we violate all His laws,

* ["A gallows, in the ordinary sense, is scarcely intended, since hanging was not a Persian punishment. The intention, no doubt, was to crucify or impale Mordecai; and the pale or cross was to be seventy-five feet high, to make the punishment more conspicuous. On the use of impalement among the Persians, see the note on chap. ii. 23." RAWLINSON.—TR.]

† ["As Ahasuerus had already consented to a general massacre of the Jews within a few months, it seemed probable that he would readily allow the immediate execution of one of them. Requests for leave to put persons to death were often made to Persian kings by their near relatives (Herod. IX. 110; Plutarch, *Artax.* 14, 15, 17, 23, *etc.*), but only rarely by others." RAWLINSON.—TR.]

and though His unchangeable holiness be against the sinner, still yearns toward us in its great love and grace. But just as Esther came boldly and yet modestly, so we also must combine with true humility a true and elevated courage, a disheartened repentance together with confiding faith.

BRENZ: "Consider a moment the happy issue that these events take, which are undertaken with faith and pious prayer. . . . How did Esther extort this from so great a king? Certainly not by outcries, nor by contempt, nor by disdain, nor by quarrels, nor by contention, nor by dishonest means; for by these practices women are wont to get blows and wounds rather than power and control; but by piety toward God, by reverence toward her husband, by modesty and all other reputable virtues. For so by serving and being obedient women rule, which is their only legitimate mode of governing."

STARKE: "The king's heart is in the hand of the Lord, as the rivers of water; He turneth it whithersoever He will (Prov. xxi. 1). My God reach Thy sceptre also to Thy bride now humbling herself before Thee.—To promise much is the universal custom of great men, but those keeping promises are few in number, (1 Macc. xi. 53). It is far easier to obtain favors by an humble and modest behaviour than by sullenness and a boasting manner (Gen. xxiii. 7 sqq.)."

Vers. 9–14. 1. Our book is distinguished by showing us the greatest and most surprising changes of fortune of opposite character in a very small compass. Esther and Mordecai, after having the most pleasing prospects held out to them, are plunged in the greatest distress; indeed they are seized with the terrors of death, and fast in sackcloth and ashes. Then again they are lifted up to the highest pinnacle of human fortune. Haman, on the contrary, the most powerful favorite of Ahasuerus, can even think of exterminating a whole people in order to satisfy his desire for revenge. The king not only agrees to all that he undertakes, but the queen also distinguishes him before all other officers in the most flattering manner. This he himself regards as the very summit of his fortune and honor; and then his fall is so sudden and great, that he finds his end on the very accursed tree which but shortly before he caused to be erected for his mortal enemy. In this way our book strikingly illustrates the double truth, that, whomsoever the Lord would raise especially high, He often humbles very low; and, on the other hand, he whom He would suddenly overthrow, is often raised to great heights. In other words, it shows us in what wonderful ways the Lord leads His own children, as well as godless sinners. But it also gives a very definite reason why the one receives such exalted station and the other such great degradation. We must not therefore think of God in an anthropopathic, *i. e.*, unholy manner, nor must we speak of "a freak of fortune." The process of humbling brings forth quite a different result in the pious person than does elevation in an ungodly one. The humiliation of Mordecai causes him to enter upon most severe and long-continued exertion, instead of remaining in a state of inactivity and reserve. He begins to exert himself in a most persistent manner to do all in his power for the deliverance of his people, without regard to his own personal cost or comfort. He even puts at stake the welfare of his beloved Esther, for the good of all the people. He prevails upon Esther, and she is willing to endeavor to save her people, even at the risk of her own life. By means of their humiliation they both were elevated to a grand height of purpose, which they had not before known. But the matter chiefly interesting is, that they submit to this humbling process. This is shown by their fast. They become conscious that in them are many things that provoke the displeasure of God, and thus they are purified by means of their sorrows. There was doubtless not wanting in them the proverbial Jewish stiff-neckedness; and this had first to be broken, before they became fitted for the good days coming, especially in manifesting humility, gratitude, and condescension towards others. Haman, on the contrary, as soon as he came from the banquet with Esther, gathers his friends and wife, boasting of his glorious riches, and the multitude of his sons, and his exalted dignity and honor, not in order to bring a thank-offering to his God, but only to impress upon them, to what recognition and distinctions of honor he can lay claim. The first and great mistake of the wicked is that all which they have accomplished and gained becomes a source of self-exaltation; the result is, that instead of finding their success more than great enough, they still find fault, indeed regard it as worthless, as nothing, so long as they have not yet attained the one thing, which now appears to them as chief. The effect is not that they reflect and become conscious of their internal want, but they accuse those circumstances that bring the want. Hence their third and most desperate mistake is, that they conceive the resolution, or are moved thereto by others, that, whatever be in their way, let it cost what it may, be it even an outrageous deed, they will remove it, so only they reach the longed-for object. If the antecedent humiliation is the proper beginning for the elevation of the pious, then the preceding elevation is already a beginning of divine judgment for the wicked. The words: "When thou dost humble me, thou dost make me great" (Ps. xviii. 36), which in the original reads: "Thy gentleness (condescension) hath made me great," has its truth well expressed in Luther's translation; and in so far he correctly interprets the text, since God condescends or humbles Himself only to those that are humbled. But the other: "Surely thou didst set them in slippery places" (namely the wicked), must mean that by simply permitting the success of their plans and their prosperity, the Lord places the feet of the wicked on ground which will turn to water under their feet (comp. Job xx. 16).

BRENZ: "Remark in Haman the stupendous and wonderful judgment of God. For the impious Haman is most exultant and fearless as regards the preservation and augmentation of his dignity and power; and he is most certain also of the destruction of Mordecai, whom he prosecutes with hatred. But behold now the end of the thing. The impious and secure Haman shall perish with sudden destruction; while the pious and afflicted Mordecai is unexpectedly raised to the highest dignity. . . . Let us therefore cast away all impious security, and fear God; so that, walking according to the calling of God, you may be preserved though the sky fall and the earth be moved."

FEUARDENT (from Rupert, *De victoria verbi*, VIII., 18): "'In order that he may give over a huge wild beast, as a fierce bear, to destruction, he first draws him to his food; so that he may no sooner hear the report, than feel the pang; no sooner see the pit, than fall into it. The cautious hunter well knows that it is more convenient to overpower the entrapped beast, than to overtake it by a doubtful chase with the dogs when frightened and running through the woods. These things are evidently to be regarded as not merely a part of the prudence of Esther, but much more of Divine Providence, which directed the prudence of the queen.'—Surely Haman errs in that boasting, since he neither recognises God as the author and bestower of so many good things, nor gives Him thanks without contumely and the mark of a most ungrateful mind. . . . . What could be more effeminate and miserable than such a spirit? Does he not seem like another Tantalus, catching at the streams that flee his lips? . . . So they who have not peace toward God and love toward their neighbor, cannot even have them toward themselves. 'Peace to those who are near and to those that are afar off,' says the Lord; 'but the wicked are like the troubled sea, that cannot rest, whose waves cast up mire and dirt' (Isa. lvii. 20). . . . Observe finally how false and vain is the confidence of impious and cruel men, who seek and hope to oppress and utterly destroy the servants of God. It is themselves that perish by the just judgment of God, and they are often caught by the very snares they lay for others; while God rescues His servants, and magnificently vindicates them. Goliath and Holofernes are slain with their own sword, and the saints triumph with their heads. The Babylonian satraps seemed to themselves secure, when the flames and the lions were about to devour Daniel and his companions; but the latter were gloriously preserved, and the former ignominiously perished by their own artifices and instruments. Pharaoh boasted, 'I will overtake (the Hebrews), I will divide the spoil' (Exod. xv. 9); but he immediately became food for the fishes, and a prey for the servants of the Lord. 'The Lord knoweth the thoughts of man, that they are foolishness.' 'He that sitteth in the heavens shall laugh at them.' These are the effects of that judgment of which the Holy Spirit speaks by the prophets: 'Evil-doers shall be cut off; but those that wait upon the Lord, they shall inherit the earth' (Ps. xxxvii. 9). Let us therefore cast away impious security, contempt of God, and inhumanity towards others; but let us walk in the love and fear of the Lord, that at length we may come to His heavenly kingdom."

2. The previous chapter has shown of what exertions and self-denial Mordecai and Esther were capable in their conflict with Haman, since the salvation of their people was at stake; the present chapter shows us the extent of the evil mind of Haman, since he was only concerned for himself. It was not enough for him to have procured an edict commanding the universal destruction of the Jews. It seemed too long a time before this should be accomplished. Neither in his eyes should Mordecai perish in the manner of the rest of the Jews. He made it a point not only to destroy Mordecai, but to expose him to public shame. So instead of abiding by the lot, the voice of his divinity, which had imposed patience on him, he took counsel with his wife and friends. Thus he reached a point in his madness of impatience and insecurity which in itself is the best proof that such a one is not far from self-destruction.

STARKE: "An envious man cannot peacefully enjoy the benefits which God gives him. Go not after thine lusts, but refrain thyself from thine appetites (Sir. xviii. 30).—It is very grievous of wives to urge their husbands to do wickedly (1 Kings xxi. 7; Sir. xxviii. 15, 16).—He who digs a pit for others will fall in himself (Sir. xxv. 11, 20).—We must not of ourselves revenge ourselves on our enemy, but first bring him before the proper tribunal (Rom. xii. 19).—When the wicked are busy to remove from their path what will mar their earthly joy, then, on the other hand, the godly should be diligent to remove that which will embitter their spiritual and heavenly joy."

PART SECOND.

THE DANGER REMOVED.

CHAPS. VI.—X.

FIRST SECTION.

The Fall of Haman.

CHAPS. VI. VII.

A.—HAMAN, EXPECTING THE HIGHEST HONOR, IS BROUGHT LOW. HE MUST GIVE THE HIGHEST HONOR TO MORDECAI.

CHAPTER VI. 1–14.

I. *Ahasuerus is reminded of Mordecai's former meritorious act and desires to know what reward has been given him.* Vers. 1–5.

1 ON that night could not the king sleep [*the* sleep of the king fled]; and he commanded [said] to bring *the* book of records [memorials] of *the* Chronicles [words of
2 the days]: and they were read[1] before the king. And it was found written, that Mordecai *had* told of [upon] Bigthana and Teresh, two of the king's chamberlains [eunuchs], *the* keepers of the door [threshold], who sought to lay hand on the king
3 Ahasuerus. And the king said, What honour and dignity [greatness] hath been done to Mordecai for [upon] this? Then [And] said the king's servants [young men] that ministered unto him [his attendants], *There* is nothing [has not *a* word
4 been] done for [with] him. And the king said, Who *is* in the court? (Now [And] Haman was [*had*] come *into* the outward court of the king's house, to speak [say] unto the king to hang Mordecai on the gallows [tree] that he had prepared for him).
5 And the king's servants [young men] said unto him, Behold, Haman standeth [*is* standing] in the court. And the king said, Let him come *in*.

II. *Haman describes the mode of honoring a deserving man, and Ahasuerus commands him to bestow such on Mordecai.* Vers. 6–11.

6 So [And] Haman came *in*. And the king said unto him, What shall be done [*is there* to do] unto [in *the case of*] the man whom the king delighteth to honour [in whose honour the king delighteth]? (Now [And] Haman thought [said] in his
7 heart, to whom would the king delight to do honour more than to myself?). And Haman answered [said to] the king, *For the* man whom the king delighteth to ho-
8 nour [in whose honour the king delighteth], Let the royal apparel be brought [let them bring, *etc.*] which the king *useth* to wear [*with* which the king has clothed *himself*], and *the* horse that the king rideth [has ridden] upon, and the crown-royal
9 which is set upon his head: And let this [the] apparel and [the] horse be delivered to [given upon] the hand of one [*a* man] of the king's *most* noble princes,[2] that they may array [and let them apparel] the man *withal* whom the king delighteth to honour [in whose honour the king delighteth], and bring him on horseback [cause him to ride on the horses] through [in] *the* street [wide *place*] of the city, and proclaim [let them call] before him, Thus shall it be done to the man whom the king
10 delighteth to honour [in whose honour the king delighteth]. Then [And] the king said to Haman, Make haste, *and* take the apparel and the horse, as thou hast said

[spoken], and do *even* so to Mordecai the Jew that sitteth [the *one* sitting] at [in]
the king's gate: let nothing fail [not *a* word fall] of all that thou hast spoken.
11 Then [And] took Haman the apparel, and the horse, and arrayed [apparelled]
Mordecai, and brought him on horseback [caused him to ride] through [in] *the*
street [wide *place*] of the city, and proclaimed [called] before him, Thus shall it be
done unto the man whom the king delighteth to honour [in whose honour the king
delighteth].

III. *The vexation of Haman is only increased through the evil prophecy of his friends.* Vers. 12–14.

12 And Mordecai came again [returned] to the king's gate: but [and] Haman
hasted [urged himself] to his house mourning, and having his head covered [veiled
13 *as to the* head]. And Haman told [recounted to] Zeresh his wife and all his friends
[lovers] every *thing* that *had* befallen him. Then [And] said his wise *men* and
Zeresh his wife unto him, If Mordecai *be* of *the* seed of the Jews, before whom thou
hast begun to fall, thou shalt not prevail against [be able to] him, but [for thou]
14 shalt surely fall before him. *And while* they *were* yet talking with him [and, *i. e.*,
then] the king's chamberlains [eunuchs] came [approached], and hasted to bring
Haman unto the banquet that Esther had prepared [made].

TEXTUAL AND GRAMMATICAL.

1 [The original is very explicit, וַיִּהְיוּ נִקְרָאִים, "and *these* were *in the act of* being called *over*."—Tr.]

2 ["The princes, the Parthemim," a term apparently of special distinction.—Tr.]

EXEGETICAL AND CRITICAL.

Vers. 1–5. As in the former chapter the danger for Mordecai rose to the highest point, and we may expect nothing more than that both opponents, if left to themselves, should destroy each other on the following morning, even before the careful Esther has as yet accomplished her mission, we now perceive how timely is the occurrence of an event in the intervening night, which not only prevents Esther's intercession for Mordecai from being too late, but also brings about the beginning of the downfall of Haman. The author ascribes this occurrence to the troubled sleep of Ahasuerus. Thus any who merely take a superficial view of things might ascribe it to chance. But to judge from what we have already seen, it is certainly not opposed to his view, that the second Targum in all things transpiring takes God into account, and represents things as if the angel of God's mercy were well informed of the lamentations of the daughters of Israel, and at God's command had disturbed the sleep of Ahasuerus.

Ver. 1. **On that night could not the king sleep**—but not because the issued edict against the Jews had caused him unrest. In consequence **he commanded to bring the book of records of the Chronicles**, in which, according to chap. ii. 23, Mordecai's deed was inscribed. He caused it to be read, not in order to find out whether the Jews had really deserved their extermination. This would have been worthy of a better king, but it is opposed by the facts in ver. 10 and chap. iii. 15, and also chap. vii. 5. His object was simply to entertain himself with the records of the past. Still it is remarkable that just that point, treating of Mordecai's act, should have been read. On any other than a providential view, one would be inclined to think that he had commanded first of all to read those passages referring to the Jews.* The use of the participle וַיִּהְיוּ נִקְרָאִים signifies that the reading lasted for some time, perhaps extended through the night. Hence we may not be astonished that when the passage referred to came to be read, Haman already waited in the outer court.

Vers. 2, 3. The name *Bigthana* reads *Bigthan* in chap. ii. 21. The question of the king: **what honour and dignity hath been done to Mordecai for this?** means, What honor and reward has been assigned him? עַל־זֶה, because of this report. עָשָׂה with עִם means: *to apportion*, to requite, (comp. 2 Sam. ii. 6; iii. 8 *et al.*).†

Ver. 4. The question: **who is in the court?** means, what officer is now present? The king desired to consult with him as to what distinction would be appropriate to Mordecai. It seems that those desiring to be admitted to the king's presence had to wait in the outer court. With reference to the king's intention to distinguish Mordecai, comp. Brisson *De reg. Pres. princ.* I., c. 135.

Ver. 5. Even though other officers were there already, still Haman stood first in choice.‡

* ["There is reason to think that the Persian kings were, in most cases, unable to read. (Rawlinson's *Ancient Monarchies*, Vol. IV., p. 18). Hence documents, which they wanted to consult, were read to them." Rawlinson.—Tr.]

† ["It was a settled principle of the Persian government that 'Royal Benefactors' were to receive an adequate reward. The names of such persons were placed on a special roll (Herod. VIII. 5), and great care was taken that they should be properly recommended. (See Herod. III. 140; V. 11; VIII. 85; Thucyd. I. 138; Xenoph. *Hel.* III. 1 and 6, *etc.*). It is a mistake, however, to suppose (Davidson) that they were always rewarded *at once*. Themistocles was inscribed on the list in B. C. 480, but did not obtain a reward till B. C. 465. Other 'benefactors' waited for months (Herod. V. 11), or perhaps years (*ib.* IX. 107) before they were recompensed. Sometimes a 'benefactor' seems to have received no reward at all (*ib.* III. 138)." Rawlinson.—Tr.]

‡ ["He was waiting in the outer court, till it should be

Doubtless he was the most acceptable to the king. יָבוֹא is a short order: "Let him come in," namely into the house of the king.

Vers. 6–11. Convinced that he only could be the man whom the king delighted to honor, Haman at once designates the very highest honor, and is immediately commanded to award it to Mordecai. Our author very strikingly portrays how Haman, in the very moment in which he expected to receive the highest distinction for himself, was most effectually and painfully brought low; and that his opponent, whom he hoped to destroy, was elevated to the highest place of honor. Both of these things, too—and this adds an additional charm to the whole—were brought about by Haman himself, by his own expressed judgment, indeed by his own hand.

Ver. 6. When the king had asked the question, Haman thought within himself (אָמַר בְּלִבּוֹ), **to whom would the king delight to do honor more than to myself?**—יוֹתֵר מִמֶּנִּי, *going beyond me*, more than myself. יוֹתֵר occurs in this form only in a later period (comp. Eccl. xii. 12, 9; also chap. ii. 15; vii. 11, 16).

Ver. 7. Haman was quickly prepared to give answer, and without any difficulty called up one distinction of honor after another. The sentence: **For the man whom the king delighteth to honor,** is placed in advance as being a theme brought up by the king and pleasant for his own ears to hear. We can replace it with the Nomin. Abs. in this way: As regards the man, *etc.* Thereafter he adds honor upon honor that should be bestowed on such a one, and seems hardly to know where to stop. But his aim is that the king should thereby designate this man to be thus honored as his second or other self, which in view of the divine dignity of the Persian kings, implied a great deal.

Ver. 8. **Let the royal apparel be brought which the king useth to wear.**—The constr. of לָבַשׁ with בְּ occurs only here and in the Arabic; in other places לָבַשׁ is followed by the accus., or by עַל with a distinct part of the body. The garment is not to be one such as the king is accustomed to wear, but as the perfect tense fully shows, one which he has worn. Hence it is not to be a common apparel for a special occasion, or the so-called Median dress, which the king himself wore, as also those distinguished by him, especially his princes (comp. Herod. III. 84; VII. 116; Xenophon's *Cyrop.* VIII. 3, 1 as also Bähr's annotation on Herod. III. 84); but it was a costly garment, whose value was much enhanced by the fact that the king had worn it. It is not expressly related that, the king gave as a present his own garments as a mark of honor, at least not by the Grecian authors. Plutarch, however, relates (in his *Artax.* 24), that Tiribazus had asked of the king that he put off his royal apparel and present it to him (Tiribazus, and doubtless as a mark of honor); but that the king had presented him with it, yet forbade him to wear it.* It is therefore to be remarked that those things which were used by the king, and which he had directly touched, especially his garments, were through him sanctified. A courtier even called the table sacred, from which Darius Codomannus had eaten, and wept when he saw Alexander the Great place his feet upon it. The steed upon which the king had ridden wore a crown, and was thereby designated as royal and sacred. נִתַּן can only be tertia præt. Niph., not prima Plur. Imperf. Kal, as in Judg. xvi. 5. אֲשֶׁר בְּרֹאשׁוֹ does not have reference to the head of a man, as if one could with Le Clerc, Rambach and others translate: "that the royal crown was placed on his head" (to this is opposed the præter נִתַּן, instead of which the Imperf. should have been chosen); but it rather means: upon the head of the horse. That the royal riding horse was thus crowned is also not expressly stated, still it is not improbable, since, according to Xenoph., *Cyrop.* I. 3, 3; viii. 3, 16, to him belonged a golden harness. Besides all this there is seen on Assyrian and Old Persian monuments, not so distinct on the latter, horses of the king, and perhaps also of princes, that wear an ornament on their heads terminating in three points, which can easily be taken for a crown.†

Ver. 9. **And let this apparel and horse be delivered to the hand of one of the king's most noble princes,** *etc.*—נָתוֹן, the infinitive, is the supplement of the optative יָבִיאוּ (comp. chap. ii. 3). *Delivered to the hand of, i. e.*, given over to, given up to. As regards הַפַּרְתְּמִים, comp. chap. i. 3. The place רְחוֹב הָעִיר, upon which the man to be honored should ride up and down, must, according to chap. iv. 6, have been before the king's gate and palace, and therefore a public thoroughfare. According to Gen. xli. 43, a similar honor was bestowed upon Joseph.

Vers. 10, 11. The king perfectly agreed to the proposition of Haman at once—and this must no doubt surprise the reader; he orders this designated honor to be shown to Mordecai. That Mordecai was a Jew and accustomed to sit in the king's gate could be well known to him from the records of the chronicle of the empire, or from the courtiers, who read the history to him, and who had doubtless also given him still

announced that the king was ready to grant audiences." RAWLINSON.—TR.]

* ["The honors here proposed have been thought 'excessive,' and certainly they are such as Persian monarchs rarely allowed to subjects. Each act would have been a capital offence if done without permission. Still there is nothing contrary to Oriental notions in their being done under sufferance." RAWLINSON.—TR.]

† ["The meaning of this clause is doubtful. Either it may be translated, 'and on whose head a royal crown is set,' the reference being to the horse, which conceivably might bear an ornament like a crown on its crest; or, 'and that a royal crown be set upon his head,' the reference being to the man, and the suggestion being not to deprive the king of his own diadem, but to place on the head of the person about to be honored a crown similar in general character to the royal one. (Compare chap. i. 11). The grammatical construction is in favor of the former rendering; but we have in evidence that Persian horses even wore crowns on their heads."—RAWLINSON. We may add that the latter idea is too fantastic for even Oriental taste.—TR.]

other information respecting Mordecai.* It is very remarkable that the king did not here remember, or at least overlooked the fact that he had decreed the destruction of the Jews, and had even given them over to Haman; but this is not entirely inexplicable, as may be seen from his usual mode of doing things.—**Let nothing fail of all that thou hast spoken,** *i. e.*, omit nothing of all these things (comp. Josh. xxi. 45; Judg. ii. 19).

Vers. 12–14. While Mordecai returns, loaded with honors, to his usual place of station, the gate of the king,† Haman, with covered head and sorrowful heart, hastens home to his friends and wife only to hear the discouraging prophecy that the unfortunate occurrence will be the beginning of his end. To cover the head was a sign of deep shame and distress (comp. 2 Sam. xv. 30; Jer. xiv. 4).‡ His friends are now called *wise men*, at least some of them, because they undertook to forecast his future. Perhaps there were among them some magicians, who, according to Cicero, *Divin.* I. 23, were a nation of wise and learned men. They very wisely concluded: **If Mordecai be of the seed of the Jews, then לֹא תוּכַל לוֹ, thou shalt not prevail against him**; then shalt not thou be the conqueror, but he (comp. Gen. xxxii. 26, נָפוֹל תִּפּוֹל), either thou wilt entirely, or at least surely fall. It may be asked, how did they arrive at such a conclusion? If they only attributed enmity on the part of Mordecai, then they needed only to recall the edict against the Jews and published by Haman. But they also attribute a superior power to him, because he is a Jew. Hence they must base themselves on something else. Most interpreters, among them also Bertheau and Keil, think that although these friends had before counselled Haman to have Mordecai, the unfortunate Jew, hung, yet now when he had become a highly honored person on the part of the king, and this too, as it were, through a miracle, the truth impresses itself upon them that the Jews must be under the especial divine protection. And indeed we find far more indicated here than a fear of the shrewdness and energy of the Jews. The fact that the Jews still existed in spite of all afflictions which they had endured must have impressed many with the conviction that there was a higher power assisting and caring for them. But these persons are more concerned now to appear very wise. Hence they act as if they had not known that Mordecai was a Jew, although Haman, in chap. v. 15, had expressly so stated.

Ver. 14. In order that the narrative may make a very strong impression, there must now follow blow upon blow in quick succession. Hardly had the prophecy been uttered before its fulfillment begins. Accordingly the eunuchs of the king arrive, who press Haman to come to the banquet of the king.

DOCTRINAL AND ETHICAL.

Ver. 1 sq. 1. Mordecai, according to chap. iv. 14, was convinced that if Esther would not undertake the rescue of her people, there would be found other means and ways. He had placed his trust less in her than in the general providence which watched over him. Now it is seen that though Esther had become willing to intercede, he was correct in his position. Even before Esther had ventured to express her request for her people, Mordecai himself was threatened with destruction; and before he could do anything to avert, or was even acquainted with his danger, it was already removed. It seems to have been a very insignificant means of which Providence availed itself for his protection. But it was one which, because it clearly lay above human co-operation, very definitely revealed the higher activity in his behalf: it was the sleeplessness of Ahasuerus. When the Lord is desirous of protecting or saving His people, something must serve Him of which men least thought before. Nothing is either too great or too small for Him.

BRENZ: "This is as it is written in the Psalm: 'He suffered no man to do them wrong; nay, He rebuked even kings for their sake.' For the pious are so great a care to God, that in order to preserve them He does not even spare kings, but brings upon them various calamities."

FEUARDENT: "Let every one bear in mind day and night that pious proposition of Augustine concerning the solicitude of God for His saints (*Conf.* iii. 11): "So day and night dost Thou watch for my safe-guard as if, forgetful of Thy whole creation in heaven and earth, Thou consideredst me alone, and hadst no care for others.'"

Berl. Bible: "O Lord, it is good to trust in Thee in the expectation of Thy help! Thou dost continually watch over the souls left in Thy care. And though Thou dost even wait until things have come to extremities, in order to cause the greater exercise of faith, so that none may despair of Thy assistance, still at the right time Thou art ever ready to help.—What indeed is more natural than that a king cannot sleep, and that he should wish something read to him? It is this altogether natural, yet wonderful leading, which causes the hearts of those who experience it to rejoice! To all other hearts this is dark. This wise, divine Providence is still unknown to those who only live in and for themselves."

2. It does not appear that Ahasuerus had a restless night because he had grievous thoughts regarding the edict of destruction against the entire Jewish peeple. We find that he is far too careless, much too indifferent and superficial, for such a state of mind (comp. chap. iii. 15; vii. 5). Still we would have naturally expected

* ["There is nothing strange in the king's knowing the nationality and position of Mordecai. His nationality would probably have been noted in the book of the chronicles; and, when told that nothing had been done for him (ver. 3), the king would naturally have asked his position." RAWLINSON.—TR.]

† ["It is quite consonant with Oriental notions that Mordecai, after receiving the extraordinary honors assigned him, should return to the palace and resume his former humble employment. Ahasuerus regarding him as sufficiently rewarded, and not yet intending to do any thing more for him." RAWLINSON.—TR.]

‡ [It was also "through shame probably; not wishing any of his acquaintance to accost him." RAWLINSON.—TR.]

it, and it would have been well for him if it had been so. Had he been concerned about the great number of subjects that would thus be murdered, it would not have been necessary for him first to be reminded of the fact, through the reading of the history of his reign, that he had once been in danger of being murdered himself. He would have spontaneously remembered that only a Mordecai saved him from his fate of destruction. It would have been quite just that he, while robbing so many of their rest and sleep, whom he had destined to a doom of death, should be sleepless not one, but many nights. Would that every one whose eyes cannot find sleep at night might ask whether he had at any time or in any manner done wrong, which he should be in haste to set right; or whether he does not still owe thanks for some benefit received! Would that all those who must be awake at night were clearly conscious of the fact that there is Another who is also awake, and that He it is who imposes upon us this sleeplessness! Only when we look up to Him can we find true rest (comp. Ps. cxix. 55).

3. It was soon after the marriage of Ahasuerus with Esther that Mordecai discovered and reported the conspiracy. Hence it was now over five years that this meritorious deed had been recorded, but not yet rewarded. Instead of reward, he was threatened with destruction. Those who are diligent for the welfare of others must often give up the hope of receiving their well-merited reward, even at the present day. What is more sorrowful still is the fact that one is often inclined to impugn both their motives and their work, as if they had not designed it or exerted themselves to effect it. Mordecai's history may be very instructive and comforting to such. Ahasuerus too may here again as elsewhere remind us of a faithful watchman, who, however it may go with him, never sleeps nor slumbers. The works of the good are not only recorded on earth, where they are often and easily forgotten, but they are above all recorded in heaven. It is because God saves men by His grace that He will render unto all according to their work—to those not obedient to the truth, but obeying unrighteousness, displeasure and wrath; and to the others according to their patience in good works, glory and honor (Rom. ii. 7). The seed that they have scattered, if it was good, is indestructible, and cannot be lost; and when the time comes, God will bring it to maturity, so that it may bear abundant fruit either to the sowers or to others (comp. Gal. vi. 9).

Brenz: "Although men are unmindful of benefits received, and, as Pindar says, old thanks sleep, still our Lord God is never forgetful." When God's time for reward has come, then even the zeal of enemies must assist Him, as we have seen in our history of Haman. However watchful and diligent our enemies may be in order to utterly destroy the pious, yet all their acts and labor form only the ground of the scene, which by the help of God is made to serve in perfecting the web of His leadings.—Brenz: "This is the right hand of the Most High which brings it to pass that those good things occur to the pious which the wicked hope for; and to the ungodly there come those evils which they have prepared for the godly." For the wicked are only the bearers of that power which is ever desirous of evil, and yet ever produces good.

Feuardent: "In Haman thou perceivest how blind and erring is the temper of every ambitious man. He admires and regards only himself; he fancies himself worthy of all honor and reverence, and thinks that all things are due to him. He despises all others as obscure, abject and vile. It is well, however, that there is a God in heaven who laughs to scorn, contemns, judges and hurls down the proud from their seats, but glorifies the humble: so that all may learn to be wise concerning themselves, and to be content with moderate fortune. . . . . Let all the pious therefore take courage, nor ever fail or despair of divine help on account of the rage and greatest power or violence of tyrants. For Christ still lives; He reigns, and will forever reign; and He puts all His enemies under His feet."

Starke: "Princes should have diligent care that none who have deserved well of the State or of themselves are left to go unrewarded (Gen. xli. 42; Dan. ii. 48). God knows our acts of kindness; and though we may regard them as lost or ignored, yet He can bring them to the light at the proper time to receive even a greater reward than if they had been immediately rewarded (Gen. xli. 12 sq., 39 sqq.)."

Ver. 6 sq. Feuardent: "Diligently weigh the change of the right hand of the Most High. Haman had come into the court in order that by authority of the king he might destroy Mordecai by an ignominious death. Him, however, he is compelled to exhibit and proclaim to all in royal magnificence. He had come for the purpose of raising him aloft fastened upon a very high cross with the utmost shame. But on the contrary he is compelled to adorn this very man with regal splendors, to set him on the king's horse, and to herald him publicly as the monarch's most dear and honored friend. He had come with the design of bringing a capital charge against him; and he has the task of decorating his head with the royal diadem."

It seems to us to be like a divine irony in the destiny of Haman that he is himself compelled to assign the highest distinction to his mortal enemy, and that the king instructs him to impart this honor with his own hands, thus making his downfall the more striking and lamentable. But in fact this same truth is plainly shown daily over the entire ungodly world. The world must ever concede honor and glory to those who have deserved well respecting the welfare of mankind; but it is by no means its heroes and divinities who can claim this merit, though they have been regarded as the men of glory from antiquity (Gen. xi. 4).* What the latter have accomplished has been deception, wars and vain labors. It is those whom the world regards least of all fit for their work that have done most for it. And whose will be all that the world

* According to Thiersch (*Ueber den christlichen Staat*, p. 209), Napoleon maintained that a prince who followed his conscience would be a good and noble governor, but not a great man.

has brought forth and fostered, and which it regards as great and beautiful? When the judgments of God shall have been consummated upon the world, lambs will pasture upon it as if upon *their own* pasture, and the waste places of the fat ones shall strangers eat (Isa. v. 17).

Vers. 12–14. 1. When Haman had bestowed the highest dignity on Mordecai, he hastened home, sad and with covered countenance. It is a bad sign that he knew nothing better to do in such an hour. Those are upon difficult paths who feel themselves humbled when they have been obliged to show deserved honor to others. Even in the estimation of the world it would have been far better if he had endeavored to change his enemy into a friend. And had he but reflected and correctly apprehended his present position, he would have recognized the warning voice of God, which endeavored in a firm, but yet kind tone to lead him in the way of his salvation. The final judgments of God are ever preceded by other heralds. They are indeed the announcement of the beginning of the revelations of the wrath of God; but they are also proofs of the long-suffering and love of God, which would, even in the eleventh hour lead to salvation. But it is a remarkable fact that when the worldly need their wisdom most, especially they who have usually been regarded as wise, just then they are utterly bereft of counsel; and hence their proud and stubborn hearts all at once become faint.

Feuardent: "In prosperity he is highly insolent and cruel; but in adversity he is so broken and dejected that he knows not which way to turn." But his counsellors are no better off than himself. Feuardent: "His friends do not console him, nor show him any plan for escaping his danger, which nevertheless was then the most needful help for Haman; but they throw him, just hesitating between hope and fear, into despair. 'Thou wilt surely fall in his sight,' say they. Had they admonished him indeed of his many and heinous sins toward God and His servants, of his duty of recognizing the inevitable judgment of God, of repentance, of reconciliation; then perchance it may have turned out better with him."—When our author permits these advisers to give expression of the superiority of the people of God, their words are much more to the point and weighty, as Feuardent says: "The power and efficacy of truth is so great that even its enemies and all the ungodly bear testimony to it. So the magicians of Pharaoh are compelled to explain: 'This is the finger of God;' and the Egyptians cry: 'Let us flee before Israel, for the Lord fighteth for them' (Ex. viii. 19; xix. 25)."

2. What Haman fears, and what is hinted at by his advisers, is the great truth that the Lord had laid a stone in Zion, upon which those falling upon it shall be broken. But it is just those that have placed themselves upon this stone, who are secure against all assaults by the world. And what the world daily and clearly demonstrates is the fact that it is not enough to recognize or apprehend the truth; but it is necessary also to give the heart a proper position with respect to it. Happy are they who need not fear, but who can console their hearts when the Lord says: "I will bless them that bless thee, and curse them that curse thee;" "Touch not mine anointed, and do my prophets no harm" (Ps. cv. 15); "He who toucheth you, toucheth the apple of his eye" (Zech. ii. 8).

Starke: "Self-conceit, obstinacy and selfishness are three shameful and harmful evils that have plunged many into ruin (1 Tim. vi. 9). Wordly persons seek their highest good in external pomp and appearance (Ps. xlix. 12).—Self-love appropriates all things to itself, and concedes nothing to its neighbor.—Men seek perishable honor; would that they strove diligently after the imperishable honor and glory of heaven!—The manner of wicked advisers is, when the haughty fare too well, to goad them on to vindictiveness; but if something unforeseen checks them, they drive them to despair.—God is the same always; He can bring it about that neither earth nor hell can prevail against us.—The wicked are nearest destruction when they deem themselves farthest from it (Ps. lxxiii. 7, 18, 19)."

B.—ON THE VERY GALLOWS CAUSED TO BE ERECTED FOR MORDECAI, HAMAN, ACCUSED BY ESTHER, IS HIMSELF HUNG.

Chapter VII. 1–10.

I. *Esther pleads for her People, and accuses Haman.* Vers. 1–6.

1 So [And] the king and Haman came to banquet [drink] with Esther the queen.
2 And the king said again [also] unto Esther, on the second day, at *the* banquet
[feast] of wine, What *is* thy petition, queen Esther? [*ask*,] and it shall be granted
[given to] thee: and what *is* thy request? and it shall be performed, *even* to *the*
3 half of the kingdom [*ask* to *the* half of the kingdom, and it shall be done]. Then

[And] Esther the queen answered and said, If I have found favor in thy sight
[eyes], O king, and if *it* please [*be* good upon] the king, let my life [soul] be given
4 me at my petition, and my people at my request: For we are sold, I and my peo-
ple, to be destroyed [*for one* to destroy], to *be* slain [to smite], and to perish [cause
to perish]: but if [and provided] we had been sold for bondmen and bondwomen,
I had held my tongue [hushed], although [for] the enemy [adversary] could not
5 countervail [*is* not equalling] the king's damage. Then [And] the king Ahasu-
erus answered [said],[1] and said unto Esther the queen, Who is he [*is* he this], and
where is he [*is* this he][2], that durst presume in his heart [whose heart has filled
6 him] to do so? And Esther said, *The* [a man][3] adversary and enemy *is* this
wicked Haman.[4] Then [And] Haman was afraid [terrified] before the king and
the queen.

II. *Ahasuerus, extremely enraged, causes the Death of Haman.* Vers. 7–10.

7 And the king, arising [arose] from *the* banquet of wine in his wrath, *went* into
the palace-garden: and Haman stood *up* to make request for his life [soul] to
[from] Esther the queen; for he saw that *there* was evil determined [finished]
8 against him by [from with] the king. Then [And] the king returned out of the
palace-garden into the place of the banquet [feast] of wine; and Haman *was* fallen
[falling] upon the bed whereon Esther *was*. Then said the king, Will *he* [*Is it* to]
force the queen also before [with] me in the house? *As* the word went out of the
9 king's mouth, [and] they covered Haman's face. And Harbonah, one of the
chamberlains [eunuchs], said before the king, Behold also, the gallows [tree] fifty
cubits high,[5] which Haman *had* made for Mordecai, who had spoken [spoke] good
for [upon] the king standeth in *the* house of Haman. Then [And] the king
10 said, Hang him thereon. So [And] they hanged Haman on the gallows [tree]
that he *had* prepared for Mordecai. Then [And] *was* the king's wrath pacified
[subsided].

TEXTUAL AND GRAMMATICAL.

1 [Ver. 5. The Chaldaizing influence upon the language is evident in this vague repetition of the verb אמר, which eventually led to its use in the sense of commanding.—Tr.]

2 [Ver. 5. The pron. הוּא here very nearly approaches a copula.—Tr.]

3 [Ver. 6. אִישׁ here is more than the ordinary apposition of class; it is almost a demonstrative like *iste.*—Tr.]

4 [Ver. 6. The original is very intense: *Haman, this bad man.* Doubtless her finger pointed to him.—Tr.]

5 [Ver. 9. The position of this clause in the original is more striking, being at the end of the sentence.—Tr.]

EXEGETICAL AND CRITICAL.

Vers. 1–6. What here follows seems a thing to be expected as a matter of course, yet the manner of its occurrence, particularly the rapidity with which events succeed each other, as well as their magnitude and importance, imparts a certain charm to the narrative. Esther now steps unreservedly forward at the banquet that she has prepared and to which she has invited Haman (in chap. vi. 14), and boldly presents her accusation and request. The king is quite prepared to give a correct decision in the case.

Ver. 1. **So the king and Haman came to banquet with Esther the queen.**—לִשְׁתּוֹת stands for: *in order to participate in the* מִשְׁתֶּה. The drinking after the feast, מִשְׁתֵּה הַיַּיִן (comp. chap. v. 6) was probably regarded as the chief matter at the time. But Esther petitioned (ver. 3): **let my life be given at my petition, and my people at my request.**—The בְּ is the so-called בְּ *pretii*, "about," "for." Her petition is seemingly the ransom which she proffers: "my people" means in short: *for the life of my people.* She bases her petition in ver. 4 on the words: **For we are sold, I and my people, to be destroyed,** *etc.*—She has all the more occasion for the expression נִמְכַּרְנוּ, since she and her people were left to the mercy of Haman for the sum of money he had promised the king if the Jews should be destroyed (chap. iii. 9; iv. 7). לְהַשְׁמִיד and the following active infinitives are clearly substitutes for the passive form, precisely as in the royal order (chap. iii. 13).* She also adds, however: **But if we had been sold for bondmen and bondwomen, I had held my tongue, although the enemy could not countervail the king's damage,** and she thereby indicates that it concerns not only her own, but also the king's interest. אִלּוּ, contracted from אִם לוּ, as in Eccl. vi. 6, also common in the Aramaic language,

* ["Esther here quotes the exact words of the edict issued for the destruction of the Jews. Thus the king would not fail to understand her, and to learn for the first time that his favorite was a Jewess." Rawlinson.—Tr.]

introduces an event in a hypothetical manner as being more desirable, and is followed by the perfect, if instead another event than the one anticipated has occurred. In the next sentence usually the perfect follows with ו *consec.* Here, however, the ו is absent because Esther does not desire to say what she would do, but what she would have done: "I had held my tongue, although," *etc.* The sentence: כִּי אֵין הַצָּר שֹׁוֶה, means according to R. Sal. ben-Melech and Rambach: The enemy can by no means equal, compensate or make good by his money the loss which the king suffers by our destruction. Similar also are the views of Clericus and others, who suggest an intermediate thought enlarging the meaning, such as: "But I dare not be silent." Though even such an addition were in itself not doubtful, still שָׁוָה in the Kal, with בְּ, does not mean *compensare* (to compensate), but to be equal to, or to be worth as much as some other thing (comp. Prov. iii. 15; viii. 11). The assumption of Gesenius, that the expression: "The enemy is not equal to the damage to the king," is only another form of sentence for: "The enemy cannot make good the damage to the king," is very improbable. Hence Bertheau and Keil interpret it: "The enemy is not worthy of the king's damage," *i. e.* is not of sufficient account that I should grieve or distract the king. They insist that נֵזֶק does not only mean *pecuniary loss*, as is commonly assumed from Ezra iv. 13, 22, but according to the Targums means also *bodily harm* (comp. Targ. Ps. xci. 7; Gen. xxvi. 11; 1 Chron. xvi. 22). Still the thought thus gained is not quite satisfactory. It would have mattered little, not whether Haman, but whether the Jews were worthy of the king's displeasure. Certain it is that Esther expressed herself in very brief words, and such as implied more. Perhaps we may enlarge their sense thus: I would have held my tongue; for the punishment of the enemy is not worthy of, is less important than the averting of the damage which the king will suffer, now that the Jews are ordered to be destroyed; but this he would not have suffered if they had been sold as slaves, and hence had realized a large sum. In this way the chief thought is made to be the loss which the king would sustain if a whole people were destroyed; and Esther's keeping out of sight her special concern about the destruction of the Jews, which would have been very shrewd in her under any circumstances, becomes particularly so in the present instance and before Ahasuerus. The ancient translators, it seems, were at a loss here, and hence offer us but little help.

Ver. 5 with its twice-repeated וַיֹּאמֶר: **Then the king Ahasuerus answered, and said unto Esther the queen,** by its solemn title: "The king to the queen," indicates the great importance of these words and of the moment. The king of the great empire here addressed her, who was a daughter of her people, but also the queen in this great realm. At the same time the twice-repeated: "he said," reveals the agitation of the king, to which also corresponds the double question: **Who and where is he?** אֲשֶׁר מְלָאוֹ לִבּוֹ: **that durst presume in his heart to do so.**—We might expect it to read: "Who had filled his heart," *viz.* with the thought to do so. But it is the heart from which proceed the thoughts, and which determines the rest of the man to conclusive purposes (Isaiah xliv. 20; Eccl. viii. 11; Matt. xv. 19).*

Ver. 6. Esther still hesitates to name Haman, but at last brings the predicate into prominence: **The adversary and enemy is this wicked Haman.**—She does not say: "The evil-disposed person," *viz.* of whom she is speaking, but without the article, אִישׁ צַר, in order to make as strikingly prominent as possible the conception of the man so inimical. Haman trembled; for נִבְעַת means more than that he was simply alarmed (comp. 1 Chron. xxi. 30; Dan. viii. 17, and בִּעוּתִים, Ps. lxxxviii. 17; Job vi. 4).

Vers. 7–10. Thereupon the king became at once terribly angry. Because of his agitation he went aside for a moment, but soon returned, and at once gave order for the execution of Haman. —**Into the palace-garden** (comp. chap. i. 5), which was the place to which he retired. This is strikingly expressed by קָם. He did this in order to recover from the first burst of anger, and to consider what was to be done with Haman. Haman remained standing **to make request of his life to Esther.**—עַל־נַפְשׁוֹ, properly, "because of his life" (בִּקֵּשׁ with עַל, as in chap. iv. 8), since he saw that on the part of the king there was no more hope for him if Esther would not intercede for him; strictly: **that evil was determined against him by the king,** *fully determined* (כָּלָה as in 1 Sam. xxv. 17; Ezra v. 13).

Ver. 8. **Was fallen,** *i. e.* had kneeled down (נָפַל as in Josh. vii. 10 and elsewhere) **upon the bed whereon Esther was** (sat), hence as a petitioner he fell at her feet.† The king, however, soon returned and said—since he could not control his anger, but now manifested it more terribly: **Will he force the queen also before me in the house?**—The infin. לִכְבּוֹשׁ is here placed, as if he were understood as asking a question. But it may also be made stronger (comp. 1 Chron. xv. 2, *etc.*), viz. to trample under foot, to subjugate. If the question had only been whether the queen could be forced sexually, then Ahasuerus could not have asked such a question so lightly. It would only have been an expression of his highest displeasure and wrath. If Esther were honest and just, she must of necessity have exonerated Haman from such an evil design. The whole situation of things makes such a foul purpose highly improbable, indeed impossible. Or perhaps Ahasuerus was only asking whether, if one would attain anything from the queen, it was

* ["Ahasuerus could not really have doubted; but he affects to doubt, that he may express his anger at the act, apart from all personal considerations." RAWLINSON.—TR.]

† ["Like the Greeks and Romans, the Persians reclined at their meals on sofas or couches (Herod. ix. 80, 82; Xenoph. *Cyrop.* VIII. 8, 16, *etc.*"). RAWLINSON.—TR.]

necessary to make request with such force.* We can readily think that Esther sought to withdraw from Haman, but that he, as it were, forcibly detained her. The word of which it is now said: **As the word went out of the king's mouth, they covered Haman's face,** cannot mean the question that just preceded. Then it would be "*this* word;" but this is another word. We may consider that this word, possibly with a little addition, quite intelligible to the officers, was to them a command to take Haman out of his sight. The subject of חָפוּ is those whose duty it was to execute such commands, the servants of the king. The covering of the face was probably the beginning of the execution of the death-sentence (comp. Curtius vi. 8, 22: "They brought Philetas with covered head into the palace"). Even old interpreters, such as Brentius, Rickel, Feuardent, remind us of the sentence in Cicero *pro C. Rabirio* IV. 13: "Lictor, bind his hands, veil his head, hang him on the hapless tree."†

Ver. 9. In order that it might appear very strikingly what our history here would teach—that he who dug a pit for others, especially for pious Jews, shall fall into it himself; or yet more definitely that inimical heathendom shall perish by its own devices, it must be so ordered that one of the officers shall bring it about to have Haman hung upon the same gallows which he had caused to be erected for Mordecai. And in order to show how much hated this enemy of the Jews was, one of the king's officers must point out this very tree of death. This person was Harbonah, doubtless the one mentioned in chap. i. 10, one of the eunuchs of the king, *i. e.* of the higher officers who waited on the king. The word גַּם with which he begins: **Behold also, the gallows fifty cubits high, which Haman had made for Mordecai,** *etc.*, may not imply that the other servants or even Harbonah himself had already brought accusations against Haman, and in addition would also reproach him with the erection of this gallows (Bertheau, Keil); but from Harbonah's view, it points out the most appropriate means at hand offered by the prepared gallows for the fate of Haman. This is more significant against Haman. In giving prominence to the fact that Mordecai was the one who spoke well of the king by revealing the plot against the king's life (comp. chap. ii. 22; vi. 2), he intimates that it was more fit for Haman to grace the gallows than the one for whom it was originally erected.

DOCTRINAL AND ETHICAL.

Vers. 1 sqq. 1. How very carefully Esther brings her petition before the king, even though the king for the second time has accepted her invitation! She waits until the king himself inquires into it anew, and until he has even obligated himself to her to the half of his kingdom; she so frames her speech that her more personal interest, which in the present instance would have been of paramount importance in the eyes of the king, is presented equally with, indeed in advance of, all others. She avoids at once opposing herself against Haman; and finally she seeks to take the king on his weak side by giving prominence to the fact that in the destruction of the Jews the king would sustain a great loss. It was to her still a question whether Ahasuerus would permit her to interfere in the business of government—indeed whether he would grant her a hearing while opposed to so powerful a rival. But she acted at last with fear and trembling—although she was assured of the best ally as being with her—not only Ahasuerus, but also God's love. Her petition, moreover, had the very best effect. Thus the Lord, who leads the hearts of men and of kings like streams of water, has His help prepared for us, when we in our little faith stand trembling; and often where we hardly dared hope or advance, He gives us the greatest success. All depends upon this, that our hesitation be not of unbelief, but that we have fears only from our own power, capability, or worthiness; and that we seek not so much to promote our own cause as rather God's, and ours through Him.

Starke: "Trembling soul, if this heathen king is so trustworthy in his promises, then your heavenly King is far more faithful. The former promises only to give the half of his kingdom—but He to give you the whole kingdom (Luke xii. 32; xxii. 29). Truth may be crushed to the earth, but it dies not; it can be avoided or offended, yet it will finally come to light and triumph."

2. Haman, from the very outset, had moved toward the fulfilment of his wishes with the greatest assurance. Even after being inquired of by the king as to what should be done to the man whom the king would especially honor, he had answered with the greatest confidence. Doubtless he thought that, because of the friendship, or because of the weakness of the king, all things were for him permissible, and he hoped every thing for himself. Yet if he had but reflected, he must have acknowledged that this foundation was unsafe, and that it was easy for another to gain the favor of the king against himself. But this is the common curse of human self-confidence that it places us in a state of insecurity. He who has succeeded in gaining the favor of the great is very liable to think that now he will also easily govern the servants of his Lord.

3. Truly it is a distressing condition in which Haman finds himself at the table of Esther. Outwardly he receives the highest distinction and is made happy, but inwardly there already comes a painful presentiment of his downfall. He is indeed already bound by the cord that shall plunge him into destruction.

Feuardent: "But in all this the first notable thing is how far apart stand the judgments of the Almighty and those of this world, since those whom the world esteems most happy and fortunate are truly most unhappy and unfortunate before God. . . . . Men, indeed, seeing only what

* ["Of course the king did not believe his own words. But he meant to tax Haman with a further offence in not sufficiently respecting the person of the queen; and he thereby suggested to the attendants his instant execution." Rawlinson.—Tr.]

† ["The Macedonians and the Romans are known to have commonly muffled the heads of prisoners before executing them; but it is not mentioned elsewhere than here as a Persian custom." Rawlinson.—Tr.]

appears, and judging according to the outward semblance, would have boldly pronounced no man more fortunate than Haman. But in fact and in God's view, who sees the heart, he was of all men the most miserable. For he was inflated with ambition, he was hot with envy, he was bursting with hate, and went to the banquet in the most disturbed state of mind. There rankled in the bottom of his heart the thought of that fresh honor which he had lately been forced to confer upon his enemy; and he was moreover goaded to desperation by what his friends had told him to his face—that he himself, having once begun to fall before the Jew, would forever be his inferior, and that Mordecai would increase in glory and honor."

Haman, at the table of Esther, is but a picture of all wicked ones at the table of fortune. The change of circumstances now manifest, it is true, was unique, and seemed as if purposely selected for him.—FEUARDENT: "A little while ago all fell prostrate before Haman, but now he quails before a feeble woman. He who persecuted the Jews worse than a dog or a serpent, now becomes a suppliant to a Jewess. He who had procured a cruel slaughter for all the Hebrews is now anxious to save his own life. He who could not endure Mordecai now intercedes with his domestic." The old reverse substantially recurs: "At the feast he who was unwilling to afford a crumb of bread to Lazarus, asked to be cooled by the finger of Lazarus dipped in water." This change will be most striking when Christ shall lay all His enemies at His feet.

On ver. 8. 1. The only means left to Haman to be tried for his salvation evidently was that he should fall at the feet of Esther and implore her pardon. But it was just this which Ahasuerus, now returning from the garden, interpreted as a great crime, and so it filled the measure of his sin. When once the season of divine grace and forbearance allotted to sinners is closed, when punitive justice arises against them, then it seems as if they can undertake nothing but what will aggravate their case and hasten their own destruction. As Ahasuerus did in this case, so did all those who stood by the side of Haman and had given him their confidence. Now that he is so near his downfall, these are inclined to use every thing against the offender by which he might obtain deliverance. They know him too well to be ignorant of the tricks and deceptions of which he is capable. Petitions for pardon—and even repentance—is in such cases often thought to be only the repentance of Cain, affording no guarantee of genuine reform. Possibly these judges go too far in their sentence, but God's justice employs them as channels against the offenders.

FEUARDENT: "The king indeed is unjust in fixing this calumny upon Haman—but God is just who permits the righteous penalty to fall upon him for his lies and calumnies, inasmuch as he would have brought violence upon other virgins or matrons, and would have plunged the whole people of God into ruin. Accordingly it is written: "By what one sinneth, by that also shall he be punished;" and again: "With what measure ye mete, it shall be measured unto you again."

2. The question raised by ancient interpreters whether it was not the duty of Esther to exonerate Haman from the accusation by the king, and to second his request for pardon, can only be satisfactorily answered by making the proper distinction between the views of such points in the Old and in the New Testaments. Upon New Testament grounds, the answer would undoubtedly be in the affirmative. It is no greater offence than one which the Christian, though he have suffered the most grievous insults and offensive acts, should be prepared to pardon, in a spirit free from hatred or revenge. Now whether the king, here acting in his judicial capacity, could entertain her request, would have been a different matter. Taking, however, the Old Testament view, the answer would most certainly be, No; and this the more, inasmuch as there was not yet a more satisfactory means of averting evil than the destructive judgments of God upon Haman, who, as an Agagite and an Amalekite, was regarded as representing the cause of evil in opposition to the cause of God and of His people (comp. Doct. hist. thoughts on Neh. iii. 36 sqq.). Further, in Esther's conduct is plainly shown the important fact that, when the season of grace is expired, Justice desires no interruption through petitions for mercy. This truth must be taken to heart, and we must not bewail its force. When Christians see the wicked perish, let them weep over their fate. But we must rejoice over the divine judgments upon iniquity. This serves to strengthen our faith in a holy, ever active God. Our own opposition to iniquity must be as unrelenting as was that of Esther against Haman.

STARKE: "It is barely credible that the king should have thought further upon this matter—have perceived the wonderful dealings of God. Neither can we believe that he was thereby led to know the true God. Esther, however, and Mordecai, together with many of the Jews, must have been gloriously strengthened in their faith. Jehovah's judgments are just (Rev. xix. 2). Let the Christian here notice the goodness and truthfulness of God (Rom. xi. 22), and let both be to him a warning voice!"

On vers. 9, 10. Bitter and sarcastic must it have struck upon the ears of Haman when Harbonah, one of the eunuchs, who up to this time had humbly shown him all desired honor, remarked, now that the doomed man was led away: "Behold also, the gallows fifty cubits high, which Haman had made for Mordecai, who had spoken good for the king, standeth in the house of Haman." Must it then be that this despicable creature should raise his foot against the dead lion? See how in this moment he turns toward the newly rising sun with praises in his mouth! Must this miserable slave also add to the already great misfortune of Haman—that he should be hung on just this gallows which he had intended for the Jews! Poor Haman! Didst thou not know that in such ways as were thine thou hadst no really true friend? Didst thou not perceive that a selfish spirit and hypocrisy formed thy body guard? Not know that those who externally bowed the knee to thee, inwardly gnashed their teeth against thee? True friendship and fellowship can only exist between those who are together united to God. Even then we may often discover the overweening egotism which again loosens such bonds. Where this common bond is wanting, there separation must ensue; there, in fact, each goes his own way. If in such a case all the secret endeavors and aims could be exposed, we would discover a "war of all against all." It is frequently seen that apparent friends afterward become executioners, who, by their mockery, add to the misery of the culprit. In the future also it will be found that the enemies of the people of God will themselves destroy each other in order that judgment on them may be perfect. There is a universal just government of the world on the part of God. He who is capable of so shameful an act as not only to wish to destroy his enemy, but also to cover him with the greatest possible ignominy, must not be surprised if in his own well deserved misfortune great shame shall also accompany his own end. Whoever digs a pit for others, will himself fall into it. This proverb verifies itself in its fullest sense. It has the ring of Satanic mockery when Harbonah says: "And the gallows also stand ready, and that, too, before Haman's own house." There are many people who hesitate not to utter it mockingly, and how good were it for all those who are in danger of entering the way of destruction, should they hear it said loud enough for them to hear, and should they repeat it to themselves: "Also the gallows stand ready without."

STARKE: "It must also so happen in the just judgment of God that since the highest minister of State had caused the highest gallows to be erected in accordance with his greatness of feeling and State position and honors, before which all bowed in adoration to the earth, he should himself be elevated above all other people that were hung."

SECOND SECTION.

The Deliverance of the Jews.

CHAPTERS VIII. IX.

A.—ESTHER AND MORDECAI PROCURE PERMISSION FOR THEIR PEOPLE TO STAND ON THEIR OWN DEFENCE.

CHAP. VIII. 1–17.

I. *Esther and Mordecai receive authority to order all things needful for the deliverance of the Jews.*
Vers. 1–8.

1 ON that day did the king Ahasuerus give *the* house of Haman, the Jews' enemy,
unto Esther the queen: and Mordecai came before the king; for Esther had told
2 what he *was* unto her. And the king took [removed] off his ring [signet], which
he had taken [caused to pass] from Haman, and gave it unto Mordecai. And Es-
3 ther set Mordecai over *the* house of Haman. And Esther spake *yet* again [added
and spoke] before the king, and fell *down* at [before] his feet, and besought him
with tears [wept and supplicated to him] to put away [cause to pass] *the* mischief
[evil] of Haman the Agagite, and his device that he *had* devised against the Jews.
4 Then [And] the king held out the golden sceptre toward [to] Esther. So [And]
5 Esther arose, and stood before the king, And said, If *it* please [*be* good upon] the
king, and if I have found favor in his sight [before him], and the thing [word] *seem*
right before the king, and I *be* pleasing [good] in his eyes, let it be written to re-
verse the letters [books] devised by [of *the* devising of] Haman *the* son of Ham-
medatha [the Medatha] the Agagite, which he wrote to destroy the Jews which
6 [who] *are* in all the king's provinces: For how can I *endure to* see [and (*i. e.*, when)
I see (*i. e.*, look) on] the evil that shall come unto my people [my people shall find]?
or [and] how can I *endure to* see [and (*i.e.*, when) I see (*i. e.*, look) on] *the* destruc-
7 tion of my kindred? Then [And] the king Ahasuerus said unto Esther the
queen, and to Mordecai the Jew, Behold, I have given Esther *the* house of Haman,
and him they have hanged upon the gallows [tree], because [upon that] he laid
8 [sent *forth*] his hand *upon* the Jews. Write ye also [And write YE] for [upon] the

Jews, as it liketh you [*is* the good in your eyes], in the king's name, and seal it with the king's ring [signet]: for *the* writing which is written in the king's name, and sealed with the king's ring [signet], may no *man* [*there is* no *one* to] reverse.

II. *Mordecai authorizes the Jews to make preparations for a common defence.* Vers. 9–14.

9 Then [And] were the king's scribes called at that time in the third month, that *is*,
the month Sivan, on *the* three and twentieth [twenty] *day* thereof [in it]: and it
was written, according to all that Mordecai commanded, unto the Jews, and to the
lieutenants [satraps], and the deputies [pashas], and [*the*] rulers [princes] of the
provinces which *are* from India [Hodu], [and] unto Ethiopia [Cush], a hundred
[and] twenty and seven provinces, unto every province [province and (*i. e.*, by) pro-
vince], according to the writing thereof, and *unto* every people [people and (*i. e.*, by)
people] after [according to] their language [tongue], and to the Jews according to
10 their writing, and according to their language [tongue]. And he wrote in the king
Ahasuerus' name, and sealed *it* with the king's ring [signet]; and sent letters
[books] by posts [*the* hand of the runners] on horseback [the horses], *and* riders on
[of] mules [the steed], camels [the mules], *and* young dromedaries [sons of the
11 mares]: Wherein [Which] the king granted [gave to] the Jews which [who] *were*
in every city [and (*i. e.*, by) city] to gather [congregate] themselves *together*, and
to stand for [upon] their life [soul], to destroy, to slay [smite], and to cause to pe-
rish, all [every] *the* power of *the* people and province that *would* assault them, *both*
12 little ones and women, and *to take* [*he gave*] the spoil of them for a prey. *Upon* one
day, in all *the* provinces of king Ahasuerus, *namely, upon the* thirteenth [thirteen]
13 *day* of [to] *the* twelfth [twelve] month, which [that] *is the* month Adar. *The* copy
of the writing, for a commandment [law] to be given in every province [and (*i. e.*,
by) province] *was* published [revealed] unto all people [the peoples], and that the
Jews should [*for* the Jews to] be ready against [to] that day to avenge themselves
14 on [from] their enemies. *So* the posts [runners] that rode upon [riders of] mules
and camels [the steed] went out, being hastened and pressed on by the king's com-
mandment [word]. And the decree [law] was given at [in] Shushan the palace
[citadel].

III. *Mordecai's honor and the joy of the Jews.* Vers. 15–17.

15 And Mordecai went out from the presence of [before] the king in royal apparel of
blue [violet] and white [linen], and *with* a great crown of gold, and *with* a garment
[robe] of fine linen [byssus] and purple: and the city of Shushan rejoiced [shouted]
16 and was glad. The Jews had [To the Jews was] light, and gladness, and joy, and
17 honour. And in every province and in every city [and (*i. e.*, by) city], whitherso-
ever [which] the king's commandment [word] and his decree [law] came [*was* ap-
proaching], the Jews had [*was* to the Jews] joy [gladness] and gladness [joy], a
feast and a good day. And many of [from] the people [peoples] of the land be-
came Jews [Judaized themselves]; for *the* fear of the Jews fell upon them.

EXEGETICAL AND CRITICAL.

It seems almost self-evident after what occurred in chap. vii. that now, next to Esther, Mordecai should also come to great distinction. Whether, however, they would be able fully to reverse the fate that threatened the Jews, remained uncertain in view of the difficulty of the situation. Even after Mordecai had taken his own protective measures, up to the very hour when success was assured, uncertainty continued. In chap. viii. it is to be shown first what authority he received and what measures of policy he adopted.

Vers. 1–8. First, Mordecai's *authority*. On the very day in which Haman fell the king presented the queen with his house. Justly enough the Targums understand by the term "*house*," also the *people* in it, and the entire possessions belonging thereto. It was usual for Persian kings to possess themselves of the property of those who had been punished with death (Josephus, *Antiq.* XI. 1, 3; 4, 6). Mordecai **came before the king**, *i. e.* he was made one of the officers who saw the face of the king (comp. chap. i. 10, 4; vii. 9). He owed his position, not merely to his merit, as having himself been of service to the king, and now meriting the title *benefactor of the king* (Herod. VIII. 85), but because of his relation to Esther (chap. ii. 7). Indeed **the king took off his ring** (ver. 2, וַיָּפַר, as in chap. iii. 10), his seal-ring, **which he had taken from Haman, and gave it unto Mordecai.**—הֶעֱבִיר מִן, as in Jon. iii. 6;

he made him prime minister (Gen. xli. 42; 1 Macc. vi. 15; comp. chap. iii. 10).* In addition Esther placed him over the house of Haman, *i. e.* left to him the honorable and lucrative management of the large estate thus reverting to her, in fact made him her governor of the house. Both henceforth enjoyed a brilliant position; but they were not misled thereby into evil. The remarks with reference to the present prosperity of Esther and Mordecai are evidently made with regard to what followed. They did not take their ease at the expense of the needed care over their people; these were not forgotten. On the contrary they believed it incumbent upon them to do all in their power to make their people happy and prosperous. The mourning of Esther was still great; it did not cease until full deliverance came to them.

Ver. 3. **And Esther spake yet again before the king, and fell down at his feet, and besought him with tears.**†—She thus caused him to understand distinctly that she was by no means satisfied with what had been done. In so far as Esther had implored him in a general manner to cause **to be put away,** to neutralize, to annul (הֶעֱבִיר) **the mischief of Haman** (which he expected to inflict upon the Jews), **and his device** that he had devised against the Jews (comp. Jer. xviii. 11; Ezek. xxxviii. 10), the king showed his willingness to comply, and as in chap. iv. 11; v. 2, he again stretched forth the golden sceptre toward her, so that she could take courage to arise and stand before him. Still it was necessary to find out the ways and means how the thing should be begun.

Ver. 5. Esther suggested: **If it please the king** (comp. chap. i. 19; v. 4, 8; vii. 3); and further on feeling the doubtful character of her proposition, she added: **and the thing seem right,** advisable to him. כָּשֵׁר = to succeed, to accomplish, and in this sense has reference to seed which has sprouted well (Eccl. xi. 6, in the Hiphil, Eccl. x. 10); it is a later word of which elsewhere we only find the noun כִּשְׁרוֹן (Eccl. ii. 21; iv. 4; v. 10). **Let it be written,** or commanded by an edict, as in chap. iii. 9, **to reverse the letters** (לְהָשִׁיב, to cause to change from the state of being to non-existence) **devised by Haman.**—As is often the case, here the substance of a letter is indicated by an apposition, מַחֲשֶׁבֶת הָמָן (comp. chap. iii. 8 sq. and 12 sqq.). But in order the more certainly to carry through this doubtful proposal, she adds in ver. 6: **For how can I endure to see evil that shall come unto my people? or how can I endure to see the destruction of my kindred?**—With reference to the connection of אוּכַל וְרָאִיתִי, we may indicate that one of the verbs, instead of being in the Infin. (with לְ) is subordinate to the other as a finite verb (with וְ), comp. Ewald, § 285 *c*. Still לֹא אוּכַל itself means: "I cannot endure it," or "I will not be able to stand it" (comp. Isai. i. 13), and the term וְרָאִיתִי is equal to "when I shall have seen." רָאָה with בְּ indicates to look upon some one with interest, be it that of pleasure, as is usual, or of pain or sorrow, as is the case here; comp. in this relation Gen. xii. 1.

Vers. 7, 8. In order to indicate in advance that his good will abounds towards Esther and Mordecai, and that he would grant them all that the law would sanction in favor of the Jews, the king here reminds them of what he had so far done for Esther and Mordecai. Since, however, he could not directly annul his first decrees, but could simply make them powerless in effect, he commands them not to send new orders to the governors—in this manner a suspension or recall of the first edict could not be accomplished—but to send an edict to the Jews themselves, commanding them to prepare for their defence. The sentence: **For the writing which is written in the king's name, and sealed with the king's ring, may no man reverse,** may have the sense, and so it is generally held, that the simple recall of the first edicts was not possible. אֵין לְהָשִׁיב may indicate a reflection upon לְהָשִׁיב in Esther's petition in ver. 5.* But since these words so nearly correspond to what precedes: "Let it be written in the name of the king, and seal it with the king's ring," it is clearer and more natural to understand him to say: The new edict to the Jews will be just as authoritative and irreversible as was the former one to the governors. This must equally be obeyed with that. Of course the confirmation belongs still to the words of the king. The phraseology speaks only in an objective sense of the "king," because it refers to a general rule. The infin. absol. Niph. וְנַחְתּוֹם is used instead of the perfect [by an ellipsis of the substantive verb].

Vers. 9–14. These contain the *measures* of Mordecai.† In the same manner as did Haman (chap. iii. 12–15) on the 13th of the first month, so Mordecai wrote to and "commanded the Jews and the rulers of the provinces," on the 23d of the third month, *i. e.* Sivan. This was fully two

* ["A pleasure-seeking Persian king, like Xerxes, was glad to be relieved of the toil of governing, and willingly committed to one favorite after another the task of issuing and signing with the royal signet the decrees by which the government was administered. That the official entrusted with these high powers might be a eunuch, appears from Diodorus (XVI. 50). RAWLINSON.—TR.]

† [From the statement of ver. 4 that the king again held out to her the golden sceptre, "we must understand that Esther had once more intruded on Ahasuerus unsummoned." RAWLINSON.—TR.]

* ["The answer of Ahasuerus is a refusal, but one softened as much as possible. He first dwells on the proofs which he had just given of his friendly feeling towards the Jews (ver. 7). He then suggests that something may be done to help them without revoking the decree (ver. 8). Finally, he excuses himself by appealing to the well-known immutability of Persian law." RAWLINSON.—TR.]

† ["The suggestion of Ahasuerus quickened the inventive powers of Esther and Mordecai. The scribes were at once summoned, and a decree issued, not revoking the former one, but allowing the Jews to stand on their defence, and to kill all who attacked them. It has been pronounced incredible that any king would thus have sanctioned civil war in all the great cities of his empire; but some even of the more sceptical critics allow that *Xerxes* might not improbably have done so (De Wette, *Einleitung*, p. 198 *a*)." RAWLINSON.—TR.]

months later, although Haman's fall must have occurred soon after the edict of extermination was published. No doubt Mordecai thought it expedient first to establish himself in his new position before taking such steps and proposing such measures. He wrote to the Jews, but so that the governors became acquainted with the nature of this order, and were obliged to forward it in their extensive provinces to every single Jewish community (comp. chap. i. 1).

The subject of וַיִּכְתֹּב in ver. 10 is the one transmitting or originating the writing, *i. e.* Mordecai. In order to speedily make known the edict so as to free the Jews from their anxiety, and avert the evil in time, he dispatched the messengers with the greatest speed. רָצִים, *i. e.* couriers, בַּסּוּסִים, *i. e.* on horses, **by posts on horseback, and riders on mules, and young dromedaries.**—רֶכֶשׁ, in distinction from סוּס, is the saddle-horse (dromedary), the race-horse (1 Kings v. 8), and is here used in a collective sense. אֲחַשְׁתְּרָנִים (vers. 10–14) are not "asses," according to the modern Persian *estar*, which in the Sanscrit = *acvatara*, and hence may have been *acpatara* in old Persian; but they were princely, royal horses, hence belonging to the court, from *kshatra*, "royal," king, according to Haug, in Ewald's *Bibl. Jahrb.* V., p. 154. רַמָּךְ = the Syriac *ramco*, "herd," particularly a herd of horses, with which we may also compare the word *ramakat*, "stud," in the Arabic.

Ver. 11. Mordecai wrote that **the king granted the Jews which were in every city to gather themselves together, and to stand for their life**, *i. e.* to defend themselves (comp. Dan. xii. 1), **to destroy, to slay, and to cause to perish all the power**, which like an army would raise itself against them (חַיִל), **of the people and province that would assault them, both little ones and women, and to take the spoil of them for a prey.**—This too was to take place on the day already designated in chap. iii. 13, *viz.* the thirteenth day of the twelfth month. The reduplication of the expression "to destroy," *etc.*, refers to chap. iii. 13. The same should be granted the Jews which, according to Haman's edict, was allowed the heathen. The Jews were permitted to apply the *jus talionis*. The case then stood that the governors and other authorities were by no means obligated to assist in the preparation for the destruction of the Jews, nor yet to obstruct or hinder the resistance which the Jews would offer to their assailants, as might seem to be implied in the first edict. For then the second edict, which was equally authoritative, would have been little respected; but they could leave the case to the people, whether they would attack the Jews and risk a conflict, and they need not afterward punish such Jews as had slain their enemies. But still more. It was permitted the Jews to assemble and prepare and arm for their common defence in advance, so that they might act as one man against all the assaults and reverses, which in case of their standing disunited would surely have befallen them. לְהִקָּהֵל (to collect), placed in advance here, was especially important (comp. its prominence in chap. ix. 2, 15, 16, 18). Without this the Jews would not have possessed more than the simple right of self-defence, which, under any circumstances, they would have availed themselves of. Besides, even in the Persian empire the larger portion of the inhabitants seem to have possessed humanity enough to feel the disreputableness of an attack upon the Jews for the purpose of rapine, and they were little inclined to participate therein. On ver. 13 comp. chap. iii. 14 *b*, and on ver. 14, chap. iii. 15.

Vers. 15–17. The effect of this new measure was to produce great and general joy, and to bring great honor to Mordecai. He went forth from the presence of the king **in royal apparel of blue and white** (comp. chap. i. 6), **and with a great crown of gold,* and with a garment of fine linen and purple†** (תַּכְרִיךְ ἁπ. λεγ., in Aramaic תַּכְרִיכָא). He was thus adorned doubtless to show what honor had been shown him by the king, but more particularly to make it manifest how he had succeeded in the matter of the Jews, and at the same time to publish his joyous feelings thereat. Importance attaches here not to the royal garment, which had already been given him in chap. vi. 8 sq., but to the State robes of the first minister at court, which, it appears, Mordecai had not put on at the time of his elevation (vers. 1–2), but which he put on after his care for his people was removed. Then the city of Shushan, *i. e.*, its inhabitants one and all, and not the Jews alone, of whom there is separate mention made in ver. 16, **rejoiced** (צהל is not exactly to cry aloud, comp. Isa. xxiv. 14) **and was glad.**—Hence they had deprecated the massacre awaiting the Jews, and perhaps apprehended with fear the great disorders and dangers that would ensue. But the Jews, ver. 16—*i. e.*, those living in Shushan—for the others are mentioned in ver. 17, had light and joy in contrast to the darkening of their future fate (אוֹרָה, found in the fem. in Ps. xxxix. 12; in Isa. xxvi. 19, pl. אורת), and gladness, and joy, and honor.

Ver. 17. So also the joy spread to those without, who were so exceedingly distressed through Haman's edict (chap. ix. 3). They indulged in feasts, and in a good, joyous day, *i. e.*, a holiday (comp. chap. ix. 19, 22). But this was not all. Many of the people of the land became Jews (מִתְיַהֲדִים, derived from יְהוּדִי, and found only here), because the fear of the Jews, and doubtless also of the mighty and powerful God of the Jews, ruling over their destiny, and not so much the fear of Mordecai and Esther, had fallen upon them (comp. Ex. xv. 16; Deut. xi. 25).‡

* ["Not a crown like the king's (כֶּתֶר), but a mere golden band or coronet (עֲטָרָה)." Rawlinson.—Tr.]

† ["The tunic or minor robe of the king was of purple, striped with white (Xenoph. *Cyrop.* VIII. 3, § 13; Plutarch, *Alex.* § 51; Q. Curt. III. 5)." Rawlinson.—Tr.]

‡ ["Mordecai's power might by itself have caused some fear, but the chief alarm felt probably was lest the Jews, when the day came for revenging themselves, should account the large class of indifferent persons among their enemies. Persons of this class avoided the danger by becoming Jews." Rawlinson.—Tr.]

DOCTRINAL AND ETHICAL.

On ver. 1 sqq. 1. If in the present case the danger that threatened the Jews had not been so imminent and the disposition of both Esther and Mordecai so patriotic, then they might possibly have become proud in view of the wealth and high life and station that they now enjoyed, or they might have grown indifferent or reserved with respect to the distress of their countrymen. It is too frequent an occurrence that upstarts fear to lose caste by paying regard to former relations. Hence they are quick to forget and neglect their previous friends. There is no question that the attainment of honor and wealth will bring a blessing only when these become an incentive to good works, especially in promoting God's kingdom. There is connected with their enjoyment sufficient discontent, envy and misery, and also enough trouble and curses. In general, Christians who have come to power are more timid in taking care of their friends than worldly people are. Hence the latter can more safely count on the applause of the great mass of men. But the world will not thank the former for their timidity, and God will hold them to account.

Feuardent: "We are taught by Mordecai's example that even pious men sometimes come to the head of affairs, and are safely entrusted with the reins of government; and that God adorns with this glory on earth those whom He will afterwards crown in heaven likewise. They are promoted, however, not so much for their own sake as that they may aid and promote the church and people of God, and may free and console those in affliction."

Starke: "We should have sympathy for oppressed brethren in the faith (1 Pet. iii. 8; Col. iii. 12; Gal. vi. 10). The innocence of the guiltless should be protected (Sir. iv. 9; 1 Sam. xx. 32). He who has no pity for the pious and innocent when they are in danger is not worthy of the name of a man, much less that of a Christian; for we are members of one body (1 Cor. xii. 12)."

2. Although Haman had been removed and Mordecai raised to his present station, yet the people still stood in jeopardy of their lives. Since the edict issued against them was irrevocable, their case was still critical. There were not many perhaps who deemed it possible that any means could be found to avert the threatened calamity. Mordecai himself may have long been in doubt regarding the way to be pursued out of the difficulty. And even after it suggested itself to him, it may have seemed improbable that it should lead to success. All depended on the question whether the assailants would not be too numerous for the Jews to overpower. This could not be previously ascertained. It may afford us light to know that he waited two months after his elevation before he issued the new edict. The period until then was one of dark foreboding to the Jews. But the pious Jews doubtless knew how to comfort themselves. "God often delays help, not because He will render none, but in order to exercise our faith, and to stimulate us the more to call upon Him. Then also the help granted will make the deliverance more sweet, and transform a great distress into a great joy" (*Berl. Bible*).

Mordecai, for his part, doubtless held fast to the thought that one must not despair of the salvation of God's people, and that though the danger be ever so great, God is infinitely greater, and that it is man's duty to do all in his power for himself. With respect to Esther, it was something extraordinary that she, although by descent nothing but a poor Jewess, should propose to the great king of the Persians, the mighty and proud Ahasuerus, that he would revoke in one way or another an edict whose irrevocable character as a Persian dogma was fixed. Really this was a demand to divest himself of that higher divine glory (*δόξα*) which the faith of the people had surrounded him with. It was to run the risk of unsettling the faith of the people in himself, and to expose himself to State disturbances. The difficulties surrounding him may even remind us of the problem that presented itself to Christ, when He, in the face of the sentence of condemnation upon the sinner on the part of justice, still made provision for grace. Esther might have feared that though her power over Ahasuerus had become great, still he might resent such boldness, and indignantly turn her away, refuse her request, and, if possible, become still more embittered against the Jews. Whatever considerations, however, may have arisen in her heart at the time, still she was doubtlessly incited by the predominant thought that the higher position one holds, the greater are the responsibilities connected therewith; that the more influence one wields, the greater must also be the courage to sustain it, so that one must not hesitate to strive after the highest aims and to tread the most difficult paths in the line of duty. But this correct view, this beautiful conviction, could not have been possible unless she had been first in possession of a pure love for her work. As is the case with men, so it was also with her, as a woman, that a true and correct conviction depended upon the state of her heart. If, in the following chapter, she manifests a sharp contrast with the heathen according to the Jewish Old Testament view, which threatened to cause her to err in the Christian view, and to bring vengeance and hate into play, yet, on the other hand, she reveals toward her people a love so strong, so self-sacrificing, and so bold, that it seems as if she had heard and apprehended the great question: "This I did for thee; what doest thou for me?" She here shows that mercy which is appropriate to him who recognizes how great the mercy was that met him.

3. It is a great and precious word which Esther utters in justification of her large and bold request: "How can I endure to see all the evil which will come upon my people, and how shall I bear to see the destruction of my friends?" She here openly expresses the fact that, though she is now greatly elevated, yet she is not able to sever the bond that unites her to her kindred. But, still more, she asserts that her life, though embellished with all the glory that Ahasuerus could bestow, has no value to her if she cannot also know that the lives of her kindred are safe from harm. All this was so well expressed by

her that her word is very appropriate in pointing for our comfort to that Prince who in reality makes this sentiment His own—who, though in the form of God, thought it not robbery to be equal with God, but laid aside His glory, and became obedient to death, even the death of the cross. But it is also appropriate as an exhortation for us, which should impel us in our circumstances to more and more approach her in this duty. It would be little credit to us should we prefer only those who are alike spiritually-minded with ourselves, and should we neglect or ignore those who are related to us according to the body, and should we look upon the perdition of so many souls with indifference.

On vers. 7–14. The great excitement which now took place in Shushan, beginning among the scribes of the king and spreading through all the one hundred and twenty-seven provinces of the great Persian empire, from India to Ethiopia, by means of the couriers who rode the best and fleetest horses of the king's stud, and which seized all satraps and governors, but particularly all Jewish communities, may, as a first effect, have provoked much inquiry respecting the meaning of the message, and then great astonishment at it. It is, however, hardly possible that any one already comprehended the significance of the event. What was visible was seemingly only a shell in which lay secreted a seed capable of infinite developments, a new universal law, or rather a new and glorious gospel which should henceforth rule over the world's history and expand to ever increasing authority. The Jews were to have the right to arm themselves against the day of attack on the part of the heathen. This implied that though externally dependent, still among and in themselves they should have freedom and the right to observe their laws and religion. This again prophetically indicates that the kingdoms of the world, although outwardly powerful, should inwardly lay themselves more and more open to the power of the kingdom of God. The Jews should now be empowered to take their defence against their enemies into their own hands. Thus it was implied that, in spite of the restricted sphere to which they were consigned, they still had a right to self-exertion. This mode of action upon attack only left them in an externally insufficient position for successful defence. Yet even in this was contained the prophecy that the people of God are permitted, in an inward and higher sense, themselves to do the best for victory over their enemies, and this the more since the means of the world's empires are here insufficient. Both the right to exist and to be active in the new sphere which they should enter, though as yet existing in embryo, was never sanctioned here. And if Judaism even to-day expects to find in the book of Esther that which will afford it joy, then we must go still further and apprehend its deeper and more glorious import for Christianity and the Christian church.

On vers. 15–17. Mordecai, after having attained all his requests, went out from the king clothed in royal garments, adorned with a large golden crown upon his head. And in all the land and cities, wherever the new law was promulgated, joy and rejoicing arose among the Jews. A great festival day had come for them. We do not know in how far their joy was pure. If it only arose because they could now make the necessary preparations to defend themselves from the attacks of their assailants, then no one will begrudge them their joy. It was certainly a time of deliverance for them. It is just such times as these that have made great impressions not only upon the Jews, but likewise upon the heathen surrounding them. As in the case of the exodus of the Jews from Egypt (Ex. xii. 38; Numb. x. 29), so also here many of the people of the land joined themselves to the Jews, indeed were converted to Judaism. Prophecies such as Isa. xiv. 1; xliv. 5 began to be in part realized. Periods of deliverance are chiefly periods of the extension of God's kingdom. Would that we might realize this in our times of trouble! Since the time of sorrow must of necessity have an end and make way for a time of deliverance, we may very properly rejoice in prospect of the future growth in the church, however threatening the outlook may be. It is on this account that our Lord exhorts us to raise the head when all these things are in process of fulfilment.

The points most important in our chapter are given in brief terms closely following each other. There is God's watchful and energetic care for His instruments for good. Esther and Mordecai are in advance established in their influential position, so that they may the more effectually execute His will. Then comes His care for His people, from whom He averts the threatening danger, and lastly the world is cared for.

Brenz: "What an example is here presented to us of the issue of the greatest dangers which may threaten God's people or church. But what is said of the safety of the universal church, the same holds true of every private individual who is a member of the church. 'I pray not for them alone,' says Christ, 'but for those who through their word shall believe in me.'"

Starke: "It is a small thing for God to turn the seasons of sorrow of the pious into hours of joy (Ps. xxx. 12; John xvi. 20). God helps His people (Luke i. 52) and causes them to rejoice over their enemies (Ps. xcii. 12)."

B.—THE JEWS DESTROY THEIR ENEMIES, AND AT MORDECAI'S REQUEST ESTABLISH THE FESTIVAL OF PURIM.

CHAP. IX. 1–32.

I. *The common defence of the Jews is very successful.* Vers. 1–15.

1 Now [And] in *the* twelfth [twelve] month, that *is the* month Adar, on *the* thir-
teenth [thirteen] day of the same [in it], when [that] the king's commandment
[word] and his decree [law] drew near to be put in the execution [done], in the day
that *the* enemies of the Jews hoped to have power over [on] them, (though it [and
(*i. e.*, then) that] it was turned *to the contrary* that the Jews [themselves] had rule
2 [should have power] over [on] them that hated them [their haters]), the Jews
gathered [congregated] themselves *together* in their cities, throughout [in] all *the*
provinces of the king Ahasuerus, to lay [send *forth*] hand on such as sought their
hurt [on the seekers of their evil]; and no man *could* withstand [stood in *the* face
3 of] them; for *the* fear of them fell upon all people [the peoples]. And all *the*
rulers [princes] of the provinces, and the lieutenants [satraps], and the deputies
[pashas], and [*the*] officers of the king [doers of the work which *was* to the king],
4 helped [*were* lifting] the Jews; because the fear of Mordecai fell upon them. For
Mordecai *was* great in the king's house, and his fame [hearing] went [*was* going]
out throughout [in] all the provinces; for this [the] man Mordecai waxed greater
5 and greater [*was* going and great]. Thus [And] the Jews smote [on] all their ene-
mies *with the* stroke [smiting] of *the* sword, and slaughter and destruction, and did
what they would [according to their pleasure] unto those that hated them [on their
6 haters]. And in Shushan the palace [citadel] the Jews slew and destroyed five
7, 8 hundred men. And Parshandatha, and Dalphon, and Aspatha, and Poratha,
9 and Adalia, and Aridatha, and Parmashta, and Arisai, and Aridai, and Vajezatha,
10 the ten sons of Haman, *the* son of Hammedatha [the Medatha], *the* enemy of the
11 Jews, slew they; but [and] on the spoil laid [sent *forth*] they not their hand. On
that day *the* number of those that were slain [the slain *ones*] in Shushan the palace
12 [citadel] was brought [came] before the king. And the king said unto Esther the
queen, The Jews have slain and destroyed five hundred men in Shushan the palace
[citadel], and *the* ten sons of Haman; what have they done in *the* rest of the king's
provinces? Now [And] what *is* thy petition? and it shall be granted [given to]
13 thee; or [and] what *is* thy request further [again]? and it shall be done. Then
[And] said Esther, If it please [*be* good upon] the king, let it be granted [given] to
the Jews which [who] *are* in Shushan to do to-morrow also according unto this
day's [to-day's] decree [law], and let Haman's ten sons be hanged [let them hang]
14 upon the gallows [tree]. And the king commanded [said] it so to be done; and
15 *the* decree [law] was given at Shushan; and they hanged Haman's ten sons. For
[And] the Jews that *were* in Shushan gathered [congregated] themselves *together* on
the fourteenth day also of *the* month Adar, and slew [smote] three hundred men
[males] at Shushan; but [and] on the prey [booty] they laid not their hand.

II. *At the desire of Mordecai the Jews resolve to celebrate the* 14*th and* 15*th of the month Adar as Purim.* Vers. 16–28.

16 But [And] the other [remainder of the] Jews that *were* in the king's provinces
gathered [congregated] themselves *together*, and stood [*there was a* standing] for
[upon] their lives [soul], and *had* rest from their enemies, and slew [*there was a*
smiting] of [in] their foes seventy and five thousand (but they laid not their hands
17 [hand] on the prey [booty]). On *the* thirteenth day of *the* month Adar: and on

the fourteenth *day* of the same [in it] rested they [*there was a* resting], and made
18 [*there was a* making] it *a* day of feasting [banquet] and gladness. But [And] the
Jews that *were* at Shushan assembled [congregated] *together* on *the* thirteenth *day*
thereof [in it], and on *the* fourteenth thereof [in it]; and on *the* fifteenth *day* of the
same [in it] they rested [*there was a* resting], and made [*a* making] it *a* day of
19 feasting [banquet] and gladness. Therefore the Jews of the villages [country *places*],
that dwelt in *the* unwalled towns [cities of the country *places*], made [*were* making]
the fourteenth day of the month Adar *a day of* gladness and feasting [banquet], and
20 *a* good day, and of sending portions one [*a* man] to another [his neighbor]. And
Mordecai wrote these things [words], and sent letters [books] unto all the Jews
that *were* in all *the* provinces of the king Ahasuerus, *both* [the] nigh and [the] far,
21 to stablish *this* among [upon] them, that they should keep [to be making] *the* four-
teenth day of *the* month Adar, and *the* fifteenth day of the same [in it] yearly, [in
22 every year and (*i. e.*, by) year], as the days wherein the Jews rested from their
enemies, and the month which was turned unto them from sorrow to joy [gladness],
and from mourning *into a* good day; that they should make [to make] them days
of feasting [banquet] and joy [gladness], and of sending portions one [*a* man] to
23 another [his neighbor], and gifts to the poor. And the Jews undertook [*each* re-
ceived] to do as they *had* begun [what they *had* begun to do], and as [what] Mor-
24 decai *had* written unto them; because Haman *the* son of Hammedatha [the Me-
datha] the Agagite, *the* enemy of all the Jews, *had* devised against the Jews to
destroy them, and *had* cast Pur (that *is*, the lot) to consume [discomfit] them, and
25 to destroy them: but [and] when *Esther* [it] came before the king, he com-
manded [said] by [with the] letters [books], *that* his wicked [evil] device, which
he devised against the Jews, should return upon his *own* head, and *that* he [him]
26 and his sons should be hanged [they should hang] on the gallows [tree]. Where-
fore [Therefore] they called these days Purim, after [upon] the name of [upon]
Pur: therefore for [upon] all *the* words of this letter, and *of that* which [and what]
they *had* seen concerning this matter [upon thus], and which [what] had come
27 unto them. The Jews ordained [established], and took [*each* received] upon them,
and upon their seed, and upon all such as joined [the *ones* joining] themselves unto
[upon] them, so as [and] it should not fail [pass], that they would keep [to be
making] these two days according to their writing, and according to their *appointed*
28 time, [in] every year [and (*i. e.*, by) year]; and *that* these days *should be* [these
days *were*] remembered and kept [made] throughout [in] every generation [and
(*i. e.*, by) generation], every family [family and (*i. e.*, by) family], every province
[province and (*i. e.*, by) province], and every city [city and (*i. e.*, by) city]; and
that these days of Purim should not fail [pass] from among [*the* midst of] the Jews,
nor the memorial [remembrance] of them perish [cease] from their seed.

III. *At the request of Esther the Jews also resolve to commemorate the feast of Purim with fasting and mourning.* Vers. 29–32.

29 Then [And] Esther the queen, *the* daughter of Abihail, and Mordecai the Jew,
wrote with all authority, to confirm [establish] this second letter of [the] Purim.
30 And he sent *the* letters [books] unto all the Jews, to *the* hundred twenty and seven
31 provinces of *the* kingdom of Ahasuerus, *with* words of peace and truth, to confirm
[establish] these days of [the] Purim in their times *appointed*, according as Morde-
cai the Jew and Esther the queen *had* enjoined [established upon] them, and as
they *had* decreed [established] for [upon] themselves [their soul], and for [upon]
32 their seed, *the* matters [words] of the fastings and their cry. And *the* decree [say-
ing] of Esther confirmed [established] these matters [words] of [the] Purim; and
it was written in the book.

SUPPLEMENT.

DISTINCTION AND POWER OF MORDECAI IN THE MIGHTY PERSIAN EMPIRE.

CHAPTER X. 1–3.

1 AND the king Ahasuerus laid [put] a tribute upon the land, and *upon the* isles of
2 the sea. And all *the* acts [work] of his power [authority] and of his might, and *the* declaration [spreading] of *the* greatness of Mordecai, *whereunto* the king advanced him [whom the king made great], *are* they not written in [upon] *the* book of *the* Chronicles [words of the days] of the kings of Media [Madai] and Persia [Paras]?
3 For Mordecai the Jew *was* next [second] unto [the] king Ahasuerus, and great among [to] the Jews, and accepted of [to] *the* multitude of his brethren, seeking *the* wealth of [good to] his people, and speaking peace to all his seed.

EXEGETICAL AND CRITICAL.

The author here gives us the last and most important part of the solution, the success which followed the measures of Mordecai for the deliverance of the Jews. Thus his history takes such a turn that the great Persian heathen empire, which at first rejoiced with feasting and hilarity, now suffers a great defeat. Moreover this occurs by the very Jewish nation which Haman and similar enemies hoped to destroy. The time of joyous feasting now came to the Jews and to those who had joined them. Mordecai's measure for the removal of the danger was quite sufficient. This was true first (vers. 1–5) in the Persian empire in general.

Ver. 1. **Now in the twelfth month, that is, the month Adar, on the thirteenth day of the same, when**—אֲשֶׁר may here be taken as the accus. of time, in which, or where, **the king's commandment and his decree drew near to be put into execution,** *i. e.*, in which the king's word and law should be carried out, **in the day that the enemies of the Jews hoped to have power over them (though it was turned to the contrary so that the Jews had rule over them that hated them).** The infin. absol. וְנַהֲפוֹךְ הוּא may be made to depend, as a continuation of the preceding perfect upon אֲשֶׁר. Then הוּא will stand as a neuter for the thing which their enemies hoped to accomplish on the thirteenth. וְנַהֲפוֹךְ may also serve as a remark inserted as a casual intermediate expression, then הוּא will probably refer back to יוֹם, comp. ver. 22: "As the day was turned unto them (so) that," *etc.* As this remark does not anticipate, and in advance indicate the result afterward realized, but only speaks of change brought about by the issue of the second royal edict, שָׁלַט stands the second time for the "might" or "power" which now awaited the Jews according to right and law, but had not yet been realized. הֵמָּה added to the subject, serves to make a sharp contrast between the Jews and their enemies, so that it may be translated *ipsi*, (themselves) comp. Ewald, § 314 *a*. In ver. 2 follows the mention of a fixed time: **The Jews gathered themselves together in their cities,** *i. e.*, those in which they were more numerous, but yet dwelt mixed up with the heathen inhabitants. They gathered themselves, **to lay hand on such as sought their hurt,** *i. e.*, according to chap. viii. 11, such as attacked them to destroy them. **And no man could withstand them,**—so עָמַד בִּפְנֵי (comp. Josh. x. 8; xxi. 42; xxiii. 9), because fear of them, or their fear had fallen upon all the people (comp. chap. viii. 17).*

Ver. 3. All the princes, the satraps, and governors, and also other persons of rank whom it is unnecessary here to name (comp. chap. iii. 9), assisted the Jews. מְנַשְּׂאִים, as in Ezek. i. 4.†

Ver. 4. These were especially influenced by the fear of Mordecai, who now became more and more powerful and authoritative, (comp. 1 Chron. xvii. 12, where we find instead of גָּדוֹל the intrans. partic. גָּדֵל).

Ver. 5. Thus the Jews inflicted a great defeat

* ["The Jews apparently did not remain wholly on the defensive. Their enemies were no doubt well known to them, and were prepared for the struggle which it was seen must come. Sometimes the one side, sometimes the other, would commence the attack." RAWLINSON.—TR.]

† ["This is very important. It has been stated that according to the narrative of Esther the Jews were allowed to kill '75,000 *Persians*;' and this (supposed) feature of the narrative has been pronounced 'incredible.' The present verse shows that the real Persians, who formed the standing army which kept the empire in subjection, and were at the disposal of the various governors of the province, took the Jews' side. Their enemies were almost entirely to be found among the idolatrous people of the subject nations, for whose lives neither the Persians generally, nor their monarchs, cared greatly." RAWLINSON.—TR.]

upon all their enemies with the sword, slaughter and destruction: they carried out the right of retaliation which had been accorded them in ch. viii. 11. הִכָּה with בְּ is to *smite*, to defeat some one (2 Sam. xxiii. 10; xxiv. 17; Num. xxii. 6). מַכַּת can only depend upon הִכָּה; הֶרֶג and אַבְדָן both belong to מכת (comp. chap. ix. 5, where מַכַּת־הֶרֶב corresponds to הִשְׁמִיד).

Vers. 6–15. The defence of the Jews succeeded especially well in Shushan. Ver. 6. **And in Shushan the palace the Jews slew and destroyed five hundred men.*** The infin. abs. וְאַבֵּד as a supplement to the foregoing perfect expresses: "they slew and destroyed."

Ver. 7. The insertion of the names of the ten sons of Haman who were also destroyed, corresponds to the author's method of exactness, and his disposition to mention names, as is seen in chap. i. 14. Jewish rabbis have found these names indicative of representative importance, and have taken the individual traits to mean something prophetic. This peculiar mode of writing, corresponding so well to the style of later mystical modes of interpretation of later Jewish theology, may have been inherent in its spirit, or it may have been because they find the "minuscule" letter ת in the first, שׁ in the seventh, and ז in the tenth name, and also the "majuscule" letter ו in the tenth name.† According to statements made by Buxtorf (*Synag. Jud.*, p. 588) the mode of writing should be a sign that the ten sons were suspended in a perpendicular line, one over the other, or an omen that after their fall they should never more rise to glory. The Jews did not take the booty of their enemies as was permitted them to do in the edict of chap. viii. 11. This, however, was the order given to their enemies in the edict of Haman, chap. iii. 13, and the author here gives it prominent mention, in order to show that there was no intention on the part of the Jews, to gratify a low avaricious disposition, but only to defend themselves.

Vers. 11–15. After Ahasuerus had discovered the number of those who had perished in Shushan, he stated the same to Esther, adding: **What have they done in the rest of the king's provinces?** *i. e.*, how many must they not have destroyed there; this he said in order to prove to her that he had granted a great favor to the Jews, and hence that he was well-disposed toward them (comp. chap. viii. 7, 8). But to the same intent he also adds the promise following: **Now what is thy petition? and it shall be granted thee.**—Perhaps he recognized the fact that, if the Jews had to do with so many opponents, they could hardly have mastered them, and even now great danger threatened them on the part of those remaining, if they could not hunt down such in their hiding places (and there must have been many in so large a city) and destroy them utterly. וְיִנָּתֵן, masc. or rather neuter, with reference to מַה, while in chap. vii. 2 we find the fem. וְתִנָּתֵן in relation to שְׁאֵלָתֵךְ. The necessity of extending the privilege granted the Jews to the following day, must be evident, since Esther (chap. viii. 11) on her part, without consulting Mordecai, still further requested it. **And let Haman's ten sons be hanged upon the gallows,** *i. e.*, crucify the dead bodies in order to increase the disgrace of their execution, but more in order to augment the fear of the Jews. This was the Hebrew and Persian custom (see Ezra vi. 11 [comp. Plutarch, *Artax.* 17]).

Ver. 14. The king acceded to Esther's request, and so another edict was issued. This contained principally or exclusively a renewed permission for the Jews. This must be publicly proclaimed. With respect to the sons of Haman a simple command was sufficient. The words, **and they hanged Haman's ten sons,** by no means indicates the substance or consequence of the law; opposed to this are the accents and the perfect תָּלוּ. But since the publication of a law was the consequence of the king's acquiescence, so it was also with the hanging of Haman's sons.

Vers. 16–28. *The establishment of Purim.*—In vers. 16–19 we find the historical introduction to the new edict of Mordecai, in vers. 20–23 an index of contents, and in vers. 24–28, still further, a supplement, confirmatory of what preceded, and which seems to have been taken from some other writing.

The statement in ver. 16: **But the other Jews**—separate from those in Shushan, *etc.*—again connects with what preceded in vers. 1 and 2, in order first, to add the number of those whom they had slain, and next to give due mention to the day of their conflict as well as to the fact that the 14th was for them already a day of rest.* The author adds after the phrase **and stood for their lives** (comp. chap. viii. 11): **and had rest from their enemies.**—נוֹחַ is instead of the more usual נוּחַ, Infin. Absol. as in Num. xi. 25. And though he is interested to publish the result for which the Jews stood, namely, that they slew 75,000 of their enemies, yet he is more busied with the main thought that, these outside Jews, in distinction from those in Shushan, had peace soon after their first defence. The perfect

* ["By 'Shushan the palace' or 'the fort,' we are probably to understand the whole of the upper town, which occupied an area of above a hundred acres, and contained, no doubt, many residences besides the actual palace. It is not likely that the Jews would have ventured to shed blood within the palace precincts." RAWLINSON.—TR.]

† ["Excepting Adalia, all these names are readily traceable to Old Persian roots. *Parshandatha* is 'given to Persia,' or 'to the Persians;' *Dalphon*, which in Persian must have been *Darphon* or *Darpon*, is probably the Persian representative of the Sansc. *darpin*, 'arrogant;' *Aspatha* is from *aspa*, 'horse,' and would probably mean 'horseman;' *Poratha* is apparently from *paru*, 'much, great,' and *ratha*, 'a chariot,' and would mean 'having many chariots;' *Aridatha* is from the roots *ari* 'very,' and *da*, 'to give,' and would mean 'liberal' (comp. Phradates). *Parmashta* is a little doubtful, but may be from *fra*, an intensive particle, and *mathista*, 'greatest' (comp. Lat. *præmagnus*). *Arisai* has the intensive *ari* prefixed to a root *saya*, which is perhaps 'to conquer' or 'to go;' and *Aridai* has the same intensive prefixed to the root *da*, 'to give.' Finally, *Vajezatha* comprises two elements, *vaya*, 'the wind,' and *zatha*, (comp. Zend. *zyat*), 'powerful;' and would mean 'strong as the wind' (comp. Chitratachma, 'strong as the leopard;' Tritantæchmes, 'strong as Tritan, *i. e.*, Feridem)." RAWLINSON.—TR.]

* [*Shushan* here is "probably the lower town, which lay east of the upper one and was of about the same size." RAWLINSON.—TR.]

in vers. 16, 17, as also in ver. 18, is continued by subordinated infinitives (comp. Ewald, § 351 *c*). The statement that the outside Jews had rest already on the 14th of Adar, is here the main point. The other, in ver. 18, that the Jews in Shushan first had peace and joy on the fifteenth, is subordinate. This relation is best expressed by the word "while," by which ver. 19, with its עַל־כֵּן, may be joined to vers. 16 and 17: **Therefore the Jews of the villages, that dwelt in the unwalled towns, made the fourteenth day of the month Adar a day of gladness and feasting,** *etc.*—It does not matter much about the first season of joy, as stated in ver. 17, but it is important that this season had now become a custom of the people, and must have existed down to the time of our author. As evidence of this we have the partic. עֹשִׂים, and also the particles עַל־כֵּן, which latter is generally employed in an explanation as to how a custom originated. It seems, therefore, that for a long time there existed a difference of time as respects the day of the feast of Purim. It appears that the Jews in the smaller villages had one day, and those residing in the larger cities, *i. e.*, also in Jerusalem (according to some MSS. of the Septuagint version *αἱ κατοικοῦντες ἐν ταῖς μητροπόλεσιν*) had another. The writing of Mordecai, mentioned in the following verses, which ordered a uniform celebration, *viz.*, of two days (on the 14th and 15th of Adar) soon restored uniformity. But its acceptance had as a first consequence that, only those chief communities in the larger cities (vers. 23, 27), obeyed the order, but the smaller bodies still retained the 14th Adar as the chief day of the feast. To assume a contradiction between vers. 23 and 27 (as does Bertheau) would be unwarranted even if the section beginning with ver. 20 be not an addition by our author, but by some later person. At the time of Josephus it seems that the season of celebration was uniform (comp. *Antiq.* VI. 13). According to the Mishna (*Megilla,* 1) this difference only exists that the book of Esther should be read on the 14th in the smaller towns, but on the 15th in the ancient walled cities of Palestine הַפְּרוֹזִים, with the Kethib, is the plural of פְּרוֹז, *countryman.* The Keri is the same as Deut. iii. 5, and 1 Sam. vi. 18. There could have been another form from פְּרָז such as פָּרוֹז, as in קָטוֹן beside קָטָן. מִשְׁלֹחַ is the accus., dependent on עֹשִׂים: **And of sending portions one to another.**—According to ver. 22 (comp. Neh. viii. 10) one made presents in these feasts, similar to the sacrificial feasts, to those less wealthy, but also to others to whom one desired to signify a joyous mind.

Vers. 20–23. The writing which Mordecai sent to all the Jews, doubtless contained the substance of our book of Esther, הַדְּבָרִים הָאֵלֶּה; *i. e.*, it recounted the danger which had threatened the Jews, and the way in which they were preserved from destruction; for this was needful to state here, in order to give cause and color to the feast ordered by Mordecai. But this did not, therefore, need to include the whole book of Esther.

Ver. 21. Mordecai's purpose was: **To stablish this among them, that they should keep the,** *etc.*—קַיֵּם besides this place (verses 20–32) occurs only in Ruth iv. 7; Ezra xiii. 6; Ps. cxix. 28, 106; and used with עַל it signifies to establish something as binding upon some one, so that it shall become a duty obligatory on him. עָשָׂה with יוֹם here seems to mean (comp. ver. 27), to *celebrate* a day. The phrase לִהְיוֹת עֹשִׂים, following upon the long intervening sentences of ver. 21, is again taken up in ver. 22 by לַעֲשׂוֹת אוֹתָם יְמֵי מִשְׁתֶּה and still more enlarged. The result was (ver. 23) that what the Jews had begun to do (ver. 22) and what Mordecai wrote to them to do was by them established as a valid and permanent custom. קִבֵּל, to "accept" (ch. ix. 4), here means, according to later linguistic usage, to *recognize* something as a valid tradition or law. The sing. form is explained by the fact that the verb precedes its subject, according to Gesen. § 114. [Rather it denotes a *distribution* or individual sense.—Tr.]

Vers. 24–28. Now in order both to give the name of the feast just mentioned as well as its duration through two days, our author again briefly repeats the substance of the historical basis in vers. 24 and 25. He also makes brief mention of the facts decisive of the name, and then refers us in ver. 26 to Mordecai's letter and the experiences of the Jews as forming its basis. In ver. 24 we find Haman's intention to destroy the Jews (comp. chap. iii. 1, 6 sqq.), and he then points to the feast of Pur or casting of lots (chap. iii. 7). לְהֻמָּם, "to destroy them," from an older word, הָמַם, which generally describes confusion and anguish such as comes from God (Ex. xiv. 24; Deut. ii. 15), but which here may have been selected as a play upon the name of Haman. As regards the edict so friendly to the Jews in ver. 25, comp. chap. viii. 8 sqq.—**But when** (it) **came before the king,** *etc.* The suffix of the word בְּבֹאָהּ can have no reference to Esther; she is not mentioned in this connection (so opposed to the Targum, Syriac and most interpreters), but can only be taken as a neuter (as for example in Ezek. xxxiii. 33), (so Bertheau and Keil); and this the more in keeping with the intention of Haman, which is placed in its proper light.—**He commanded by letters that,** *etc.*—אָמַר עִם־הַסֵּפֶר for: "to command by writing," occurs only in this place. It is also peculiar in this section that the command: **that his wicked device, which he devised against the Jews, should return upon his own head,** is given in direct speech, while usually in the rest of the book the infin. with לְ is employed. Finally the author also mentions the execution of Haman and his sons, on which see chap. vii. 10 and ix. 6 sqq. In ver. 26 follows the declaration of the name of the day of the celebration, to which the author here designed to give prominence; but this is followed by the statement, after עַל־כֵּן, that this should last two days. What is simply indicated by the particles עַל־כֵּן is further enlarged upon by עַל־כָּל־דִּבְרֵי **Therefore for all the words of this letter** (of Mordecai in accordance with ver. 20), and (of all that) **which they had seen concerning the matter** (עַל־כָּכָה, concerning the so and thus), **and which had come unto them;** hence also because their own experience fully corroborated the substance of Mordecai's letter. In ver. 27 follows after עַל־כֵּן the concluding sentence: **The Jews ordained, and took upon them, and upon their seed, and upon all such as joined themselves unto them** (*i. e.* all proselytes), **so as it should not fail** (but be unalterably established, לֹא יַעֲבוֹר, as in chap. i. 19), **that they would keep these two days according to their writing, and according to their appointed time every year** (year after year).—עָשָׂה following upon ver. 21 is easily comprehensible. Their writing and determination of time can only have come to them from Mordecai's. In ver. 28 there follows the further injunction: **And that these days should be remembered and kept throughout every generation,** *etc.* The partic. נִזְכָּרִים, *etc.*, depend upon לִהְיוֹת in the preceding verse. סוֹף מִן = "to have an end," *to cease.*

Vers. 29–32. In order more firmly to establish the new law, and the confirmation of a new custom, which thus far had only been observed by Mordecai and Esther, that is, to connect a day of fasting and mourning with the days of the feast of Purim, a second letter was published. This time it was Queen Esther who composed the letter, hence the femin. וַתִּכְתֹּב. Mordecai is also mentioned; but possibly he was only added to give the letter authority and legality, as being the highest functionary in the realm, and to add the writings mentioned in ver. 30. It was especially Esther's concern that the fasts and wailings which had their origin with herself at the time of the decisive step should serve as a reminder of the great distress so happily overcome. According to chap. ii. 15 she was the daughter of Abihail, and on account of the solemnity of the occasion she is expressly designated as such. אֶת־כָּל־תֹּקֶף, "with all strength" (power). תֹּקֶף occurs only here, in chap. x. 2 and Dan. xi. 17, and would signify the great emphasis that Esther laid on the season of fasting and mourning no less than on the celebration of the joyous feast. The object of לְקַיֵּם, "to make valid as a law," **this second letter of Purim** (the first was that of Mordecai in ver. 20), is also the object of the preceding וַתִּכְתֹּב. By the word "this" the author designates the second letter, since he has in mind not to give its substance, but simply to indicate its existence.

Ver. 30 explains somewhat why Mordecai is also mentioned in ver. 29 along with Esther: **And he sent the letters unto all the Jews.** The subject can here only be Mordecai himself. The סְפָרִים, however, which he sent were not copies of Esther's letter (Keil), but writings accompanying it. These may have had the object of further confirming and explaining the facts on account of which fasts and seasons of mourning should be instituted, and of giving a historic sketch of the fast and mourning of the Jews living in Shushan. The words: **And he sent the letters unto all the Jews to the hundred twenty and seven provinces,** are in apposition to **the kingdom of Ahasuerus.**—The contents of the writing are briefly designated as words of peace, *i. e.* as words that meant well, which aimed at the welfare of Israel by thus recommending a good custom for general observance, and which were based on truth.

Ver. 31. The aim of both Esther and Mordecai's letters was: **to confirm these days of Purim in their times appointed.**—This does not mean that it had reference only to certain periods or divisions of the days of Purim in which fasts and mourning should take place, and for which arrangements should be made (Bertheau and also Keil); for that would have been expressed otherwise and more definitely; but it gives the proper validity to the selected days of the feast of Purim, the 14th and 15th Adar. The main thing, however, is contained in the following: **According as Mordecai the Jew and Esther the queen had enjoined them, and as they had decreed for themselves and for their seed, the matters of the fastings and their cry.**—Hence they would also establish the feast of Purim for themselves, so that they might join fasting and lamentation to the feast, as Mordecai and Esther had previously done. The suffix of עֲלֵיהֶם may also refer to the above-mentioned days of Purim (not as to their definite time, Bertheau and Keil; for this is only mentioned incidentally); but since קִיֵּם with עַל always means *to make a thing obligatory*, it is naturally referred to Esther and Mordecai. It is true there follows the phrase עַל־נַפְשָׁם; but we may understand this in the sense of עֲלֵיהֶם when preceding וְעַל־זַרְעָם. There cannot well be any other subject intended by קִיְּמוּ than (against Keil) the above-mentioned Mordecai and Esther. עַל־זַרְעָם is a *zeugmatic* mode of expression. It has practical reference to Mordecai's posterity since Esther, as regards her descendants, could not well hope to see them perpetuate Jewish customs.

Ver. 32 strengthens the foregoing greatly.—**And the decree of Esther confirmed these matters of Purim,** those, namely, that had reference to the fasts and mourning.—**And it was written in the book,** of course not in Esther's letter, nor in Mordecai's writing accompanying the decree, which would be designated by the plural סְפָרִים; but it was written in the book indicated in ver. 20, in which Mordecai wrote concerning these events, and which is not identical with our Esther-book, but may have served as one of its sources.* The day of fasting and mourning is not definitely fixed nor stated here; but it was probably the 13th of Adar, which Haman had set apart for the destruction of the Jews, and which the Jews celebrate as תַּעֲנִית אֶסְתֵּר, *Esther's fast*, although in the period of the Talmud there is mention made of a three days' fast, which was observed after that of Purim.

Chap. x. Our book aims not only to present the deliverance, but also the elevation of Judaism in the time and midst of the great and powerful heathenism of the period of Ahasuerus. It would represent the latter in the person of Haman, the enemy to Judaism, and the former in the person of Mordecai. Hence at its close it speaks once more of Mordecai's greatness and honor.—**And the king Ahasuerus laid a tribute upon the land, and upon the isles of the sea.**—The Kethib אחשרש is an orthographical mistake for אֲחַשְׁוֵרֹשׁ. מַס, "a levy," tribute (a tribute-service), here means a *tax* levied, and this for the reason that tribute-service belonged to products or moneys which were rendered to the king.† It may be asked why this remark occurs in our book, which, according to all that has gone before, does not belong to the history of Ahasuerus, but has to do with quite another matter. Keil thinks the author wished briefly to indicate at the close whence Ahasuerus derived the means to support such magnificent state as was described at the beginning of our book. But this inference would be superfluous, and would come somewhat late here. The only safe answer is given us by the manner in which the author, in ver. 2, connects the power of Ahasuerus with the greatness of Mordecai. The greater the power of Ahasuerus and his wealth, the more powerful the dignity of Ahasuerus. It is as if the author would tell us: Ahasuerus had power extending over the whole earth, and he caused its wealth to flow into his treasury, and hence made himself felt as the head and lord of the entire power of the earth. It is worth while in this connection to observe the comprehensive statement עַל־הָאָרֶץ וְאִיֵּי הַיָּם. But this concentration of universal sway in himself did not avail for the suppression of an externally despicable Judaism; it rather served for the recognition and elevation of the latter, since, according to the Providence recognized in our book, Mordecai, the Jew, became the second ruler after Ahasuerus. Although it seemed as if the people of God had been stricken out of the list of people of the earth, still, in Mordecai, because of his relation to Ahasuerus, it became possessed of the wealth of the peoples of the earth.‡

Ver. 2. The author does not designate either the wealth or the power of Ahasuerus or of Mordecai more minutely, but rather refers, for particulars on both to the archives of the empire of the Medes and Persians.* It is enough for him to be able to refer to these, and it is especially honorable for Mordecai's cause, that even the archives of heathen kings must remember him. For פָּרָשָׁה, "clear statement," *summary*, comp. chap. ix. 7.

Ver. 3. Here the author must once more give prominence to the fact that Mordecai, the Jew, who for him stands as the representative of Judaism, stood next to king Ahasuerus, since therefrom it follows that the greatness of the one was also that of the other.

מִשְׁנֶה, "the second," here means the first minister (comp. 2 Chron. xxviii. 7), and hence indicates that Mordecai was great among the Jews, and favored among the multitude of his brethren; *i. e.*, that he really occupied a representative position among them.† On רָצוּי comp. Deut. xxxiii. 24. The expression רֹב אֶחָיו is not to be taken in a limited sense, as if he would say less than: "*all* his brethren;" but may be explained, as Bertheau justly remarks, from the poetic elevation to which his speech rises at its close. The additional sentence also: **Seeking the wealth of his people, and speaking peace to all his seed**, is quite in place here, in so far as it indicates that what came to Mordecai also redounded to the good of his entire people. זַרְעוֹ, in parallelism with עַמּוֹ, is the *family* to which he belongs, as in 2 Kings xi. 1; Is. lxi. 9, and not his *posterity*.

DOCTRINAL AND ETHICAL.

On ver. 1. The day in which the enemies of the Jews expected to see the realization of their hopes, became instead for the Jews a day of victory, and for their enemies a day of reverse and defeat. This, under existing circumstances, seemed to be a change which could only be brought about, as it were, by a miracle. It was indeed one of those Providences by means of which it has pleased God to reveal Himself from time to time in an especially remarkable manner. At all events, the prophets had foretold such occurrences as a matter surely to be expected. When the captivity of Israel shall have

* ["As *book* elsewhere in Esther (סֵפֶר, in the sing.) always means a particular book—"the book of the chronicles of the kings of Media and Persia (ch. ii. 23; vi. 1; q. 2), it seems best to give it the same sense here." RAWLINSON.—TR.]

† ["Some fresh arrangement of the tribute is likely to have followed on the return of Xerxes from Greece. His exchequer would be exhausted, and steps would have to be taken to replenish it. The expression in the original does not necessarily imply the first imposition of a tribute." RAWLINSON.—TR.]

‡ [Upon the expression *isles of the sea*, in this connection, Rawlinson remarks: "Cyprus, Aradus, the island of Tyre, Platea, *etc.*, remained in the hands of the Persians after the victories of the Greeks, and may be the 'isles' here intended. Or Xerxes may have ignored the loss of the Ægean Islands, and have 'laid' his tribute upon them, though he might not be able to exact it."—TR.]

* ["In the latter years of Xerxes his 'power and might' were chiefly shown in the erection of magnificent buildings, more especially at Persepolis. He abstained from military expeditions." "Media takes precedence of Persia (contrary to chap. i. 3, 14, 18, *etc.*), because the kingdom of Media had preceded that of Persia, and in the 'Book of the Chronicles' its history came first." RAWLINSON.—TR.]

† ["It has been objected that Artabanus, the captain of the guard, and not Mordecai, was Xerxes' chief favorite in his twelfth and thirteenth years. But this view rests upon the false chronology of Ctesias, who gives Xerxes 13 years only, instead of the 21 of Ptolemy, Manetho, and the generality of the Greek writers. Artabanus was favorite towards the close of Xerxes' reign, *i. e.*, in his 20th and 21st years." RAWLINSON.—TR.]

reached its culmination, when the people of God are on the point of expiring under the rod of their drivers, then, instead of really perishing, they should become captors for their captors and taskmasters for their drivers (Is. xiv. 2). What is here shown in a small prelude, according to such prophecy, should attain a much larger circumference and a much greater glory. Our book itself, according to its deeper significance, points in a manner typical or prophetical to this great and glorious final history. As a matter of fact, this change of affairs was itself deeply grounded in the nature and circumstances of things. So certain as the God of Israel was the only true God, whose kingdom shall not be destroyed, but through all apparent reverses shall continually rise to new and greater victories, so likewise to His people—so long as it is the sole bearer of His sway, the grave, which threatens to swallow it up, shall ever be a place of revivification and resurrection. And to-day also His empire must continue; and that which thought to overcome its power must itself be overcome, and either be absorbed or consigned to destruction. All the days of persecution for God's kingdom are days indeed in which its enemies hope to overcome it, but it always turns out that such enemies are themselves conquered at last.

Brenz: "We have above such an example in Haman, who was himself hung on the cross which he had prepared for Mordecai. So the Egyptians were themselves overwhelmed in the sea to which they had driven the Israelites in order to overwhelm them. So also Saul, who had driven David over to the Philistines, that they might destroy him, was himself destroyed by the Philistines."

On vers. 2–4. At the time of the deliverance from Egypt and the entrance into Canaan, the Lord showed abundantly that He was able to make His people a great nation despite the most powerful of their enemies. Now in its exile He again showed them that, as for Himself, He now no longer had need of them as a people, at least as a politically independent one. The great deeds that were then done were edifying and elevating in tendency; what He now did was momentous and instructive. It was plainly evident that He could accomplish His purpose aside from external means or political circumstances. It is still more manifest than it then was that it has pleased Him to be powerful in those who are weak, and great in those who have little influence. In those days he prepared as His instruments the chief persons and princes of His own people, who were in an especial manner filled with the Spirit. Now, however, he employs instead the satraps and governors of Persia, little as they were willing or fit for such work. Together with and among kings, such as Cyrus and Ahasuerus, they must also further God's purposes. There was a time when the Lord had caused fear and terror to fall upon the peoples before Israel, especially those who stood opposed in war, so that they fled from before them (comp. Deut. ii. 25). Now, however, the princes and governors, who had great fear, were obliged to protect the rights of the subjects of the king, and thus they protected Israel. This corresponded entirely to His greatness. Therein is shown His claim as the God of all men. This is itself further evinced by the fact that, if His people will only become more spiritual, as is His wish, and partake of His nature, He will by no means leave them fatherless. But the more spiritual His kingdom, *i. e.*, His people, will become, the more will He assist them to arrive at truth, justice, and security through the world while in it.

On vers. 5–11. 1. We now know a different and better mode of conquering enemies than by the sword and through bloodshed. We know that love only will gain the victory over hate. The people of God is strongest where it is given over to sacrifice and suffering. But we know further that this spiritual mode of combat and victory has become possible only since the time when we received spiritual strength and weapons. In the Old Testament time one could only speak of an external victory over opponents, but not of an internal one. Hence we find it explicable why Israel was compelled to fight such sanguinary battles and merciless wars of destruction. What is most striking in our history is the fact that the Jews, although living in circumstances in which they did not need to wield the sword, nevertheless seized the sword. Though they were no more a people in a political sense, and hence could not procure help for themselves, still they acted as a separate political community. The cause that made them wield the sword of destruction with much the greater pleasure and satisfaction was the fact that Esther stood at their head, and instead of bespeaking a shortening of the work of blood, she promoted it. It is observable also that after the destruction of so many enemies, instead of expressing pain that it needed so severe a conflict, she manifested only joy over their success. But we may nevertheless ask whether condemnation of the then Jews, whom one judges so severely often, as well as criticism of the author, who must have thought and felt as they did, does not proceed from a too rigid doctrinal stand-point, which is inclined to measure every thing by an arbitrary standard, without sufficient regard for circumstances. We would doubtless excuse the then expressions of vindictiveness, were it not for the principle that seems to be involved. For in a real war, in which the patriotic feeling has supreme control, and the weakening of an enemy is a duty of self-preservation, we find such feelings as are exhibited in Judaism and Esther very natural, to say the least. We also perceive the same sentiments often displayed by Israel in its earlier conflicts, without taking so serious an account of them. But the main objection really fails. For the carnage was not of their free will, but a matter of stern necessity. It resulted from the peculiar situation of the case; in fact it was so ordered by the government that the Jews should seize the sword. They were not only entitled, but actually necessitated in this case to return to their political independence. Hence the older interpreters very properly lay great stress upon the fact that the Jews did not venture this of themselves, but at the instance of higher authority. Starke also says: "It is one thing to take revenge of one's self, another to do so on the order of authority; not the latter, but the former, is forbidden. The simple command of a government will justify such an act only in so far as it is a guaranty against pure thirst for revenge. Every thing here depends upon the disposition of mind. But we would certainly misjudge the temper of the then Jews were we to assume that because the people were but a religious community, we are at liberty to apply a Christian standard to them. It would be unjust to deny them the privilege, which they as an independent people formerly enjoyed, of rejoicing in a victory over their enemies; and it would be little to the purpose, if instead of aiming at their conversion, we acquiesced in their destruction. Instead of justifying the complaint that, we do not pay sufficient regard to those Old Testament national conditions, we must also remember that Old Testament saints could not well avoid often taking a stand-point opposed to their enemies, just as we are still allowed to assume a position at variance with those in enmity against God. Besides, we are not to forget that, for those who will not join themselves to the kingdom or people of God, whatever its form or degree of development, this very hostility is a ground of condemnation. All things that cannot be employed for a good end will finally issue in destruction and extinction. This is still true, and will be true until the end of time. In the same manner even the angels in heaven could not have acted differently from Esther with regard to those enemies in the city of Shushan. We would be more just to Esther, to the Jews spoken of in our book, and to the book itself, if, in what was done in Shushan as well as in all Persia, we would see an anticipation of the judgments connected and parallel with the progress of the kingdom of God on earth, and especially of the final judgment. If the animus of the O. T. with respect to the destruction of enemies seems to us terribly vindictive, rather than mild, yet this may not only be excusable, but may even be a prophetic intimation. The fact, so prominently and emphatically expressed, in the present instance, that the Jews did not stretch out their hands after the goods (spoil) of their enemies, proves to us that they meant to conduct this contest as a measure of self-protection, or better as a holy war, the sole purpose of which was the removal of their enemies.

Brenz: "This example, however, is set before us not that we should take it upon ourselves to avenge injuries, according to our own judgment, but that we may recognize the severity of the divine wrath against the impious persecutor of the people of God, and that in persecution we might most confidently expect deliverance through faith, and be obedient to the calls of God."

2. That the sons of Haman should also suffer was agreeable to Persian law, according to which, in many cases, the whole circle of relationship of a criminal must suffer death with him (comp. Amm. Marcell. xxiii. 6). Nor was this mode of proceeding contrary to the Mosaic code. The law that the children should not die for their fathers (more correctly: *at the same time*), Deut. xxiv. 16, was only applicable to those cases in which the children had no part in the crime of their parents (comp. 2 Kings xiv. 6; 2 Chron. xxv. 4). Doubtless the sons of Haman belonged to those who were inimical to the Jews and attacked them; indeed they may have been their bitterest enemies. It is fair to suppose them in the same state of mind with their father, so that Isa. xiv. 21 came true in their case. Esther requested that, after they were executed, they should also be hung. That the Jews really executed this climax of punishment, may indicate the especially severe judgment that will overtake those who are the principal agents of Antichrist on earth; and this illustrates the truth that opposition against whatever is antagonistic to goodness and piety, must rise till it reaches its overwhelming acme. This is a principle valid even for Christians, that they must be in a hostile attitude to evil to the last degree.

Brenz: "This is written in admonition of parents, in order that they may be incited to cultivate piety, lest along with themselves they may also drag their children down into destruction. Such severity of God is stated in the Decalogue: 'Visiting the iniquity of the fathers upon the children to the third and fourth generation of those that hate me' (comp. John. xviii. 17 sq.)."

On vers. 11–32. 1. In the first pages of our book Ahasuerus, together with the representatives of his empire, indeed heathendom itself, celebrated a great feast. Here, at the end, however, it is for the Jewish people to celebrate a feast. The way of the world begins with pleasure and mirth, but does not end so. The way of God's people leads through sorrow, but at its end is the great feast which is described by Zech. in chap. xiv., as a feast of tabernacles; since it will be celebrated in the tabernacles of undisturbed peace. This, according to Isa. xxv. 6 sqq., may also be the celebrating feast of salvation and consolation, in which God will wipe away all tears from all eyes. We here have to do with the celebration of a feast in time. This obviously differs greatly from the heathen festival. When in later centuries Purim was celebrated with heathenish abandon and luxury, when it seemed to the Jews that they regarded it as a duty to so intoxicate themselves so that they could not distinguish between the names of Mordecai and Haman, this became a striking proof to how low a level, even to heathenism, Judaism had sunk.

The festivals that the people of the Lord as such celebrate, have quite a different purpose from those of heathendom. Ahasuerus aimed to show the riches of his glorious kingdom. God's people desire first of all to praise God's grace. They would give thanks for the gifts bestowed upon them. They would secure and keep what they already have by rendering thanks and praise to God as its author. Their's are feasts of gratitude. Hence these also have a different character from the others. The pious cannot manifest their spirit of gratitude to God for all His benefits without also proving this by benefaction to their brethren in the faith. The love of God has kindled love to their fellows in their hearts; this would prove itself in deeds of kindness and benevolence. They would confess their allegiance to God as to one mild and kindly; they would else deny Him were they not to give sway, on their part, to mildness and kindliness. Their festivals, therefore, are seasons of refreshing, but especially so to the poorer brethren among them (comp. vers. 19, 22). At the same time there is joined to their spirit of rejoicing one of great seriousness. They cannot enjoy their deliverance without also looking back upon the sorrow that preceded it. They can only appreciate the former by taking a full view of the latter. They do not forget that though salvation is theirs, still there are even yet abundant causes for sorrow and grief. The chief cause of this is the remains of sin in them. As the *Mazzoth* (unleavened) days are followed by the serious Paschal sacrifice, and as the joy of the feast of tabernacles is preceded by the repentance of the fast of the day of atonement, so also here the joyous feast of Purim is connected with a preparation of fasting and mourning (comp. ver. 31). In eternity also will this transition hold true.

STARKE: "It is the privilege of God's children to rejoice in the Lord (Deut. xii. 15; Phil. iv. 4). When God presents us with days of joy and blessing, we should also remember the poor, (Sir. xiv. 4; Ps. xxii. 27 sqq.)."

2. In Deut xiii. 1, it is commanded neither to add to nor to take from the law. If then the Jewish people nevertheless added another feast to those already existing then, doubtless they took into account the principle that what one is encouraged to do in view of a certain law is not so much an addition as an outflow of the same. At any rate the Jewish church already began in this manner to assume a freer position with respect to the Law. And this, if the interior impulse be true, not so much to the letter as rather to the spirit, would be still loyal; nor could it very easily transform the "writing," spoken of in vers. 21, 27, into an objectionable system of statute law.

STARKE: "We can well receive or retain good church ceremonies, if only they are not opposed to the Word of God, in view of our Christian freedom. Even the holidays ordered by the authorities of one's country should be celebrated in a becoming manner (Zech. vii. 2–5)."

On chap. x. That next to the great power of Ahasuerus, having such extensive dominions, all subject to taxation, the greatness of the Jew Mordecai should have been handed down to the memory of all times in the books of record of remarkable events of the Medes and Persians, was a great honor to the Jews. To this day they rejoice over his elevation. But they may well look to it to see whether they may now claim him as their own. That which God especially honored and protected in Mordecai and the then Judaism, was their fidelity to Him and His law. And only where these are found will we find a church that may receive the book of Esther as a prophecy of its victory and continuance in spite of all oppressions on the part of the world.

BRENZ: "The Jews, because they rejected Christ, the true seed of Abraham, are now no longer the people of God, no more His Church, but belong to Ishmael and Esau, who always have persecuted the true seed of Abraham. And since they persecute the true Israel, *i. e.*, Christians with the same enmity with which Haman once persecuted them, it is clear that they are themselves the kindred and allies of Haman the Amalekite."

Only where we suffer like Mordecai may one take comfort, as is so convincingly expressed in our book in the thought that the crown is at the end of the cross.

FEUARDENT: "Mordecai, in order to vindicate the glory of God and his countrymen from the Hamanites, endured the hatred of many. He afflicted himself with fastings, prayers, sackcloth, cryings, and lamentations; he constantly spurned that impious man; and was at last adjudged to suffer on the ignominious cross. Now, however, by the singular favor of God he is crowned beyond all men (Ahasuerus alone excepted) with glory and honor even in this world."

THE END.